POLITICS
and
MODERNITY

A *History of the Human Sciences* Special Issue

edited by

IRVING VELODY

and

ROBIN WILLIAMS

SAGE Publications
London • Newbury Park • New Delhi

First published as *History of the Human Sciences*, volume 5 issue 3, August 1992
Reprinted as *Politics and Modernity* 1993

SAGE Publications Ltd
6 Bonhill Street
London EC2A 4PU

SAGE Publications Inc
2455 Teller Road
Newbury Park, California 91320

SAGE Publications India Pvt Ltd
32, M-Block Market
Greater Kailash - I
New Delhi 110 048

Contributions and correspondence for *History of the Human Sciences* should be sent to the Editorial Assistant at:

University of Durham
Centre for the History of the Human Sciences
Elvet Riverside
New Elvet
Durham DH1 3JT, UK

ISBN 0 8039 8826 5

Typeset by Type Study, Scarborough
Printed in the UK by The Cromwell Press Ltd,
Broughton Gifford, Melksham, Wiltshire

POLITICS *and* MODERNITY

CONTENTS

INTRODUCTION
Rationality deferred   1

TRACY B. STRONG
'What have we to do with morals?' Nietzsche and Weber on history
and ethics   9

MARK E. WARREN
Max Weber's Nietzschean conception of power   19

REVIEW ARTICLES

PETER BARHAM
'The next village': modernity, memory and the Holocaust   39

ZYGMUNT BAUMAN
Philosophy as the mirror of time   57

RONALD BEINER
Thin ice   65

IAN BURKITT
Beyond the 'iron cage': Anthony Giddens on modernity and the self   71

DIANA COOLE
Modernity and its Other(s)   81

GEOFFREY HAWTHORN
Is postmodern politics politics?   93

PETER LASSMAN
The idea of the political   99

CHARLES MARTINDALE
Tradition and modernity   105

DAVID OWEN
The judgement of Nietzsche:
philosophy, politics, modernity   121

RAYMOND PLANT
Political theory without foundations   137

JEREMY RAYNER
Therapy for an imaginary invalid:
Charles Taylor and the malaise of modernity   145

JOHN SHOTTER
Is Bhaskar's critical realism only a theoretical realism?   157

CHARLES TURNER
Organicism, pluralism and civil association; some neglected political
thinkers   175

CONTRIBUTORS   185

POLITICS
and
MODERNITY

HISTORY OF THE HUMAN SCIENCES   Vol. 5 No. 3
© 1992 SAGE (London, Newbury Park and New Delhi)   pp. 1–7

Rationality deferred: an introduction to the politics of modernity

Epistemological Utopia: the belief in a higher-order reality undiscernible to the naked eye. (From a recently discovered *Dictionary of Postmodernist Terms*; and with apologies to Leszek Kolakowski)

Discussion of the politics of modernity entails the assessment of politics, here taken as the world of political theory; and the understanding of modernity, considered as essentially the province of sociology.

At first sight this division offers a clear enough definition of boundaries and resources. Where politics marks out the possibilities of defining the political dimension of human endeavour, sociology offers the picture of the social framework within which politics operates. Well and good! From this point sociology elaborates its account of modernity as the world of technology and industrial organization, with its human arrangements in terms of institutions, bureaucracies, family structure, identities, classes and forms of control; together with its definition of culture, ideologies, social knowledge and the formulation of identity. Within this space political theory marks out the forms and explanation of political action with its focus on justice and the good.

It seems then that the modernist debate in political theory between liberals and communitarians may now proceed apace, protagonists able to extract from the findings of sociology the database to make relevant points where required. However, the debate between liberal theorists like John Rawls and communitarians like Michael Walzer has been clouded, not to say confused, by other developments which have come to play a subversive role in both the sociological and political understanding of human knowledge and activity.

✻ ✻ ✻

These problems and difficulties find a particular expression in the work of one of the originators of contemporary sociology, Max Weber. It is, of course, general knowledge that Weber's work on the unique development of western social institutions is marked both by a substantive concern with rationality and by a methodological commitment to social science as focused inevitably on *meaningful* social activity, and with the rigorous, that is to say, scientific explanation of such social action.

The arduous but ultimately successful incorporation of Weber into a canonical account of sociology's rise and development found its cynosure in Talcott Parsons' great work of theoretical synthesis *The Structure of Social Action*; and whatever doubts may have arisen about this work since its publication in 1937, the fixed place of Weber in the sociological firmament has remained unquestioned. Indeed his star has begun to shine more brightly ever since.

As Eugène Fleischmann noted in his path-breaking essay 'De Weber à Nietzsche', the standard interpretation of Weber takes his work to be at one with a more general view of sociology as concerned with the study and, further, frankly evolutionary progression of human societies. Such study is made feasible through the development of a framework of universal categories and causal processes. For many interpreters of Weber, that framework could be found in the categories and lists of social institutions and types of action in the pages of *Economy and Society*. The fact that this catalogue lacked one central feature, namely a mechanism which could hold this portmanteau of formulations together, acted only as a spur to complete this great work.

However, it has been the efforts of a range of scholars to begin to question this view of Weber at two points: first the picture of Weber as essentially a sociologist rather than a political thinker; and second the version of Weber's work that sees him as a progenitor of the form of standard sociology sketched above. The crucial strategy, which was for so long a politically difficult move to make, has been to place Weber's investigations not against the background of Marx – a background which at least promotes Weber at a stroke into the ranks of the great sociologists – but rather to discern his work to be as much a response to Nietzsche.

Since Fleischmann's exploration, the examination of Weber's concern with politics has been developed especially by Wilhelm Hennis and Robert Eden; and the link between Nietzsche, Weber and politics has been taken further by Mark Warren and Tracy Strong among others. The acceptance of Weber's legitimacy as a political thinker has received additional support within the academic world with the forthcoming publication by Cambridge University Press of *Max Weber: Political Writings*. It had long been recognized that Weber's accounts of forms of authority were key concepts in political sociology, but it has taken rather more time to perceive the significance of his lecture 'Politics as a Vocation' as dealing with more than the problems of professionalization in the modern world.

In *Political Judgement*, Ronald Beiner notes the tragic character of the political domain caught in Weber's expression of the unresolvable conflict between the ethic of responsibility and the ethic of conviction (of ultimate ends) – and further, that they are the only categories 'we have available to catch the full phenomenal content of political action and discourse'. There are immediate consequences for both sociology and political science in Weber's views. For the former, Weber's methodological denial of the applications of sociological analysis to the solution of conflicts of value determines a clear limitation to the scope of sociology; politics cannot be reduced to sociology. However, it also follows that the realm of political science must equally lack a determinate framework to deal with opposing accounts of political values and goods, for where these are based on a version of Rawlsian rational choice theory, they fall under the parallel prohibition of deducing such goods from formal rational-legal procedures. On the other hand, political theorizing which wants in some sense to base these qualities on a more or less well-defined notion of social needs, communitarianism, simply repeats the problems which arise in the reductionist programme in sociology.

Thus the return to Weber's texts both encompasses a reassessment of his sense of the tasks and limits of social science, and, in a characteristically Nietzschean way, poses the question of the incommensurability of competing political ethics along with the impossibility of exploiting sociology in order to elicit a firm foundation for these values – or indeed any other social values. For Weber as for Nietzsche such values are not founded in nature, culture or reason.

✳   ✳   ✳

But to continue the discussion on the objectives and findings of sociology and politics, while the nominal boundaries between the disciplines appear to offer terms for a discussion on related but clearly separable fields of investigation, the very nature of sociology as a modernist undertaking raises a particular problem about who commands which resources. As Sheldon Wolin noted long ago in *Politics and Vision*, sociology's objective of explaining all that is social inevitably subsumes the political within its remit. From Marx through Durkheim to Parsons, the political world can be no more than an aspect of the social; there is no special quality which distinguishes political behaviour from any other social phenomenon. Indeed the imperialistic drive within this discipline was clearly marked out by Mannheim with his programme in *Ideology and Utopia* for a science of politics: a *social* science of politics.

Yet apart from a brief period once signalled as the 'Behavioural Revolution in Politics' (Wolin again), political theory has been strong enough to survive on its own, indeed to flourish. Given that the academic traditions of politics departments are sufficiently entrenched to carry forward a powerful tradition and canon of representative thinkers and central topics, there is also a negative reason for the stemming of the tide of sociology. To put it briefly, the sociological analysis of politics has failed to advance and in many ways is in retreat; and this is symptomatic of a more widespread malaise – the problem of the indefinite deferral of rationality.

*   *   *

What is it then to speak of rationality deferred? Here I want to advert to Kolakowski's brilliant formulation of utopian epistemologies – the cognitive version of the belief in a higher-order reality undiscernible to the naked eye. For the problem in the standard tradition of sociology is not only the search for the perfectibility of man within some possible good society. It is also the presumption that the quest for social knowledge is to be founded on the secure basis of an inner mechanism operating beneath those surface and superficial appearances of social 'reality'. My reason for calling this tradition 'modernist' is to note and signal the battery of assumptions which conceive of an inner mechanism causally explaining the outer manifestations of our behaviour, together with the developmental presuppositions that go with such theorizing. And finally to take note of the identification, if only in a general way, of the consonance of sociology's own development with the wider progress of human knowledge. For if sociology does develop it must develop as a rational quest for knowledge.

That Weber himself is caught between a perspectival view of modern society and the demands of a rigorous science itself chained to the requirements of universal rationality cannot be denied. Indeed it is the existence of a range of conflicting postures within Weber's texts which have both enabled his incorporation into a 'greater' sociology and have frustrated all attempts to produce the 'final' Weber. What certainly is the case, however, is that social science generally has been moved by the quest to discern the rational ordering of society at some level whether this is in the social system, the agent's minds and consciousnesses or (as with Giddens) through some inarticulate combination of the two. The central problem for sociology has been the failure to confirm any such mechanisms. But – as Kolakowski notes – utopias are very resistant to reality.

The technique of the great sociological tradition is in essence, then, to proffer formal rational explanations for social occurrences, the rational basis of which the human participant may well not fully comprehend. This rational generative mechanism (be it the social relations of production or whatever) at least offers the promise that the rational core of events is available for inspection even if in some odd way the concrete social processes themselves fail to measure up to expectation. For Parsons, modernity just has to have the kind of characteristics (universalism and so on) which he found in his pattern-variables.

Values, meanings, individual ends, political activity: all are subsumable under more powerful causal and thus explanatory mechanisms, mechanisms which account for the rise and subsistence of such phenomena within society. But this is precisely the move which Nietzsche went to such lengths to criticize and destroy in the *Genealogy of Morals*, and it is precisely here that the reinterpretation of Weber takes his work in a direction contrary to the canonical account.

To mention one particular issue which throws some light on the character of the difficulty, consider Bauman's study *Modernity and the Holocaust*. If the development of rational bureaucratic structures is characteristic of the modernity programme in western societies, what, asks Bauman, are we to make of the fact that the liquidation of whole populations was effectively carried out under the aegis of such structures? Bauman's question points not only to a major ambivalence concerning the West, but a parallel uncertainty in the very tools of analysis used to understand the Holocaust. Within a tradition of progress, development and the steady extension of the political structures of liberal democracy how was such a state of affairs possible?

It is only the political naivety of social science that makes this a question at all. Further, it is the peculiar nature of standard sociology which suggests that this is a question relating to Weber's account of western society. It is solely the premise that societies progress which makes the Holocaust appear as an aberration, a momentary hiccup in the evolution of rational-legal structures. But no such possibilities are foreclosed in Weber's own work. Profiting perhaps from the same Nietzschean insights, a similar exploration of the assumptions of rational social organization can be found in Foucault's *Madness and Civilization*.

However, such distancing from the claims of rationality is unusual; in sociology epistemological utopianism is the rule, and in effect such approaches, if unable to discern the requisite rational features on the surface of society itself, are persuaded of their existence in another region. It is in this sense that we may speak of the modernist sociological enterprise as characteristically concerned with the indefinite postponement of rationality: rationality deferred.

* * *

The outcome of this discussion must be to raise doubts about the adequacy of much of the sociological analysis and description of our present world, whether that be called modern, postmodern or some other unhappy neologism (postfordism comes to mind). In any case, the shortcomings clearly imply that the space for politics has not been filled or taken hostage by sociology. But does it follow that the official versions of political theory are secured and well founded?

Perhaps this postponement of rationality has all along been the difficulty – why not rationality now! This could be taken as the slogan for liberal theorists, and, above all, of John Rawls in *A Theory of Justice*, in which the formal rational requirements for a political order which can implement justice are clearly laid out. It is certainly worth noting that such a move is no longer possible in sociology. Apart from Marx's communistic musing, no serious thinker would now offer a theory in which formal rationality is available here and now. This particular quality must either be put off to the future (with the implied transparency of social order) or be deferred to a theoretical level – Kolakowski's epistemic utopianism. Yet however unsympathetic sociologists may be to Rawls' conception of the political species, the alternative communitarian approaches have the misfortune, as Geoffrey Hawthorn points out, of appearing as amateur sociology. But reinventing social theory through the imperatives of political analysis certainly does nothing to resolve the so far unresolvable problems of social science. Even the quasi-postmodernism of Rorty falls into this trap where (in 'The Priority of Democracy to Philosophy') rejecting the classical stance of political theory to deal with the realities of politics, he calls up the resources of some unnamed kind of social anthropology. But of course, as this paper argues throughout, there is no such 'untainted' brand of knowledge available to do this work.

Apart from these more general considerations, can standard political theory serve the interests and sufficiently express the needs and rights of groups whose existence was barely recognized at the inception of these theoretical develop-ments? I have in mind the goals of feminist writers in the field of political theory who, as Diana Coole has argued, question the adequacy of the Rawlsean rational agent to express these particular issues – in terms of rights, liberties and opportunities – which especially concern feminists. Here, in particular, the connection of power and authority with gender relations in both private and public contexts, which are so salient for feminists, appear as residual elements in the traditions of modernism. It seems no accident that Coole's inquiry finds its parallel in sociology where the social analysis of the position of women has been frequently reclassified as a minor subproblem in the wider (and it is claimed theoretically more legitimate) category of social class.

It is here that the systematic treatment of western intellectual traditions offered by MacIntyre in the studies beginning with *After Virtue*, the work of Charles Taylor especially in *Sources of the Self*, and the many essays and explorations from Richard Rorty begin to raise a mirroring of doubts about the traditions on offer from politics. Curiously these doubts themselves have strong parallels with my earlier questions on the adequacy of sociology to deal with politics. For whatever the differences between them (and the religiosity in MacIntyre and Taylor has little fit with Rorty's postmodern bourgeois liberalism) they are certainly at one in discarding both the standard procedures of social science *and* the formulas of institutionalized political theory.

The most cogent account of the problems of the modernist tradition is expressed in Rorty's well-known paper 'Postmodern Bourgeois Liberalism', where Rorty rapidly displays the traits of the types of argument involved in the formalist and rationalist accounts of the political life. However, it is MacIntyre's special virtue to have recognized quite precisely the weakness of social science foundationalist explanations in general and of the political in particular; then to have offered instead a novel conceptual device (novel in political theory at least) of the narrative account of agency. Rorty's investigation leaves us with the question of just what can any *a priori*, unrooted, rational concept of the political really offer us in the concrete world. For Rorty, it is certainly not a case of rationality now, nor even tomorrow; rather it is adieu! While Rorty remains something of an exception in his complete abandonment of any recognizable claim to the rational, more typically we find, as with MacIntyre (there is of course a parallel with Habermas here), a far more complex version of rationality offered. Here, again, we seem to find agreement among these writers that the forms of assessment and analysis which we associate with Weber's purposive rationality are inadequate to found a deductive or axiomatic political science.

*   *   *

Whether such writers should be classified as postmodernists is another matter. Ronald Beiner shows a more helpful way of viewing these critiques of modernity, suggesting that to view Kolakowski as a postmodernist means no more than recognizing his assent to the general objections to foundationalism. And perhaps much the same may be said of Weber and the so-called communitarianism of MacIntyre and Taylor. For while it is far from clear that there is any agreement on the alternatives to MacIntyre's 'Encyclopedism', as he terms the range of standard social and political science procedures, there is now little question that those strategies appear increasingly unconvincing and implausible. Here Kolakowski's critical assessment of the field of utopian epistemologies finds its most powerful effect and chimes with Lyotard's scepticism towards grand narratives.

It is here too that Nietzsche's Weber, with all his inconsistencies, is most revealing. For Weber's man of science, certainly a self-reflection, recognizes the fragile character of the investigator's resources with admonitions against a variety of Faustian temptations; but this is framed within a wider picture of the likely demise of that true vocational character of the pursuit of knowledge. Yet it is the case that the expansion of bureaucratization and the steady 'americanization' of the university system have failed to stem the critical assessment of that very encyclopedism, rationalism and scientization of the human sciences which Weber continuously rejected. Rather, Weber's recognition of the temporality of the moment of purposive rationality and the disembedding of political values has gained momentum as the second millennium of western culture draws to its close; and with its closure offers a renewal of that disciplining of the intellectual self that concerned the very heart of Weber's work.

Irving Velody
University of Durham, March 1992

HISTORY OF THE HUMAN SCIENCES   Vol. 5 No. 3
© 1992 SAGE (London, Newbury Park and New Delhi)   pp. 9–18

'What have we to do with morals?' Nietzsche and Weber on history and ethics

TRACY B. STRONG

You are . . . men of sin, whom destiny . . .
Has caused to belch you up.

(Shakespeare, The Tempest)

In the last two decades the English-language study of Max Weber has been transformed. The Weber of Talcott Parsons and Edward Shils was a model postwar social scientist, intent on preserving the boundaries between facts and values, so as never to lend the authority and prestige of knowledge to the dangerous drives potentially present in the political realm. This Weber, it is safe to say, is no longer with us.

The sources of the transformation were several but they all derived from those who sought to preserve what I might call the Europeanness of Weber and to keep him from being naturalized an American. Leo Strauss hinted that what he called Weber's 'noble nihilism'[1] removed Weber from a lighthearted adherence to the supposed 'Is–Ought' distinction;[2] Wolfgang Mommsen analyzed the openness of Weber's thought to the dark developments of the 1930s and 1940s and Arthur Mitzman explored the darkness in Weber's person.[3] A younger generation of scholars, tuned to different frequencies from their reading of analytic and ordinary language philosophy and from the developments in the philosophy and history of science we associate with Thomas Kuhn, found a Weber very different from the rather staid figure of the 1950s.[4] This Weber carried his knowledge like a sword to the modern world, to wound it as much as he was wounded by it.

Who was the different Weber? In one form or another he appeared, shall we say, as a Nietzschean Weber.[5] He was a Weber who sought to grasp the full significance of his historical throwness as a western bourgeois[6] without ever seeking to escape from his historical condition; he was a Weber who thought the world to be ultimately chaos that had to be tamed by the person of knowledge; he was a man who had only scorn for those who could not face the moral nihilism of the present 'like men'.

But there was also in this Weber a kind of curious hanging back:

> It is true that the path of human destiny must break on those who gaze upon a portion of it with heartrending dismay. But anyone so affected would do well to keep his small personal commentaries to himself, as one does before the sight of the ocean and the high mountains, unless he knows himself to be called and gifted for an artistic formation or a prophetic claim [zu künstlerischer Formung oder zu prophetischer Förderung].[7]

Weber is often compared favorably to Nietzsche for precisely this kind of remark. It may be that he was conscious of the dangers to and of western civilization in the fin-de-siècle: but (it is said) he showed a sense of proportion, an 'inner distance'.[8] And indeed, just at the moment that the force and logic of his argument have led him to the space in which the prophetic or artistic voice is appropriate, Weber pulls back. The tension here is between what his learning has enforced on him and the finding of words sufficient to that understanding. At this moment, and at similar moments at the end of the 'Vocation' essays, Weber expresses a caution about saying more, as if anything that he might say would necessarily be wrong, or irresponsible, or misunderstood. His stance seems to be that of one who is not entitled to such speech. If Weber spent his life in part coming to terms not only with Marx but most especially with Nietzsche,[9] what is it that leads him at junctions like this to be so resistant to sounding like Nietzsche?[10]

Wolfgang Schluchter has explored this topic in a preliminary manner in an essay on the 'Wissenschaft als Beruf' address.[11] It is central, it seems to me, to understanding the relation and difference between Weber and Nietzsche. I should like to explore it somewhat further in the context closest to it, namely each writer's major 'meta-ethical' (dare one use such a term with these men?) writing.

'Die Wirtschaftsethik der Weltreligionen' and *Zur Genealogie der Moral* are obviously the texts in question. Nietzsche's presence in the former text has often been remarked on, but there has been, to my knowledge, no real comparison of the two writings, with the partial exception of two pages in Bryan Turner's *For Weber*.[12]

Let me briefly assert here about Nietzsche what I have written at greater length elsewhere. The *Genealogy of Morals* presents its reader with a picture of the developmental structure of what Nietzsche understands as the moral way of grasping the world. It is not for him the case that morality is bunk, a fake. It is rather (all too) real. After a servile moral way of being in the world made it impossible for the masterly moral way to continue, it came to dominate the world, if only out of lack of opposition. Morality is in fact the way that *we* grasp the world, Nietzsche says, and we will continue to do so for the reasons that we first did. It allows us to make sense of the world; it justifies our position in the world to us (including our unhappinesses). If we did not experience the world morally, Nietzsche asserts, we would run the risk of not experiencing it at all – we lose the selves that we are. We think, Nietzsche suggests, that anything is better than the loss of one's self.

The attack in the *Genealogy* is thus not a facile 'morals is bunk' approach. Rather Nietzsche is desperately concerned that in a day and age after the death of God, i.e. in an age in which moral justification is even less restrained by a non-human dimension than it has been in the past, humans who approach the world morally will come to justify anything. It is precisely because Socrates had it right – no one does what s/he thinks is evil – that anything will be declared and justified as good.[13]

Where does Weber stand in relation to considerations such as these? I want to argue that Weber's apparent moderation may be more of a source of anxiety to us than appears at first glance.

The article known as the 'Economic Ethic of the World Religions' (given in the Gerth and Mills translation as 'The Social Psychology of World Religions') appeared in the *Archiv für Sozialwissenschaft* in separate parts, starting in the year 1915. In this article, Weber sought to explore in the various world religions the 'direction giving elements in the mode of life [Lebensfuehrung] of various social strata' which have given the practical ethics of those strata their most distinctive elements.[14]

The initial focus appears to be classificatory: Weber identifies the principal strata in six creeds whose styles of life have been at least predominantly decisive for certain religions. Religion, it appears, is a particular type of account that one might give to oneself to explain one's position and being in the world. It is thus quite similar to what Nietzsche means by 'morals', which, too, are a particular way of making sense of how one is in the world.

Soon, however, the essay shifts away from its apparent typological approach. Weber speaks increasingly of 'development' and of 'steps along [a] path'. And within a few pages, Weber has switched his attention to a basic distinction having to do with the approach to the 'evaluation of suffering' and the consequent forms of 'legitimation' of 'fortune [Glueck]'.

The concern with suffering, it appears, is the key experience that makes Weber's subject-matter religion. The existence of suffering leads to two responses.

First are those who do not suffer, who are 'fortunate'. Weber distinguishes between the religion of 'honor, power, property and health' and suggests that the religion of those with such attributes is 'positive'. For such individuals religion (or morality) is the account they give to themselves of the world such that their happiness in the world is justified. In contrast, he then asserts that 'the paths which lead to the subversion of this stand are complex: they lead to the religious transfiguration of suffering'.[15] Those for whom suffering is so transfigured are said to be 'in need of salvation'. A 'professional organization [Berufsmaessigen Betriebes]' grows up around the care of souls and in the service of 'specifically *plebeian* motives'. Next, 'a significant further step along this path was taken when, under the pressure of a typical and ever-recurrent distress, the religiosity of a savior developed itself'. This view is itself naturally linked, Weber asserts, to a 'rational world-view' which in turn 'not rarely furnished suffering with a positive valuation, something which originally had been quite foreign to it'.[16]

It does not take much to see that Weber has here at least partially reproduced the schematic of the first essay in the *Genealogy of Morals*. He has presented two different forms of valuation, suggested that the first 'positive one' (which corresponds to Nietzsche's 'master morality') is relatively simple, and that the second ('slave morality' for Nietzsche) is not only more 'complex' but brings about a transvaluation of suffering. Nietzsche had of course also argued that slave morality was by far the more complex morality and that it would develop through 'ressentiment' and ascetic priests.

This distinction provides the energy for the rest of the essay. Various practices of various religions are used to illustrate the ramifications of this central distinction. The transvaluative or transfigurative mode is associated with 'plebeian motives'. The next step is the development of the idea of a savior, and that in turn, Weber indicates, presupposes a 'rational world-view'.[17]

Weber makes clear that he is elaborating on and to some degree correcting Nietzsche's analysis when he continues (in a passage simply mistranslated in Gerth and Mills):

> The power of this particular configuration of affairs grew greatly because of the increasing need to come up with an ethical 'meaning' for the division of fortunes between men along with the growing rationality of this conception of the world. The increasing rationalization of the ethico-religious understanding and the elimination of the primitive made for ever greater difficulties for this theodicy. Individual 'undeserved' suffering was all-too-common. Good [das Beste] happened all-too-often not to the best but to the bad [die Schlechten], not only in terms of a 'slave morality' but also in the terms of a masterly stratum. . . . The development of a rational religious ethic has positive roots in the inner conditions of those social strata that are less valued.[18]

Nietzsche's analysis has been parallel and at this stage he makes a key move. Nietzsche too had argued that one of the components of slave morality is to render the world calculable, rational. (If there is a savior, then one knows that if one does such-and-such acts, forgiveness or redemption will be attained – the world makes sense.) Nietzsche additionally suggests at this point (along with

Marx and Hegel) that in the struggle between the two world-views the victory is to the slaves. The thirteenth chapter of the first essay of the *Genealogy* sets out the mechanism and the rest of the book is written to a considerable degree as if master morality is no longer a factor.

Weber here allows that 'ressentiment' (the driving force in Nietzsche's progression from guilt to bad conscience to ascetic ideals) can play a role, but only along with 'other factors'. He even allows a role for what Nietzsche would call 'ascetic priests', those for whom the energy of ressentiment has provided a means to control and direct masses of people.[19]

So: no apparently single factor explanation will be permitted by Weber, but at the same time he will indicate that there might be a common element to apparently very different forms of behavior. Weber's basic move here seems so to complicate the Nietzschean categories as to make them disappear under the accumulation of historical specifics. For instance, a veritable litany of different desires for salvation appears. Nine sequential sentences start with 'One could wish to be saved from . . .'; and the conclusion first appears to be that there are many more varieties of hope for redemption, still uncharted.

However, having said this, Weber reasserts the actuality of a general stand: all of the desires for salvation derive from the experience of the 'senseless'; and all of them imply a demand that the world should 'somehow be a meaningful "cosmos"'.[20]

Thus far the parallels with the *Genealogy* remain strong. Both Nietzsche and Weber find the origins of morality/religion in the inability of people not to make sense of the world. Morality/religion show themselves in several different forms as a way of making the world make sense.[21]

But here Weber begins to diverge from the thrust of Nietzsche's essay. Whereas Nietzsche takes up the question of what happens when the will to truth (to make sense of the world) becomes conscious of itself (i.e. after the death of God),[22] eventually to conclude that we are without logical recourse against our condition, Weber suggests that it is the nature of religions to produce stratification and strata differentiation:

> The important fact of experience of the unequal religious qualifications of individuals stands for us right at and as the beginning of the history of religions. . . . From this there develops in all intensive religions a tendency towards a kind of status stratification.[23]

Weber finds himself caught. In the name of historical intellectual honesty he finds it necessary to correct the thrust of Nietzsche's essay, an essay he himself has called 'brilliant [glaenzend]'. At the same time he is caught up in the torrent unleashed by Nietzsche's polemic. Each time he uses the word 'nevertheless' it is a sign both of his being swept along and of his perceived need to resist the consequences of Nietzsche's grasp of the world.[24]

Weber, however, is determined to resist Nietzsche's final conclusion that the logic of the moral realm is that one would rather 'will nothing, than not will'.[25] In order to make it possible for value to be (re)introduced into the world, Weber now takes the argument in a new direction.

This new direction rests on the centrality that the analysis of redemption has accorded to rationality and to the progressive rationalization and disenchantment of the world. Weber wants to make use of the energy behind the desire for redemption. Nietzsche, on the other hand, at the same point of his analysis devoted an entire chapter of *Zarathustra* to the demonstration that the idea of redemption was something to be moved away from.[26] The motivation of the whole thrust of the rest of Weber's essay is to move religion and religious energy as much as possible *into* the world, or more accurately, to show that religion can be moved into the world and, with Protestantism, has been so moved.

This motivation, in fact, controls all of the *Religionssoziologie*:

> The son of the modern European civilization [Kulturwelt] will unavoidably and properly handle questions of universal history by asking himself the following: which concatenation of circumstances has led to the fact that precisely and only in the world of the West have appeared cultural phenomena which – at least we like to think – lie in a pattern of development which has *universal* meaning and value.[27]

Each of the major studies of different religions comes back to the point in this paragraph. How and to what degree do developments in that religion lie in a pattern which has universal meaning? The logic of the sociology of religion, both in the text that we have been considering and in the long section of *Economy and Society* devoted to this topic, moves from 'religious needs' to a consideration of the secular realm. Thus at the end of the 'Economic Ethic' essay, Weber asserts that we are to be interested in religions insofar as they are 'related to economic rationalism'.[28] And he proceeds rapidly to introduce the basic forms of legitimate authority and to discuss them in terms familiar from several other places in his work. In fact, the words 'religion' and 'religious' do not appear in the last five pages of the essay at all, and appear only once (in a discussion of traditionalism) after the discussions of charisma and rational-legal authority are introduced.

What has happened? I can only point to an answer here but it must contain something like the following.[29] Weber, no less than Nietzsche, sees humans as historical beings. The central characteristic of western humans (and he thinks this characteristic is increasingly universal to all humans) is that they live in a disenchanted, rationalized world. The analysis of this world – sketched out in the 'Economic Ethic' essay and elaborated throughout his work – is thus a coming-to-know of ourselves, an acknowledgment of the kinds of beings that we are.

What do we find? We find that we are creatures who live under the conditions of the general rationalization of social relationships, what he calls 'the bureaucratization of all forms of domination'. In general – this is the conclusion of the two 'Vocation' essays – there is no alternative but to accept this lot and take it upon ourselves. It is the destiny the sea has tossed up.

However, there are limits. By 'bureaucratization of all forms of domination', Weber does not mean simply the system of organization by which large institutions govern their day-to-day affairs. Rather, he notes,[30] bureaucracy is the typical expression of the forms of legitimacy in which obedience is due to and rests on norms rather than on persons. It is thus the form of 'Herrschaft' in which commands are linked to and are experienced as coming from abstract and non-human entities, from roles, not from persons. Indeed, the elimination of irrationality in the world is also the elimination of relations between persons as a basis of society.

Bureaucracy, Weber then claims, has nothing to do with the truly political, for 'politics means conflict'. However, 'bureaucracy failed *completely* whenever it was expected to deal with political problems'. The two forms are 'inherently alien' to each other.[31]

This seems to be because bureaucracy effaces or disguises that there is ruling going on at all. Officials, even at the highest level, tend to think of themselves merely as the first officers of their enterprise. Rule replaces ruling.[32] Indeed, what has happened appears to be that the administrative sphere has taken over the apparatus that was evolved in the Church. The institutions first evolved in the Church now serve as the model for the State. Weber writes that:

> . . . the official – at least in the fully developed modern state – is not considered the personal servant of the ruler. Likewise the bishop, the priest and the preacher are no longer, as in early Christian times, carriers of a purely personal charisma, and have become officials in the service of a functional purpose, a purpose which in the present-day 'church' appears at once impersonalized and ideologically sanctified.[33]

In a world that is disenchanted, politics has been lost. From his 'Inaugural Lecture' to the end of his life Weber sought to recover the political, that is the magical, the non-rationalized. What he saw in his studies of religion, I think, is that religious needs had secularized themselves. They had done so in two ways: one was by empowering rationalized institutional structures; but the second was to have legitimated ethically the salvation/redeemer desire. The main reason why Weber cannot accept Nietzsche's demand for a complete transfiguration of the structures of morality is that he hopes that in the desire for a redeemer which a secularized religious ethic may still induce, a people will find the energy to respond to a new leader.

If this is true, one must then ask oneself if Weber's vision is not in the end more dangerous, more permissive, open to more temptations and to greater self-dishonesty than was Nietzsche's. Nietzsche was not crazy to have found the moral impulse dangerous in our day and age. Incremental reform may fail to meet the demands of the day.

University of California, San Diego

NOTES

1 Strauss (1965: 48).
2 For reflections on the fate of this distinction in academia, see Strong (1990: Chs 1 and 4).
3 Mommsen (1959) and Mitzman (1969).
4 See the 'Epilogue' to the new edition of my *Friedrich Nietzsche and the Politics of Transfiguration* (Strong, 1988). In the English language, I am thinking of the work of Lawrence Scaff, Robert Eden, Frederic Jameson, Bryan Turner, Wolfgang Schluchter, Gunther Roth and others.
5 Strauss (1965) with his usual perspicacity saw this relationship, even if he got both Weber and Nietzsche slightly on the bias (as I think he does). On Strauss as a Nietzschean, see the excellent work by Drury (1985).
6 See Strong (1985a: 153 ff.).
7 See Max Weber's *Gesammelte Aufsätze zur Religionssoziologie*, Vol. I (Weber, 1947: 239), hereafter cited as *GAR* I; 'Vorbemerkung', p. 14. Another English version can be found in Parsons' translation of Weber's *The Protestant Ethic and the Spirit of Capitalism* (Weber, 1958b: 29), hereafter cited as *PESC*. Contrary to the impression Parsons gives, the 'Vorbemerkung' is intended as an introduction to the entire *GAR*, not just to the *PESC*.
8 See the interesting essay by David Owen (1991).
9 cf. Baumgarten (1964: 554) and see most especially Eden (1984).
10 Without sharing his attempt to take such considerations in a Kantian direction, I find much of importance along these lines in Goldmann (1989: especially 70–2).
11 Schluchter (1979: 65–116, especially 65–6).
12 Turner (1981: 157–8). See Fleishman (1964).
13 See Strong (1990: 164–7). In relation to Nietzsche specifically, these ideas are developed in Strong (1988: especially Chs 4 and 8).
14 *GAR* I (Weber, 1947: 239). Translation by Gerth and Mills, 'The Social Psychology of World Religions' (Weber, 1958a: 268), hereafter cited as *GM*.
15 The German here is itself tortuous: 'Verschlungener sind dagegen die Wege, welche zur Umkehrung dieses Standpunktes: zur religioesen Verklaerung des Leidens also, fuehren' (*GAR* I: 242; *GM*: 271).
16 *GAR* I: 244–5; *GM*: 273–4 (translation modified).
17 *GAR* I: 244; *GM*: 273.
18 *GAR* I: 246, 248. The translation in *GM*: 275, 276 hides the reference to the categories of the *Genealogy of Morals* and leaves out 'the elimination of'.
19 *GAR* I: 248; *GM*: 277.
20 *GAR* I: 252–3; *GM*: 280–1.
21 See Strong (1985b).
22 This is the topic of the third essay in *GM*, culminating in Ch. 27.
23 *GAR* I: 259; *GM*: 287.

24 Robert Eden, starting from an analysis of *Beyond Good and Evil* and the 'Vocation' essays, has arrived at a conclusion similar to this one. See Eden (1987: 406–7).
25 My translation of the last sentence of the *Genealogy*.
26 See the detailed analysis in Strong (1988: Ch. 8; 1989).
27 *GAR* I: 1. Different wording appears in Parsons' translation of *PESC*: see note 7.
28 *GAR* I: 265; GM: 293.
29 In the next few paragraphs I draw on material in my 'Entitlement and Legitimacy' paper (Strong, 1985a).
30 *Economy and Society* (Weber, 1978: 954), hereafter cited as *ES*.
31 Weber, 1972: 329, note 1, 351 (*ES*: 1399, 1417).
32 *ES*: 958.
33 *ES*: 959.

BIBLIOGRAPHY

Baumgarten, E., ed. (1964) *Max Weber, Werk und Person*. Tübingen: Mohr.

Drury, S. (1985) *The Political Ideas of Leo Strauss*. Basingstoke, Hants: Macmillan.

Eden, R. (1984) *Political Leadership and Nihilism: A Study of Weber and Nietzsche*. Gainesville, FL: University of Florida Presses.

Eden, R. (1987) 'Weber and Nietzsche: Questioning the Liberation of Social Science from Historicism', in W. Mommsen and Jürgen Osterhammel (eds) *Max Weber and His Contemporaries*, pp. 405–21. London: Allen & Unwin.

Fleishman, E. (1964) 'De Weber à Nietzsche', *Archives européennes de la sociologie* 5: 190–238.

Goldmann, H. (1989) 'The Person in Weberian Social Theory', in M. Milgate and C. B. Welch (eds) *Critical Issues in Social Thought*, pp. 76–94. London and San Diego, CA: Academic Press.

Mitzman, A. (1969) *The Iron Cage: An Historical Interpretation of Max Weber*. New York: Grosset.

Mommsen, W. (1959) *Max Weber und die deutsche Politik*. Tübingen: Mohr.

Owen, D. (1991) 'Autonomy and "Inner Distance": a Trace of Nietzsche in Weber', *History of the Human Sciences* 4(1): 79–91.

Schluchter, W. (1979) 'Value Neutrality and the Ethics of Responsibility', in G. Roth and W. Schluchter (eds) *Max Weber's Vision of History*, pp. 86–129. Berkeley and Los Angeles, CA: University of California Press.

Strauss, L. (1965 [1953]) *Natural Right and History*. Chicago: University of Chicago Press.

Strong, T. B. (1985a) 'Entitlement and Legitimacy: Weber and Lenin on the Problems of Leadership', in F. Eidelin (ed.) *Constitutional Democracy: Essays Presented to Henry Ehrmann*, pp. 153–80. Boulder, CO: Westview.

Strong, T. B. (1985b) 'Texts and Pretexts: Reflections on Perspectivism in Nietzsche', *Political Theory* 13(2) (May): 164–82.

Strong, T. B. (1988) *Friedrich Nietzsche and the Politics of Transfiguration*. Berkeley and Los Angeles, CA: University of California Press.

Strong, T. B. (1989) 'Nietzsche's Political Aesthetics', in M. A. Gillespie and T. B. Strong (eds) *Nietzsche's New Seas*, pp. 153–74. Chicago: University of Chicago Press.

Strong, T. B. (1990) *The Idea of Political Theory*. Notre Dame, IN: University of Notre Dame Press.

Turner, B. S. (1981) *For Weber*. London and Boston, MA: Routledge & Kegan Paul.

Weber, M. (1947) *Gesammelte Aufsätze zur Religionssoziologie*, Vol. I. Tübingen: Mohr.

Weber, M. (1958a) 'The Social Psychology of World Religions', in H. H. Gerth and C. W. Mills (eds) *From Max Weber*, pp. 267–301. New York: Oxford University Press.

Weber, M. (1958b) *The Protestant Ethic and the Spirit of Capitalism*, trans. T. Parsons. New York: Scribners.

Weber, M. (1972) 'Parliament und Regierung in neugeordneted Deutschland', in M. Weber, *Gesammelte Politische Schriften*, ed. J. Winckelmann, pp. 306–443. Tübingen: Mohr.

Weber, M. (1978) *Economy and Society*, ed. G. Roth and C. Wittich. Berkeley, CA and London: University of California Press.

© 1992 SAGE (London, Newbury Park and New Delhi) pp. 19–37

Max Weber's Nietzschean conception of power

MARK E. WARREN

Max Weber defined power as 'the probability that one actor within a social relationship will be in a position to carry out his own will despite resistance, regardless of the basis on which this probability rests' (Weber, 1978: 53). While Weber's concept of power is not universally accepted, two key elements are replicated in virtually every definition of power as a potentially conflictual relationship between dominant and subordinate individuals (e.g. Oppenheim, 1981: 29–31). The first element is an understanding of power as an expression of the wills and capacities of individuals. The second is a distinction between relations of power and other social relationships in terms of a conflict of interest between individuals.

Most social scientists have found Weber's definition congenial. On the one hand, his definition refers power in institutions and structures to individuals and the relations between them. That is, it seems consistent with methodological individualism, and thus seems to accord with a mainstream consensus about what counts as an explanation. On the other hand, his definition has a normative bearing on liberal-democratic politics. Because it distinguishes power relations from other kinds of social relations – consensual and voluntary ones, for example – it can help to identify social relations that, just because they are relations of power, we may wish to structure by means of political rights and protections. In contrast, definitions of power so broad as to include all social relations – Nietzsche's and Foucault's cosmological definitions are examples – would seem to devalue rights and protections because they fail to distinguish between power and other kinds of social relations.

In this article I take issue with this conventional understanding of Weber's approach to power and offer an alternative account. The problem is not with the supposed advantages of Weber's definition. He did value explanatory concreteness (Hekman, 1983). And he quite explicitly fashioned his sociology to understand the limits and possibilities of individual capacities for a self-directed life, a key justification of liberal-democracy (Warren, 1988a). The problem is that Weber's definition of power has too often been assimilated to patterns of explanation that he himself rejected, patterns that also involve more general inadequacies. Weber's general formulation – that power consists in A's ability to impose his will on B despite B's resistance – has typically been elaborated by means of behavioral or rational choice methodologies. Although apparently consistent with Weber's intent, these elaborations in fact undermine his approach and produce conceptual paradoxes.

Behavioralists focus on overt conflicts between actors in which one actor can be observed to prevail. The premium here is on observation: behavioralists rely on self-reports of the interests in terms of which conflicts are defined, and on observable outcomes of conflict situations. Weber rejected behavioral explanations, however, because he viewed observations as underspecifying explanations owing to the fact that a given behavior can be motivated by a variety of meanings and intentions (Weber, 1978: 4–24).

Rational choice approaches model conflict by attributing to individuals the desire and capacity to maximize preferences in a universe of finite satisfactions. Actors have power when they have disproportionately more means to pursue their preferences, and they hold these means at the expense of others. This methodology emphasizes the heuristic power of attributing to individuals a capacity to pursue their self-interest. Weber, however, saw such attributions of rationality – already typical of contemporary economics – as reflections of culturally specific complexes of meaning which themselves need explaining (as he attempted in *The Protestant Ethic and the Spirit of Capitalism*). He viewed the use of such rational models as interpretative reconstructions of intentionality rather than general models of agency (Weber, 1949: 83, 89–90).

These departures from Weber's interpretative sociology would not be very important were it not for the fact that they introduce paradoxes into Weber's concept of power that would not otherwise exist. The paradoxes stem from the assumption in the standard appropriations of Weber that power originates, as it were, in agents who are transparent to themselves and autonomous in their identity and capacities. Power relations are assumed not to alter this transparency and autonomy.

One difficulty is that reading Weber through this assumption results in relational definitions of power that cannot also explain the organization-building qualities of power. On the face of it, social relations that build on conflicts of interest between autonomous agents would seem to be unpromising ways of coordinating complex collective actions that require a positive engagement of the capacities of individuals. As the jargon of management suggests, superiors 'motivate' their subordinates to do their jobs by appealing to their interests. Command by threat produces clumsy and half-hearted performances.

Because of such difficulties some social theorists reject the relational view of power ('power over') in favor of a conception that emphasizes the collective capacities of organizations. Talcott Parsons and Hannah Arendt, for example, argue that we should conceive power in terms of the abilities of organizations to align and coordinate the actions of individuals. As Parsons puts it, power is a general social resource 'used in the interest of collective goals' (Parsons, 1960: 181; cf. Arendt, 1969).

It is commonly and correctly noted, however, that because the organizational approach does not include a relational dimension ('power over'), it cannot identify conflicts of interest, thereby losing the normatively critical function of the concept. In contrast, the relational approach ('power over') includes the normative intuition that the concept of power ought to sort out genuinely consensual from conflictual relations. Some such critical function surely is necessary if a concept of power is to have any use for, say, democratic theory. Yet if the concept is to be useful for explanation, it certainly needs to anticipate the generative capacities of social organizations. Indeed, this is a central point of Foucault's view that in the modern era power is increasingly 'productive': power relations develop and discipline the capacities of individuals and align them with organizations (Foucault, 1983). Likewise with Weber: one of his key explanatory concerns is with the increasing dynamism and inertia of organizations based on 'rational domination'. Standard appropriations of Weber's conception of power seem to exclude this concern with the generative capacities of power – a concern Parsons and Arendt address only by dismissing critical distinctions between interests in power relations. We are thus left with a paradoxical trade-off between explanatory and normative adequacy.

The second paradox is closely related: the relational definition identifies power in terms of conflict of interest, but turns out to be insensitive to what Weber took to be the most stable and pervasive form of power, *domination*, that is, the kind of power relation in which the compliance of subordinates is voluntary, or at least not understood by them as a conflictual relation. Indeed, the paradox shows up in Weber's definition of domination as 'the probability that a command with a given specific content will be obeyed by a given group of persons' (Weber, 1978: 53). Limiting domination to the 'authoritarian power of command' within hierarchical social organizations produces this elaboration:

> [*D*]*omination* will thus mean the situation in which the manifested will (*command*) of the ruler or rulers is meant to influence the conduct of one or more others (*the ruled*) and actually does influence it in such a way that their conduct to a socially relevant degree occurs as if the ruled had made the content of the command the maxim of their conduct for its very own sake. (Weber, 1978: 946)

Notice the apparent contradiction: on the one hand, Weber refers to the intentions of agents, some of whom issue commands, and others of whom willingly obey these commands. On the other hand, his wording suggests that what defines domination is that the ruled obey commands because they find them meaningful, acting as if they had made 'the content of the command the maxim of their conduct for its very own sake'. As Dennis Wrong notes of Weber and his followers, there is a 'genuine paradox . . . in the fact that submission to legitimate authority is voluntary and yet at the same time experienced as mandatory or compulsory' (Wrong, 1980: 38–9). Domination is a kind of power relation in which individuals voluntarily acquiesce, but which they do not experience as conflicting with their interests.

It appears, then, that mainstream appropriations of Weber's definition of power fail in at least three ways. First, they fail to explain how capacities of organizations are generated by power relations. Second, they fail to explain 'deep' forms of power, domination. Third, they fail normatively: if power relations cannot be adequately identified, then the rights and protections that define distributions of power in liberal-democracies may not relate to the political realities they are supposed to regulate.

We can trace these failures to the models of agency into which Weber's definition of power is appropriated. Standard appropriations of Weber hold, in effect, that individuals can identify their interests apart from the social relations within which they are embedded. The point is methodologically rather than theoretically justified: power relations can be identified only if there are ways of identifying conflicts of interest. And the only alternative to attributing interests to individuals is to rely on self-reports, or 'revealed preferences'. For reasons of method, according to this argument, we must assume that individuals are transparent enough to themselves that they can understand their interests and judge their social relationships in terms of these interests. Rational choice theory makes this assumption a priori. Behavioral methodology does not make the assumption explicitly – indeed, there is no a priori attribution of rationality. But the methodology dictates the assumption that interests are transparent to the self, because to hold otherwise would be to attribute non-observable (and hence non-verifiable) interests (Connolly, 1983: Ch. 3; Lukes, 1974). Thus, by default, individuals are conceptualized as autonomous agents, self-contained units who command resources that are external to their self-constitution in order to maximize preferences.

Certainly part of the reason for relying on 'revealed preferences' is that we like to think of individuals as being the best judges of their own interests. The mainstream appropriations of Weber, however, transform this normatively desirable but socially contingent capacity into a methodological principle. This is something that Weber did not do, and when we understand this, the apparent paradoxes in his thinking about power – indeed, the paradoxes in thinking about power more generally – will seem less intransigent.

NIETZSCHE'S INFLUENCE

One way of getting Weber right on this issue is to interpret his conception of power in light of his Nietzschean inheritance, for this is where we find the most radical questioning of conceptions of agency. Weber is reported to have written in a letter that 'one can measure the honesty of a contemporary scholar, and above all a contemporary philosopher, in his posture toward Marx and Nietzsche' (Mitzman, 1970: 182). Marx's influence has never been much of a mystery: Weber was always in contact with contemporary socialists, and it is not difficult to see his sociology as an alternative to Marx that also incorporates him. It is different with Nietzsche. While most now agree that Nietzsche was an important figure, there is little agreement as to what his importance was. Thus we are less sure what he might have meant to Weber. To be sure, there are some clear lines of influence. Most obviously, Weber's concern with modern disenchantment and the increasing meaninglessness of rationalized culture and institutions is Nietzschean to the core (Hennis, 1988: Ch. 4; Scaff, 1984: 196; Schroeder, 1987).

But we have not yet appreciated the extent to which Weber was influenced by Nietzsche's rejection of modern understandings of agency. We find this influence above all in the ways Weber poses his questions: his sociology takes no particular kind of individuality or personality for granted, but instead asks how different kinds of agents, personalities, configurations of desire and interpretation come into being. He puts the question in part by asking how individuals' experiences, social creations, goals and reflexive capacities are formed within interpretative systems of value. As Hennis has put it, Weber is interested in the 'forms of moral constitution' of the self (Hennis, 1987: 73).[1] This is a Nietzschean problematic. Nietzsche's critique of modern culture is a result of pursuing the metaphysics of Christianity and rationalism into modern conceptions of subjectivity, so that his critique of modern values is also a critique of modern conceptions of agency. 'Metaphysical' conceptions of subjectivity involve attributing a unity to the self in terms of its interests, goals, values, meanings, or capacities. But although we may experience the self as a unity, such unity is not, in Nietzsche's view, guaranteed by transcendental certainties or by substantive unity within the self. Rather, unity is given by a projected moral ideal which is in a constant state of achievement, and the form of unity reflects the conditions under which the moral ideal is incarnated. What distinguishes modernity, Nietzsche held, is that the contingency of the self becomes apparent as a matter of sociocultural fact. He called the experience of this awareness 'nihilism', because with the disintegration of the moral identities it had taken for granted, the self loses a meaningful orientation toward the world.

Under these circumstances, Nietzsche thought, we can no longer make do with the modernist approach of using the self to measure and morally judge the world. Nietzsche's most important innovation lies at this juncture: he asks a new kind of question, and from this question follows virtually the entirety of his philosophy. His question is: How are selves – 'types' as he calls them – forged out of the practices, interpretations and conditions that make up a form of life? Practices produce the self, in Nietzsche's view, according to general existential demands for meaning – demands, as it were, for agent-unity, a center out of which the self might act with effect. We do not forge the self under conditions of our own choosing, however. Indeed, existing social relations of power present the self with dilemmas for its unity and direction, so that the kind of unity the self achieves will retain an imprint, as it were, of the power relations under which it is forged. The kind of self that results from historically contingent practices – a Christian soul, an ascetic, a rational calculator, a romantic – will have much to do with the conditions under which the practices are generated. If these conditions include oppression, power relations can become an essential part of the narrative through which the self locates its own agent-unity, in this way becoming essential to self-identity. This is, in effect, the pattern of explanation we find in Nietzsche's analysis of the 'slave type' he viewed as endemic to Christian culture: he conceives a kind of self that finds power relations essential to its identity just because it achieves identity through a scriptural narrative that developed in response to slave conditions of life. Nietzsche, in other words, provides an analysis of domination, one that Weber borrows, refines and expands in his *Sociology of Religion* (Warren, 1988b: Ch. 1; Weber, 1946: Ch. IX). This analysis, we shall see, provides a template for understanding Weber.

Nietzsche does not generalize his example into a concept of domination, leaving us to extract it from a single sustained example: his analysis of priestly power in his critique of Christianity in *On the Genealogy of Morals* and *The Antichrist*. The example is interesting not because Nietzsche gives a full account of the sociology of Christianity (Weber is much more sensitive to its historical variations), but because it provides the model of analysis upon which Weber relies, and which Weber refines and elaborates, notwithstanding his somewhat disingenuous critique of Nietzsche.[2] Nietzsche's account is well known: he portrays Christianity in terms of its interpretative constitution of the self, a constitution that permits and justifies the domination of the Church, while defining individuals in such a way that their self-identities can be maintained only by accepting the power of the Church. He looks for the origins of 'the Christian-moral hypothesis' and other ascetic ideals in the existential interest situation of those who suffer, especially at the hands of others (Warren, 1988b: Ch. 1). Suffering is not, in Nietzsche's view, problematic in itself, but rather when it is senseless, without meaning (Nietzsche, 1968a: 503–5). Meaning is not, however, a problem of representing or discovering meanings that are inherent in the world; it is not a problem of truth as traditionally understood. Instead, Nietzsche understands meaning as an experience given by individuals' abilities to interpret their situations in ways that allow them to form a 'will' – an orientation toward conditions of self-reproduction. Demands for meaning become estranged from practices and are idealized as the problem of 'truth', however, when, for reasons of experience or cultural mapping, practices become so disjoined that individuals can no longer plausibly interpret them as effects of their 'will'. It is not that humans always connect meaning to will-formation. Rather, suffering produces the problem of meaning because the 'will' that one would have formed through traditional orientations, habitually and without thinking ('instinctively', in Nietzsche's terminology), is no longer possible. This is why humans 'would rather will nothingness than not will' (1968: 533).

Suffering at the hands of others produces a problem of meaning because it violates an existential need for will-formation – a point that Nietzsche seems to have borrowed loosely from Hegel, and bequeathed directly to Weber. The key to both Nietzsche's and Weber's analyses is that *suffering structures interest situations subject to interpretation.*[3] Christianity addresses these interest situations by offering an image of the world that permits a unity of the will by providing a goal – that is, a projected (and transcendentally protected) identity in terms of which the unity of the self can be secured over and against worldly suffering. The Christian narrative about sin, punishment, the need for obedience, and behavioral conditions of salvation draws much of its strength from its internal coherence. It makes contact with the world only with respect to a few painful experiences, experiences that help to underwrite the Christian devaluation of the world. Indeed, this is a condition of its success: the Christian narrative serves those who subscribe to the story precisely because it inverts the world. Oppressors will be punished rather than saved, the 'will' that is lacking in practice is restored to individuals as children of God, the community missing on earth will exist in an afterlife, and the suffering that one experiences is nonetheless a just consequence of human sin (Nietzsche, 1968a: 482–8).

Because the projection is 'imaginary', however, it must be preserved in large part by intellectual means. This allows interpretative skill to become a means of cultural distinction, and thus for a monopoly over interpretative resources by a strata of priestly intellectuals (cf. Schluchter, 1981: 23). The priest explains otherwise meaningless experiences through a Christian schematic, in terms of which they come to make sense, and can be integrated into a sensible life-plan. In this way, Christians become dependent upon the priest's exegesis of the world for their self-identity.

The structure of the Christian world-view is uniquely suited to the kind of interpretative privilege that the priest claims for himself. The reason for this, Nietzsche points out, is that Christian interpretations – in contrast to earlier magical, mythical and philosophical modes of thought – remove all criteria of truth from the sensible world of everyday experience, with the exception of experiences of hardship and bad conscience that serve as evidence of guilt and sin. The other-worldly structure of Christianity allows priests to create the view that all natural events are conditioned by invisible laws, causalities and forces to which they alone have access (Nietzsche, 1954: 627–9; 1967: 88–91). 'When the natural causes of a deed are no longer "natural", but thought of as caused by the conceptual specters of superstition, by "God", by "spirits", by "souls", as if they were merely "moral" consequences, as reward, punishment, hint, means of education, then the presupposition of knowledge has been destroyed' (Nietzsche, 1954: 630; cf. 1967: 115–16; 1982: 58). The narrative that reads all 'natural' or experienced events in terms of a shadow world of invisible actors and fictitious happenings produces a conceptual incapacity to engage reality, and thus deepens whatever de facto, politically maintained incapacity already exists. This, Nietzsche claims, is the priest's *greatest crime against humanity* (Nietzsche, 1954: 630).

The priest's intellectual authority resides not only in his ability to locate causal agents in a non-empirical, metaphysical world but also in his interpretation of suffering and bad conscience as empirical evidence for his exegesis. Since suffering produces a hope for redemption from suffering, the priest increases the likelihood that his interpretative authority will be accepted by tying the promise of redemption to acceptance of his exegesis. In this way, control over the resources of self-identity becomes a means of power.

We can see how Nietzsche's critique of Christianity provides an analysis of power that does not find its way neatly into standard definitions. Clearly the relationship between the Church and its followers is not one of oppression, as in the case of master and slave. Slaves do not harbor illusions that their interests are the same as their masters'. Rather, the relationship is one of domination: priests exercise power through their interpretative role in defining the wills of individuals. They control, as it were, the cognitive life of individuals – not directly, of course, but through their strategic location in reproducing a system of thought against a background of needs for meaning that are heightened and even induced by oppression and suffering. In exchange for obedience, the Church provides access to means of salvation (or, as Weber adds in discussing Protestant variants, means of legitimating good fortune). What makes this particular kind of power relation one of domination – a value-rational form of legitimate domination, in Weber's terms – is that although it is *not* exercised 'against the wills' of subordinates since their 'wills' are shaped by the relationship, this relationship nonetheless has a compulsory quality: priests have control over the means of salvation, and this control is used to secure obedience (Nietzsche, 1968a: 561–5; Weber, 1978: 490–2; cf. Nietzsche, 1974: 304–10).

At the same time, Nietzsche's critique builds on, or at least presupposes, a counterfactual account of interests. The 'willfulness' of the obedience does not mean that the power relationship is in the interests of subordinates. According to Nietzsche, the priestly rulers of the Church do not simply minister to the sufferings of their followers. They exploit suffering in such a way that they gain control over the capacities of sufferers to sustain their sense of subjectivity. Nietzsche views the priest 'type' as an ideologist who employs politically produced sufferings to solidify his interpretative authority, while destroying the autonomy of his followers by disconnecting reason from worldly situations (Nietzsche, 1954: 595–8; 1968a: 561–5; 1982: 48). This is why he can claim in discussing Pauline Christianity that 'with morality it becomes easiest to lead mankind by the nose' (Nietzsche, 1954: 621). What is wrong with priestly power is that it disconnects self-identity from self-directed practices. Power relations that do not allow individuals to identify themselves in terms of a consistent pattern of effects in the world must develop imaginary identities – and this is precisely what allows for and defines a relationship of domination. The counterfactual account of interests follows: humans are in a pathological condition when their identities are not the residuals of their practices – that is, when their practices are controlled by others, and their identities are tran-scendentally guaranteed. This is, as it were, an analytic account of Nietzsche's most important normative distinction between 'strength' and 'weakness'. Domination secures weakness in the form of a self-interpretation disconnected from practices.

Before summarizing Nietzsche's contributions to Weber's approach, we need to consider briefly Nietzsche's concept of the will to power. The problem is this: if, as Nietzsche argues, the world is will to power, does this not make any particular analysis of power beside the point? The answer is no: the analyses operate on different, although interrelated, levels in Nietzsche's thought. I have argued extensively elsewhere that in characterizing the world as will to power, Nietzsche develops a general relational ontology of practices (Warren, 1988b: Ch. 4). The concept simultaneously denotes the motivation to form a will, the interpretative structures within which wills are identified, and experiential conditions and resistances. Wills, Nietzsche argues in an important aphorism in *Beyond Good and Evil*, are ex post interpretative identities that reflect a narrative continuity of practices (Nietzsche, 1968b: 215–17). One interprets consistent effects of practices in terms of a unified origin, which evolves into the interpretation 'I'. Domination, however, is based on a broken link between practices and self-identity; identities that reflect domination are, in Nietzsche's terms, 'pathological' developments of will to power.

We find, then, the distinctions necessary to a relational definition of power within Nietzsche's general ontology of power. He chooses to call all practices 'power', but then distinguishes some of these as 'pathological' – that is, configurations of practice that displace self-identity into a realm of non-contingent, transcendental identities. Nietzsche's analysis thus fits the relational definition of power. It does so, however, without producing the two paradoxes of the standard elaboration. First, we can see that the fact that there is a conflict of interest does not mitigate the organization-building qualities of power. The instability of master–slave relations as compared to the stability of the Church testifies to this. But we can also see why conceptually: hierarchical relations that engage the wills of subordinates are less costly for the dominant. Obedience secured voluntarily does not require police, guards, or overseers. It does require guidance, discipline and codes of conduct. But these are internalized as part of the same interpretative structure that provides the payoff in meaning and identity for subordinates, and so is relatively easy to enforce. The power holder becomes a source of comfort, a guide to secure the promised rewards. As we shall see, it is for parallel reasons that Weber understands the power relations of bureaucracies – 'rational domination' – to be productive and dynamic: there is no overt conflict between the wills of subordinates and the tasks to which they are assigned in bureaucratic organizations. The personalities of bureaucrats are formed through their 'calling', which they understand in terms of the role they serve in a rationalized organization. Although Weber recognizes that the Protestant sense of 'calling' has long since disappeared, that we no longer have a choice but to work for rationalized organizations, these organizations still mold identities in ways that motivate. Every good manager knows that the essence of 'productive' power relations lies in inducing subordinates to do their best with guidance, recognition and the promise of future upward mobility. In exchange, managers gain loyalty, a proper attitude, a productive team player. In Foucault's terms, power becomes productive.

From this perspective, we can also see that the second paradox of the standard definition dissolves – the fact that domination involves obedience that is experienced as simultaneously compulsory and voluntary. One obeys because doing so provides meaning, an identity, a place, a purpose. In this sense, the obedience is essential to self-identity, and one 'willingly' obeys because the will depends on it. At the same time, the consequences of disobedience – loss of salvation, security, meaning and place – are so obvious that one may experience the same commands as compulsory, in the sense that to do otherwise is unthinkable.

WEBER'S ANALYSIS OF DOMINATION

Let us take a closer look at Weber's conception of domination to see whether it really takes the Nietzschean form I am suggesting. Clearly Weber does not attempt a general ontology of power, as does Nietzsche. Weber's view of the world does, of course, include many of the attributes that would follow from holding a Nietzschean ontology. For example, he views his objects of explanation as contingent practices ('actions'). And his explanations of social structures, types of individuals and historical logics refer back to these relationships. Weber is careful not to project metaphysical conceptions of subjectivity into individuality, nor an intrinsic logic into society or historical development (Warren, 1988c: 465–71). To do so would be to circumvent their explanation, by projecting conceptual origins rather than by locating contingent constellations of events. Finally, like Nietzsche, he views conflict as endemic to social life, even if it is channelled into peaceful pursuits and friendly rivalries.

What I am concerned to show here, however, is that Weber's comments on that subset of power relations he calls 'legitimate domination' express the Nietzschean insights I have outlined. This is clear even in his initial definitions, where Weber identifies limiting types of domination in terms of how individuals understand the relationship between their interests and the powers that structure their lives. Thus Weber distinguishes between

> . . . domination by virtue of a constellation of interests (in particular: by virtue of a position of monopoly), and by virtue of authority, i.e., the power to command the duty to obey. . . . The purest type of the former is monopolistic domination in the market; of the latter, patriarchal, magisterial, or princely power. In its purest form, the first is based upon influence derived exclusively from the possession of goods or marketable skills guaranteed in some way and acting upon the conduct of those so dominated, who remain, however, formally free and are motivated simply by the pursuit of their own interests. The latter kind of domination rests upon alleged absolute duty to obey, regardless of personal motives or interests. (Weber, 1978: 943)

In both cases, individuals enter into power relations 'willingly' and this is why Weber describes these relations as domination rather than, say, oppression. The difference between the two, however, turns on the extent to which an individual's subjectivity is defined by the relationship. In the ideal type of market domination, individuals remain cognitively competent; they can distinguish their interests from the interests of those they serve. In this sense, they remain, in Weber's terms, 'formally free'. In the second case, however, interests are defined through the relationship itself, and individuals lose, as it were, the cognitive competence to identify their distinctive interests. Their subjectivity is molded in the image of the power relation.

These are, of course, limiting types, so that the 'borderline between these two types of domination is fluid' (Weber, 1978: 943). Indeed, they interact. Weber uses the example of an economic monopoly: a monopoly over goods in the market will allow a dominant party to dictate terms of trade to those who need the goods and have no alternatives. Once such interactions are established, however, domination in the market can evolve into domination by authority. For example, a dominant firm will guarantee its monopoly by integrating suppliers and retailers into the organization, so that they become part of a hierarchical bureaucracy (Weber, 1978: 943–6). The relation of domination is no longer based solely on material interests, but also on recognized authority. Indeed, Weber holds that domination will tend to evolve in this direction, so that even the formal freedom of market domination will tend to produce bureaucratic domination, which involves, among other things, a loss of the ability to distinguish one's own subjectivity outside of relations of domination.

Such a situation is expressed in Weber's more narrow and explicit definition of domination as

> ... the situation in which the manifested will (*command*) of the ruler of rulers is meant to influence the conduct of one or more others (*the ruled*) and actually does influence it in such a way that their conduct to a socially relevant degree occurs as if the ruled had made the content of the command the maxim of their conduct for its very own sake. (Weber, 1978: 946)

It is clear in this definition that Weber does not polarize agency and relations of power, but internally relates them as does Nietzsche. This shows up, for example, when Weber argues that coercion and legitimate authority interact, rather than being opposite kinds of power, as they are often understood to be (Wrong, 1980: 38–40). In many instances coercive relations form the background conditions of legitimate authority. In the case of market relations, for example, a subordinate party is forced to accept the terms of trade of the dominant party. These will be 'guaranteed' in some way affecting the subordinate party's conduct – by a legal code that secures and enforces private property, binding contracts and the like. Thus the legal structure both lays out a framework of formally free exchanges between juridically free and equal subjects, and routinizes these exchanges in ways that come to define the subject parties: retailers become branch offices of monopolistic distributors; workers become integrated into hierarchical chains of command. Free exchanges evolve into organizational hierarchies which coordinate individuals through rules, disciplines, codes of conduct and offices. They become, as it were, a way of life for the parties to the exchange, engaging and defining identities in ways that go beyond the initial motivations and add a layer of determination to the structural conditions of the exchange. Routines allow the coercive backgrounds of these exchanges to recede as individuals become integrated into the exchange in such ways that they no longer experience overt conflicts of interest. Thus for Weber, unlike most contemporary social scientists, coercion and legitimate authority are often two sides of the same coin. Here we can see that the paradox involving willing acceptance of coercive relations is not really a paradox at all, but instead describes two complementary moments of power relations that have insinuated themselves into individual identities.

Weber does not conceive individuals subject to domination as passive victims. The insinuation of power into self-identity can occur only because individuals struggle to satisfy what Weber sometimes calls 'ideal' interests through the relations in which they find themselves entangled.[4] This is not always clear in Weber's writings because he does not always use the term 'interest' carefully. Often, as in the above definitions of domination, the term simply refers to material gain. But he also makes use of a broader conception of interests, sometimes insisting that interests are never just 'material', but also affective, ideal, rational and so on (e.g. Weber, 1978: 499). It is this broader conception of interest that is implied in his definition of social action as behavior oriented toward other persons to which the actor ascribes a meaning (Weber, 1978: 4). Indeed, Weber's ontology of social action builds on an assumption that 'meaning' is a general human *need*, one closely linked to the reflexive constitution of the self. It is in this sense that interests are not only material, but also what Weber sometimes calls 'ideal': they are closely linked to a person's reflexive constitution of the self from within available material and cultural resources. This is why Weber argues that domination by virtue of material interests is much more likely to be experienced as oppressive than domination by authority, even though the latter usually includes and goes beyond the former (Weber, 1978: 946). And it most certainly explains why Weber claims that relations of domination founded on 'constellations of [material] interests' alone are unstable bases of organization: material interests are never enough to constitute 'meaning', that is, to orient/constitute the self in such a way that institutional practices can and do continue.

This same idea appears in the seemingly odd and ironically Kantian wording of Weber's definition of domination as conduct that 'occurs as if the ruled had made the content of the command the maxim of their conduct for its very own sake' (Weber, 1978: 946). This means that subordinate parties obey because their 'ideal interests' are engaged and defined through the system of attributions that legitimizes the power relation. From this perspective we can see that Weber's well-known types of legitimate domination – traditional, charismatic and rational – are distinguished by the different ways in which the subordinate parties define their identities.[5] Each constitutes different kinds of selves according to the actions that are required of them: as a member of a family or a tribe; as an instrument of God, the nation, or a leader; as an official, a legal-juridical person with rights, and so on. Insofar as subordinate parties orient their activities and explain their lives through these identities, the power relation is legitimate and justified. In each case, self-definition is integrated into the practices required by the power relation, and the stability of the power relation depends on 'meaningfully' constituted practices within the relationship such that agent-identities are formed. This point is reinforced by our intuitive understanding that a power relationship that comes into question – that is, identified *as* a power relation by subordinates – is less powerful and stable than one accepted without question.

One of the many things that Weber seems to have learned from Nietzsche and integrated into his conception of power, then, is that 'meaninglessness' is an untenable situation. Humans need to explain to themselves and others their social fortunes and misfortunes, which also means that they need to ascribe meaning to themselves as social subjects. This is true not just for those who are dominated, but also those who dominate. With respect to a dominating group, for example, Weber comments that

. . . justification of its legitimacy is much more than a matter of theoretical or philosophical speculation; it rather constitutes the basis of very real differences in the empirical structure of domination. The reason for this fact lies in the generally observable need of any power, or even of any advantage of life, to justify itself.

The fates of human beings are not equal. Men differ in their states of health or wealth or social status or what not. Simple observation shows that in every such situation he who is more favored feels the never ceasing need to look upon his position as in some way 'legitimate', upon his advantage as 'deserved', and the other's disadvantage as being brought about by the latter's 'fault'. . . .

This same need makes itself felt in the relations between positively and negatively privileged groups of human beings. Every highly privileged group develops the myth of its natural, especially its blood, superiority. Under conditions of stable distribution of power and, consequently, status order, that myth is accepted by the negatively privileged strata. (Weber, 1978: 953)

Similarly in his sociology of religion Weber claims that with the rise of rational religions, general 'religious needs' (that is, needs for meaning) are transformed into a 'need for an ethical interpretation of the "meaning" of the distribution of fortunes among men' (Weber, 1946: 270, 275). Weber's formulations imply that subordinates are never passively 'constituted' as subjects by external relations. They may accept a ruling 'myth' that legitimizes domination, but they do so only when they can define their own identities in and through it, and they often transform these myths in the process, providing a key impetus for cultural evolution.

In terms of Weber's ontology of social action, such needs are not external to social action, but part of what makes it an 'action' rather than a mere behavior. Every act has a more or less explicit set of reasons and justifications attached to it that are so fundamental as to situate the individual qua subject/agent in relation to existing material and cultural resources. Indeed, for Weber, it is not proper to speak of social action at all prior to the emergence of capacities involving an individual's reflexive monitoring of conduct in social situations, as in the case of purely traditional and affective behavior (Weber, 1978: 25). As Charles Taylor has argued, this process of monitoring one's own motives and the ability to give a meaningful account of one's conduct is what defines agent capacities (Taylor, 1985: Chs 1–2). It is here that we find Weber's counterfactual account of interests: he conceptualizes the need for meaning/subjective identity in a way that assumes the possibility of agency. The guiding normative proposition of his studies is that there is a general interest in directing and affecting one's life, an interest that is both cultivated and undermined within rationalized cultures. This interest is realized in a personality constituted by the 'consistency of its inner relationship to certain ultimate values and meanings of life, which are turned into purposes and thus into teleologically rational action' (Weber, 1975: 192; cf.

Löwith, 1982: 45–6; Portis, 1978; Schluchter, 1979: 73–4). A person has a capacity for agency when he or she can combine a consistent system of values (upon which the stability of identity and the meaningfulness of actions depends) with actual behavior, connecting values to worldly effects (Schluchter, 1979: 76–92). We see, then, that Weber has a conception of what kinds of interests are violated within power relations. In this sense, Weber's account of power, like Nietzsche's, retains its critical edge, distinguishing social relations in terms of the kinds of individuals they constitute.

Much of Weber's substantive work involves studies of these relations in terms framed by this normative potential. Rational domination displaces a potential for a value-rational monitoring of conduct which is, as it were, the progressive moment of rationalized culture. Bureaucratic rationalization in particular is problematic because it represents a potential for rational agency that is undermined by the social formations within which it developed. Thus, while bureaucracies provide identities for their members through status, offices, rational codes of conduct and the like, these identities are not integrated into the content and goals of their actions. Their actions serve the ends of the organization – making products and delivering services, for example. These are dictated by processes over which the bureaucrat has little control, such as political leaders and markets. Weber's concern with this bifurcation of interests and actions is that it destroys capacities for responsible agency by divorcing the rationality of means and the rationality of ends (Weber, 1946: Ch. IV; 1978: Appendix II). It is in this sense that domination within bureaucratic hierarchies violates an interest in, and potential for, rational agency, and why Weber saw bureaucratic power relations as the most urgent problem for western societies. Weber did not believe, of course, that bureaucratic domination could be eliminated from modern societies. For this reason he limited the goals of his political theory to containing bureaucratic rule through liberal and pluralist institutional devices, a topic I have discussed elsewhere (Warren, 1988a).

We can see, then, that Weber retains the normative thrust of the relational conception of power, that is, its concern with identifying power in terms of conflicts of interest. But he also conceptualizes power relations deeply, in terms of the ways they constitute individuals' self-understandings. This is what allows Weber to span the other great divide in standard conceptions of power: whether power should be understood 'negatively' as a conflictual relationship between individuals ('power over'), or 'positively' as an emergent organizational capacity ('power to'). From Weber's perspective, we can see that power becomes 'productive' (to use Foucault's terms) just when it becomes domination proper – that is, when it begins to work through defining subjective meanings and identities. Intuitively, we can see that unless a subordinate is *motivated* to do something there cannot be power over his or her capacities of agency. Without this, power is no longer a social relation. The capacities of agency of one person are not enlisted by another, and the relation loses its organization-building qualities.

This point is clear even in the most obvious kind of power, the threat to use violence against a subordinate (Wrong, 1980: 26). The use of violence signifies that the dominant party has become powerless because it has failed to engage the subordinate's will, and thus cannot make use of the capacities of the subordinate as an agent. This is no doubt why Hannah Arendt, an advocate of the view of power as an emergent organizational capacity, argues that 'power and violence are opposites; where one rules absolutely, the other is absent. Violence appears where power is in jeopardy, but left to its own course it ends in power's disappearance. . . . to speak of non-violent power is actually redundant' (Arendt, 1969: 56). What Arendt misses and Weber does not, however, is that the *threat* of violence, or coercion, is a background condition of all relations of power, including organizationally productive ones. What distinguishes violence and power in Weber's perspective is not that they are opposites, but that where power is *only* coercive, 'ideal' interests will not be engaged, and the subordinate's will cannot be oriented toward the organizational tasks at hand. This is why coercive relations by themselves are unstable bases for organizations. Indeed, a power structure that does not engage ideal interests may find that these interests are satisfied with alternative identities that undermine the power structure. A person might rely on identities provided by the Church, by labor unions, by resistance movements, by ethnic or racial identities, and so on, each of which provides a point of resistance. Interestingly, considerations such as these are embedded in Gramsci's notions of hegemonic and counter-hegemonic cultures: a hegemonic culture develops identities that reinforce relations of coercion, while a counter-hegemonic culture develops identities that are outside of these re-lations. In the latter case, prevailing power relations are 'stripped down' to coercion, and this is what renders them vulnerable to change.[6]

CONCLUSION

We can see, then, why the standard appropriations of Weber's relational defi-nition of power are wrong: they ascribe a transparency to agents in order to identify overt conflicts of interest. In so doing, however, they miss two import-ant dimensions of power manifest in two paradoxes. The first paradox is that this view requires that we hold that relations of overt conflict can produce organiz-ational power. Yet, on the face of it, organizational power seems to depend on cooperative relations. The second paradox is that the most effective power relations elicit voluntary obedience, an obedience which is (paradoxically) as-sured by coercive means. Both paradoxes dissolve when we look at Weber's understanding of power in light of his Nietzschean problematic. Weber, like Nietzsche, focuses on how relations of domination form the identities of the individuals involved. A relationship of domination is not one that takes place between two pre-constituted agents. Because self-experiences of agency depend on social resources, forms of agency develop within these relations themselves.

This is why experiences of agency that depend on a power relation can actually reinforce the relation against the interests of the subordinate party. Yet Weber's critical insight – one expressed by Gramsci, hinted at by Foucault and picked up by Habermas – is that relations of domination can also develop capacities for agency through (ideological) legitimations. These become promises which are materialized in expectations, often to the point of rendering relations of domination vulnerable. Neither Nietzsche nor Weber develops his conceptions of power in this direction, but they do both provide us with some of the critical resources for doing so.

Department of Government
Georgetown University, Washington DC

NOTES

1 Taylor (1990) argues in a similar vein that an intrinsic relationship exists between moral identity and human agency.

2 Weber (1946: Ch. XI; 1978: 499) mistakenly reduces Nietzsche's account of the origins of salvation religion to his account of 'ressentiment'.

3 Compare Weber's discussion of the causality of religious ideas: 'Not ideas, but material and ideal interests, directly govern men's conduct. Yet very frequently the "world images" that have been created by "ideas" have, like switchmen, determined the tracks along which action has been pushed by the dynamics of interest. "From what" and "for what" one wished to be redeemed and, let us not forget, "could be" redeemed, depended upon one's image of the world' (Weber, 1946: 280).

4 See note 3 above.

5 'Psychologically, the command may have achieved its effect upon the ruled either through empathy or through inspiration or through persuasion by rational argument, or through some combination of these three principal types of influence of one person over another' (Weber, 1978: 946).

6 Weber occasionally draws conclusions that are not unlike Gramsci's. For example, he writes that under 'conditions of stable distributions of power' justifying myths are accepted by the 'negatively privileged strata'. 'Such a situation exists as long as the masses continue in that natural state of theirs in which thought about the order of domination remains but little developed, which means, *as long as no urgent needs render the state of affairs "problematical".* But in times in which the class situation has become unambiguously and openly visible to everyone as a factor determining every man's individual fate, that very myth of the highly privileged about everyone having deserved his particular lot has often become one of the most passionately hated objects of attack' (Weber, 1978: 953); emphasis added.

BIBLIOGRAPHY

Arendt, H. (1969) *On Violence*. New York: Harcourt Brace Jovanovich.

Connolly, W. (1983) *The Terms of Political Discourse*, 2nd edn. Princeton, NJ: Princeton University Press.

Foucault, M. (1983) 'The Subject and Power', in H. Dreyfus and P. Rabinow (eds) *Michel Foucault: Beyond Structuralism and Hermeneutics*, 2nd edn, pp. 208–26. Chicago: University of Chicago Press.

Hekman, S. (1983) *Weber: The Ideal Type, and Contemporary Social Theory.* Notre Dame, IN: University of Notre Dame Press.

Hennis, W. (1987) 'Personality and Life Orders: Max Weber's Theme', in S. Whimster and S. Lash (eds) *Max Weber and Modernity*, pp. 52–74. London: Allen & Unwin.

Hennis, W. (1988) *Max Weber: Essays in Reconstruction*, trans. K. Tribe. London: Allen & Unwin.

Löwith, K. (1982) *Max Weber and Karl Marx*, trans. H. Fantel. London: Allen & Unwin.

Lukes, S. (1974) *Power: A Radical View.* London: Macmillan.

Mitzman, A. (1970) *The Iron Cage.* New York: Knopf.

Nietzsche, F. (1954) *The Antichrist*, in *The Portable Nietzsche*, ed. and trans. W. Kaufmann. New York: Viking Press.

Nietzsche, F. (1967) *The Will to Power*, ed. W. Kaufmann, trans. W. Kaufmann and R. J. Hollingdale. New York: Random House.

Nietzsche, F. (1968a) *On the Genealogy of Morals*, in *The Basic Writings of Nietzsche*, ed. and trans. W. Kaufmann. New York: Random House.

Nietzsche, F. (1968b) *Beyond Good and Evil*, in *The Basic Writings of Nietzsche*, ed. and trans. W. Kaufmann. New York: Random House.

Nietzsche, F. (1974) *The Gay Science*, trans. W. Kaufmann. New York: Random House.

Nietzsche, F. (1982) *Daybreak*, trans. R. J. Hollingdale. Cambridge: Cambridge University Press.

Oppenheim, F. (1981) *Political Concepts.* Chicago: University of Chicago Press.

Parsons, T. (1960) *Structure and Stress in Modern Societies.* New York: Free Press.

Portis, E. B. (1978) 'Max Weber's Theory of Personality', *Sociological Inquiry* 48: 113–20.

Scaff, L. (1984) 'Weber Before Weberian Sociology', *British Journal of Sociology* 35: 190–215.

Schluchter, W. (1979) 'Value Neutrality and the Ethics of Responsibility', in G. Roth and W. Schluchter, *Max Weber's Vision of History.* Berkeley and Los Angeles, CA: University of California Press.

Schluchter, W. (1981) *The Rise of Western Rationalism.* Berkeley, CA: University of California Press.

Schroeder, R. (1987) 'Nietzsche and Weber: Two "Prophets" of the Modern World', in S. Lash and S. Whimster (eds) *Max Weber, Rationality, and Modernity*, pp. 207–21. London: Allen & Unwin.

Taylor, C. (1985) *Human Agency and Language: Philosophical Papers*, Vol. 1. Cambridge: Cambridge University Press.

Taylor, C. (1990) *Sources of the Self.* Cambridge, MA: Harvard University Press.

Warren, M. (1988a) 'Max Weber's Liberalism for a Nietzschean World', *American Political Science Review* 82: 31–50.

Warren, M. (1988b) *Nietzsche and Political Thought.* Cambridge, MA: MIT Press.

Warren, M. (1988c) 'Marx and Methodological Individualism', *Philosophy of the Social Sciences* 18: 447–76.

Weber, M. (1946) *From Max Weber*, ed. and trans. H. Gerth and C. W. Mills. New York: Oxford University Press.

Weber, M. (1949) *The Methodology of the Social Sciences*, ed. and trans. E. Shils and H. Finch. New York: Free Press.

Weber, M. (1975) *Roscher and Knies: The Logical Problems of Historical Economics*, trans. G. Oakes. New York: Free Press.

Weber, M. (1978) *Economy and Society*, ed. G. Roth and C. Wittich. Berkeley: University of California Press.

Wrong, D. (1980) *Power: Its Forms, Bases, and Uses*. New York: Harper & Row.

HISTORY OF THE HUMAN SCIENCES   Vol. 5 No. 3
© 1992 SAGE (London, Newbury Park and New Delhi)   pp. 39–56

'The next village': modernity, memory and the Holocaust

PETER BARHAM

Alongside more salutary benefits, the Holocaust is one of the distinctive products of modernity, the lives not merely of individual survivors but of nations and subsequent generations have been marked by the scars of the genocide, and the remembrance of the Holocaust has entered deeply into modern politics. A number of recent publications offer the opportunity to reassess some of the problems of traumatic memory and the question of how we are to relate to the tragedies of the past.

THE MORAL VIOLATIONS OF AUSCHWITZ

Drawing on the Fortunoff Video Archive for Holocaust Testimonies established at Yale University, Lawrence Langer has produced a profound yet troubling analysis of the oral narratives of Holocaust survivors.[1] Perhaps the most shocking thing about these testimonies is that there is a powerful sense in which some four decades later most of these witnesses have never been able to leave the concentration camp; or, so far as they have left it, they have merely gone to the next village and have the camp still within view, and when the wind gets up find themselves unprotected against the onslaught of its sounds and odours. In her memoirs of her camp experiences, the *émigrée* French writer Charlotte Delbo lends a representative emphasis when she describes how she does not so much live with Auschwitz in her post-camp existence as live *beside* it.[2] Langer does not supply data on the postwar lives of the witnesses he discusses but from the detail that emerges it is plain that these are not incapacitated people and many of them have been successful in their occupations, married and brought up families. Nevertheless, despite the apparent continuity of these lives, and the solidity of their reconstructive efforts, they are in diverse ways still fettered by the power of a remembrance that asserts the inextinguishable presence of another place and time and frequently disrupts the flow of their narratives and their search for a form through which to cohere their experiences. The surviving victim may come to feel divided by a past that hinders the growth of an integrated perspective. As one witness put it, 'You have one vision of life and I have two'.[3] A process of renewal that commenced with the recapture of forgotten habits – how to use a toothbrush, toilet paper, a knife and fork – and forgotten tastes and smells – blossom, the sweet scent of rain in spring – finds itself vulnerable to the blasts of the 'counter-time' of Auschwitz, where the rain stinks of diarrhoea and the winds carry the odour of burning flesh.

The metaphor of spatial proximity helps to identify the sense of temporal dislocation and subversion that witnesses experience. Ostensibly these are stories of a progressive distancing from a set of traumatic events that happened in a time and place quite distinct from the present, but as Langer describes it the 'plot' enforces a very different kind of operation. 'The "story" is the chronological narrative, beginning with "I was born" and ending with "I was liberated".' By contrast, the 'plot':

> . . . reveals the witness seized by instead of selecting incidents, memory's confrontation with incidents embedded in moments of trauma. . . . Auschwitz as story enables us to pass through and beyond the place, horrible as it may be, while Auschwitz as plot stops the chronological clock and fixes the moment permanently in memory and imagination, immune to the vicissitudes of time.[4]

The solicitations of deep memory are invariably those of loss and defilement. Life continues, 'but in two temporal directions at once, the future unable to escape the grip of a memory laden with grief. "I have children", reports one former victim. "I have my family. But I can't take full satisfaction in the achievements of my children today because part of my present life is my remembrance, my memory of what happened then, and it casts a shadow over my life today."'[5] For Charlotte Delbo the 'counter-time' of Auschwitz exists in a hardened 'skin of memory', buried in a form of 'deep memory' distinct from the 'common memory' of her present-day self, but for Delbo herself, as for others, on occasions the skin 'bursts and gives back its contents' and for many of the witnesses whom Langer discusses, the boundary between past and present is in any case evidently much less impregnable.[6]

Witnesses are gripped by different forms of remembrance; for example, anguished memory in which memory functions not to repair the broken dialogue with an unmastered and incomprehensible past but to assault and divide, and where people are in consequence 'haunted by the untransfigured actuality of what they recall'.[7] As Langer aptly suggests, from these witnesses we learn the meaning of Nietzsche's remark that 'without forgetting it is quite impossible to *live* at all'.[8] So, for example, at a selection for work in the Kovno ghetto, Betty K. tried to conceal her child in a coat but it was discovered and taken away from her. Betty K. was then dispatched by train to a concentration camp and she describes how the train journey seemed both to initiate and to complete her life-cycle: 'The way I felt,' she says, 'I was *born* on that train and I *died* on that train.'[9] Borrowing from Maurice Blanchot, Langer speaks of the 'died event' in contrast to the 'lived event' in the experience of former victims and the paradox of how one survives a 'died event'. Under the impact of a 'died event' (the seizure of Betty K.'s child, for example), the survivor is drawn into a non-relation (the relationship to the absent child) from which she cannot be excused (for example, Betty's anguish over her responsibility for the loss of her child, 'I don't know if it was by my doing, or when it was done, or how . . .'). The person may indeed survive but the terms of existence available to her are those of living under the threat of a death or dying which has already taken place. Blanchot's thought is certainly difficult to grasp but it helps us to understand the *finality* of the 'died event' and to recognize it as a determinate ending, no matter how many new beginnings may come after it.[10]

Where anguished memory strives, albeit unsuccessfully, to discover a form for traumatic experience, and to bring the past into a more tolerable relation to the present, the voice of humiliated memory is that of unrelieved distress, enforced not merely by the unrelieved recall of past events but also by the strain between the 'choices' that former victims were driven to make and the evaluative frames in which they assess their actions now. Humiliated memory 'records those moments when history failed the individual and left him victim to what Nietzsche called the "blind power of facts . . . the tyranny of the actual". It can retreat to no ideal world of thought as consolation to carry it through the trying times.'[11] For example:

We were sleeping on the floor and next to me was another camp inmate. I don't know how old he was – he looked old. And we just got our ration of bread, and he was already so sick that he couldn't eat that bread. And I was laying next to him, waiting that he should die, so that I can [prolonged pause] *grab* his bread.[12]

Humiliated memory is *prospective* as well as retrospective. 'Everything is in *front* of me,' Leon H. says, 'I can't get rid of it.' Leon H. suffered first the murder of his mother and father; then the death of his younger brother who was late for roll-call in the camp and was beaten so badly that he died in his brother's arms; and finally the death of his older brother who, refusing to eat garbage and slowly wasting away, was judged not worth saving and left to freeze to death outside the barracks:

How can you live with that? Everybody was gone from me. . . . Since then I couldn't get somebody. I live in torture all these years. Suicide [in tears now] was on my mind. But I had family [meaning his *present* family]; I loved them so much. How do you explain that? How do you tell?[13]

As Langer describes, the contradictions and confusions of tense and chronology here dramatize how impossible it is for the victim to 'get over' his loss. The Holocaust experience 'murdered part of the future even for those who survived it' and for most of these witnesses it is an unfinished narrative in which the historical closure of 'liberation' possesses little or no significance.[14] Ostensibly these testimonies are stories about how the narrators survived but as Langer powerfully brings out they are in essence not so much stories of survival as of deprival. The real subjects of the narratives are not so much the surviving witnesses as those who perished and the lives of the witnesses are defined not merely by their own survival but by the circumstances in which those closest to them went to their doom. In their anguished probings the witnesses relentlessly interrogate the circumstances in which their relatives died, their own powerlessness, and not least their own actions throughout these hideous years, in an endless and unanswered quest for some moral resolution.

There is, however, also a troubling dimension to Langer's book that comes from the complaints he ventures about the language of contemporary moral thought. According to Langer, the survivors feel betrayed by a world which has saddled them with values that proved useless in the presence of catastrophe. So, for example, the conventional belief that individuals possess some measure of control over their destiny not infrequently proved disabling and inhibited victims from adopting a course of action that might at the very least have enhanced their chances of survival. Indeed, on crucial occasions survivors were evidently only able to take actions that turned out to save their lives by emptying their minds of conventional reasons for not doing what they were about to do.

However, Langer seems to require of a set of beliefs and values that they serve as a kind of all-weather anorak to sustain quite unpredictable and, on any reasonable understanding, non-human conditions and he considers that the testimonies he discusses raise the 'issue of whether the idea of the good life before Auschwitz, and the premises on which it was built, were of any use to the victim of the Holocaust universe'.[15] The unreconciled understandings of witnesses, he argues, do 'much to question the reality of moral theories' and to mock conceptual efforts throughout the history of western philosophy which have tried 'to determine the relationship between duty and the good life, what it is right to do and what it is good to be'.[16]

He reserves a special animus for Charles Taylor's account in *Sources of the Self* of the moral topography of human lives.[17] In contrast to naturalistic treatments of the self, Taylor claims that selves can only be understood as beings who exist in a space of concerns or questions that provides the framework or constitutive horizon in which they must orientate themselves and endeavour to find their way. At the core of the aspirations of the self in this space of questions is a 'form of craving which is ineradicable from human life' to 'seek and find an orientation to the good', and to 'be rightly placed in relation to the good'.[18] Similarly, the reason that the need to make sense of our lives as a story holds such importance for us is that we exist in a space of 'questions which only a narrative can answer. In order to have a sense of who we are, we have to have a notion of how we have become, and of where we are going.'[19]

Taylor's claim that it is impossible for us to do without frameworks is, Langer argues, not so much contradicted as discarded by most Holocaust witnesses. To step outside such constitutive horizons, Taylor writes, 'would be tantamount to stepping outside what we would recognize as integral, that is, undamaged human personhood'.[20] Former victims evidently have been forced over these horizons and their personhood has clearly been damaged but the fault, suggests Langer, 'may lie with the vocabulary of moral theory rather than with the individual who exists precariously in spite of it'.[21] On Langer's reading, Taylor is unduly preoccupied with a quest for unity as the ideal of moral identity and is in consequence blind to the harsh realities that have produced multiple or dispersed identities and the typically diminished selves of the post-Holocaust world.

But this is a curious and, in the light of Langer's achievement in this book, somewhat ironic interpretation of Taylor. In the first place, Taylor (and Langer lends somewhat grudging acknowledgement to this) helps us to understand the enormity of the violations that have been inflicted on Holocaust victims, to get a measure of what, quite beyond the direct suffering they experienced in the camps themselves, has gone desperately awry in their lives; and he does so, not as Langer thinks by positing a pristine space of moral unity, but by outlining the moral contours in which human agents inevitably have to try to make their way and from within which in most times and places human agents are able to achieve some form of at least minimally successful narrative resolution.[22] Unsurprisingly perhaps, Langer is struck most forcibly by the unreconciled understandings of his witnesses and the dismal failure of their efforts at narrative resolution. Certainly this is so but what must strike us also is the extent to which the assumptions, aspirations and cravings Taylor identifies are shared by the witnesses themselves. To put it slightly differently, it is only in the light of such assumptions, aspirations and cravings that the preoccupations and concerns of the witnesses are at all intelligible to us. Similarly, it is only by locating them – their desperate attempts to orient themselves and find answers to unanswerable questions – within the contours of the sort of moral universe that Taylor describes that we are able to give an account of what their anguish consists in; and, most importantly, it is only because these former victims implicitly locate themselves in such a universe that they suffer such anguish and humiliation.

Langer seems to ask that we try to narrow the gap that separates us (and also victims in their present-day situations) from these horrific events and revise the vocabulary of moral theory to include the situation-based ethics of the concentration camps. But it is not obvious that this is either a feasible or a desirable task. The gap which both we as audience and surviving witnesses themselves experience is a measure of the extent of the dehumanization to which victims were subjected; and hence their inevitable difficulty in understanding it, in coping with the remembrance of what became of them and how they acted, under these circumstances. The strength of Langer's study, I would argue, is that he amply demonstrates the extent and depth of the moral violations inflicted by the Holocaust. So, for example, he describes how he is tempted to see the eventual suicide of the Auschwitz survivor and Belgian writer Jean Amery as 'an admission of the final triumph of humiliated memory, that is, of the ultimate failure to escape the assaults on the moral self during his Holocaust-determined existence'.[23] However, Langer gives the impression that the experience of the camps would not have been so devastating if victims like Jean Amery had been able to shed their moral selves and sensitivities. Perhaps indeed the consequences of the Holocaust would have been less painful if they had been able to do so; but in that case the record of the Holocaust would not have been the record of a specifically human tragedy. Take away this framework and we cease to understand the Holocaust as a specifically human tragedy. It is precisely these assaults on the moral self that enable us to understand the kind of atrocity that the Holocaust was and to distinguish it from (say) the maltreatment and extermination of an equivalent number of goats.

MODERNITY AND TRADITION

In an obvious sense, of course, the unreconciled understandings of Holocaust witnesses belong to themselves alone but we can also hear in them the conflictual and sometimes anguished probings of a number of exemplary modern figures who, though they have not known the insides of the concentration camps, have experienced different moments in the dislocations and ravages of the decades that culminated in the Holocaust. In an illuminating discussion of the characteristic 'structures of consciousness' of Franz Kafka, Walter Benjamin and Gershom Scholem, Robert Alter explores the unreconciled understandings of these three 'post-traditional' Jewish writers who, situated in a liminal realm between tradition and modernity, gazed without illusion on the collapse they witnessed all about them, but were continually drawn to search in the rubble for signs of the traditional moral landscape.[24] Over the long years of their friendship, Benjamin and Scholem shared a perception of Kafka as the 'post-traditional' writer who 'above all others mapped out the spiritual territory of the modern condition'.[25] In a poem on Benjamin's autobiographical *One-Way Street* Scholem reflected:

In the old days all roads led
To God and his name, somehow.

We are not pious [Wir sind nicht fromm].
We remain in the Profane,
And where God once stood now stands: Melancholy.

For both of them, Kafka was 'the writer who gazed unblinking into the heart of this melancholy but at the same time could not help seeing the ghostly lineaments of the landscape of the old days'.[26] And in the paradox of Kafka's desolate bureaucratic universe we can detect the anguish of Langer's witnesses, torn between the untransfigured reality of their memories and the constitutive grip of traditional moral horizons, for though in Kafka's landscape the outward signs of tradition have been all but demolished, at the same time 'the classic Jewish triad of revelation, law and commentary virtually defines his imaginative world, whose protagonists at once cannot do without these categories and cannot understand them, tolerate them, live by them'.[27]

Much of Benjamin's writing in the last two decades of his life is pierced by a terrible sense of estrangement from a harmonious past, and the angel of history whom he famously describes as propelled into the future by the storm of progress, his face turned towards the receding vistas of tradition, while the pile of debris before him grows ever higher, is as Alter aptly remarks a 'kind of dumbfounded refugee from the world of religious symbolism', not an 'annunciating angelman but witnessing man, allegorically endowed with the terrible power of seeing things utterly devoid of illusion'.[28] Out of the ruins of memory, the 'detritus of history' as he termed it, Benjamin struggled to excavate a connection with the distant world of origins and the *Theses on the Philosophy of History* composed in 1940 in the months before his suicide, convey the force of an experience of the past that is at once mystical and traumatic. The historical articulation of the past, he observed, does not mean representing the past 'the way it really was', but rather is the attempt to 'seize hold of a memory as it flashes up at a moment of danger'.[29]

In a commentary on a little fiction of Kafka's, called as it happens *The Next Village*, in which a grandfather, looking back over his life, reflects on the paradox of how it seems so foreshortened that the span of a long life apparently does not allow sufficient time even for a ride over to the next village, Benjamin gives the interpretation:

> . . . the true measure of life is remembrance. Retrospectively, it traverses life with the speed of lightning. As quickly as one turns back a few pages, it has gone back from the next village to the point where the rider decided to set off. He whose life has turned into writing, like old people's, likes to read this writing only backward. Only so does he meet himself, and only so – in flight from the present – can his life be understood.[30]

Such is the power of remembrance that when we travel back with such lightning rapidity, it seems as though we have not had time to go further than the next village. Benjamin's angel was already aghast at the debris of modern history, but contemporary aspirations towards the recovery of origins must pass through the neighbouring village that is the legacy of the Holocaust. The next village, we might say, is the stuff that traumatic memories are made of. And then we might reasonably ask whether the span even of a long life allows sufficient time to come to terms with, and transcend, such memories.

'OŚWIĘCIM' AND 'AUSCHWITZ'

In Silesia in southern Poland, close to the confluence of the Sola and Vistula rivers, there is an industrial town called Oświęcim, better known in the West as Auschwitz, the name the Germans gave not merely to the town but to the complex of concentration camps established adjacent to it. According to a British journalist, present-day Auschwitz 'is a place which needs a pseudonym, for who would want to admit that they have made their home at Auschwitz? It is as if the Polish name was essential for any narrative plausibility.'[31] The questions raised by this remark embrace not only the consciousness of the people who happen to live in the town next to the concentration camps but also the actuality of Poland as the site of the Holocaust (in addition to Auschwitz-Birkenau there were, of course, a large number of other concentration and extermination camps), and therefore the legacy of the Holocaust in the Polish national consciousness or, as might be said, the condition of Poland itself as 'the next village'. Yet the writer, of course, also implies a particular stance on how we are to answer these questions, not least an attitude towards the Poles and the suggestion that there is something duplicitous or shameful about Polish dealings over the memory of the Holocaust. In doing so he touches, unwittingly perhaps, on the vexed and painful history of conflicting narratives from western and Polish sources in the assessment of the Holocaust, particularly as these concern the relations between Poles and Jews in the immediate Polish past, and the claims of Jewish memories over Polish memories. So, for example, the published memoirs of Jewish survivors from occupied Poland are unquestionably profoundly shocking, sometimes searingly so, and the perpetrators of Polish violence against the Jews evidently included rather more than the peasantry.[32]

These issues are still live ones and a collection edited by Carol Rittner and John Roth, though it treats specifically the controversy over the Carmelite convent at Auschwitz, inevitably discusses also the longer history of conflict between Polish and Jewish remembrance.[33] 'Auschwitz' and 'Oświęcim', writes Emanuel Tanay, a Jewish Holocaust survivor, one location, two memories.[34] For westerners accustomed to the remembrance of 'Auschwitz' as the symbol of the Holocaust, and the intense scholarly effort that has accompanied it, it comes as something of a shock to discover that to a considerable extent for more than 40 years at least the concept of the Holocaust did not exist in Polish consciousness. For Poles the significant focus of remembrance has been 'Oświęcim' as a national symbol of the German occupation and a memorial to the three million Poles who died (most, though not all, at German hands) during the war, and though the records and practices around 'Oświęcim' have made some acknowledgement of the Jews, they have done so fleetingly and ambiguously and can legitimately be accused of having minimalized the nature and extent of Jewish suffering, and more particulary the drastic and wholly specific designs of the Third Reich in embarking on the 'final solution' of European Jewry. 'The sad fact', remarks Stanislaw Krajewski, one of the few remaining members of the Polish-Jewish community in Poland, 'is that most Poles do not recognise the exceptional character of the Nazi project to wipe out the Jewish people. They either poorly understand, or ignore altogether, the Jewish significance of Auschwitz.'[35]

In a percipient article by a Polish scholar on Polish attitudes towards the Jews published in 1987, Aleksander Smolar stated bluntly: 'Until quite recently, and for several decades, systematic attempts were made to eliminate the Jews from Polish memory'.[36] Smolar goes on to argue that whereas in the West the cumulative evidence of the Holocaust had traumatic effects and 'revealed the ugly, irrational side of a civilization built on the premise of technical rationality', in Poland the elimination of three million Polish Jews, mostly by starvation or extermination – some 90 percent of the prewar Polish-Jewish population – never provoked a shock to the collective consciousness.[37] The peculiarity of Poland, as Smolar tellingly remarks, is that only here has anti-Semitism been perceived as compatible both with patriotism and with democracy. Indeed 'the experience at the time of war and in the immediate postwar period served mostly to strengthen old resentments and revive traditional hostility'. Moreover, the Poles 'having suffered much heavier losses than their allies in the West, and entering upon yet another era of foreign domination, have had little time to worry about a crisis of civilization, let alone indulge in Christian-European remorse with regard to the Jews'.[38] Furthermore over the decades of Soviet domination the Polish population depended very heavily on the Church as a buttress against hostile influences and the time was hardly propitious in which to excavate the roots of anti-Semitism in Polish Catholicism. And Poles had in any case other struggles of memory over forgetting to pursue, in particular the memory of the victims of Stalin at the Katyn massacre.

Judging from some of the papers in the Rittner and Roth collection, the reconciliation of Polish and Jewish memories is still a delicate matter. The Polish name for Jewish survivors, Tanay tells us, was 'Niedopalki', a colloquial term which roughly translated means 'those who have not been completely burned'.[39] Richard Rubenstein implies a debt of gratitude on the part of the majority of Poles towards the Germans for having 'solved' the Jewish problem that had caused them so much difficulty in the interwar years.[40] The history of Polish–Jewish relations in the interwar period continues to be controversial, and Polish Jews in the 1920s and 1930s certainly decried what they perceived as a

Polish economic policy of 'extermination'. However, distinguished Jewish historians such as Ezra Mendelsohn have assayed a more even-handed analysis than is found here of the struggles of Poland in its new-found independence as an impoverished, exclusivist and therefore anti-Semitic nation-state that nonetheless extended to Jews significant freedoms and opportunities for achievement (if many Jews were poor, most were better off than most Polish peasants, though this surely can only have exacerbated the traditional anti-Semitism of the peasantry), a period of Polish history which Mendelsohn summarizes as 'the best of times and the worst of times' for Jews.[41]

Moreover, in recent years, particularly under the stimulus of the Institute for Polish-Jewish Studies in Oxford, significant gains have been made in repairing the divisions between Polish and Jewish understanding both in the investigation of the long and rich history of Polish–Jewish relations across the centuries and in attempting a more sensitive and nuanced analysis of the traumas of the recent past.[42] However, it is from within Poland itself that some of the most important reassessments have emerged of the moral responsibility of the Poles for the fate of the Jews, and the 'absent community' of Polish Jewry has now come to weigh upon Polish consciousness to a considerably greater extent than previously. There is now only a very small Jewish community in Poland and to that extent the relations between Poles and Jews can be regarded as a chapter of Polish history that has been abruptly but finally finished. But what lives on, and is deeply 'unfinished', is, as Smolar puts it, 'the heritage of the past as an internal Polish problem'.[43] A collection edited by Antony Polonsky brings together contributions to a debate that was sparked off by the publication in 1987 in the Catholic intellectual weekly *Tygodnik Powszechny* of an article by Jan Błoński, Professor of the History of Polish Literature at the Jagiellonian University in Krakow, entitled (in an echo of a famous poem by Czesław Miłosz), 'Poor Poles Look at the Ghetto'.[44] Błoński's essay is in essence a moving and thoughtful meditation on Poland as a nation which exists in a moral space of questions that is indelibly marked by shameful memories. Above all, Błoński tries to retrieve the discussion of the Polish witness to the Holocaust from the debris of nationalist apologetics and return it to a familiar, if awesome, moral landscape in which human agents recognize the essential web of connections between memory and identity, and the inescapable claims of vocabularies of moral defilement, at once in their intimate applications to the insides of individual agents and to the condition of a native soil. He describes the painful discomfort of an unspoken truth he experienced at a gathering of Polish and Jewish scholars which was due, he concluded, 'to the sense of a kind of contamination, a feeling of being somehow soiled and defiled'.[45] This experience led him to reflect on the meaning of the words – 'sullied, blood-stained, desecrated' – which Miłosz applies to the native soil of Poland, and hence on the consequences of the Jewish genocide which, although not perpetrated by the Polish people, 'took place on Polish soil and . . . has tainted that soil for all time'.[46] To those who reject the notion of collective responsibility, and insist that it is enough to condemn the crimes of the past, he replies:

> Our country is not a hotel in which one launders the linen after the guests have departed. It is a home which is built above all of memory; memory is at the core of our identity. We cannot dispose of it at will, even though as individuals we are not directly responsible for the actions of the past. We must carry it within us even though it is unpleasant or painful. We must also strive to expiate it.[47]

And to those who argue that his admonitions imply Polish participation in the Jewish genocide he answers that 'participation and shared responsibility are not the same thing'.[48] The Polish responsibility that concerns Błoński is not criminal but moral responsibility, 'centred on indifference, indifference at the time of the Holocaust', the result of which was that 'Jews died with a feeling of solitude, with a feeling of having been abandoned'.[49] Perhaps the most searing reflection on the neighbourliness of indifferent witness, and 'the loneliness of dying men', is Czeslaw Miłosz's poem on the destruction of the Warsaw Ghetto, 'Campo di Fiori':

> Sometimes the wind from burning houses
> would bring the kites along
> and people on the merry-go-round
> caught the flying charred bits.
> This wind from the burning houses
> blew open the girls' skirts
> and the happy throngs laughed
> on a beautiful Warsaw Sunday.

(trans. A. Gillon)

As one Polish historian has remarked, at stake in the search for the lost history of Polish–Jewish relations is 'the Polish people's choice between freedom, which requires as full a recognition as possible of history, and imprisonment as people desperately committed to nationalistic myths'.[50] One of the particular strengths of Polonsky's collection is that alongside a number of fine pieces entrusted to the reckoning with Polish nationalism and the 'difficult questioning of the Polish heroic and tragic self-image',[51] there are others (notably by Władysław Siła-Nowicki and Witold Rymanowski) which in various ways rebuff Błoński's moral overtures and in one case declare him 'guilty of the offence of slandering the Polish nation in accordance with article 270' of the penal code.[52] As the Polish-Jewish sociologist, Zygmunt Bauman, recognized, Błoński and his critics have tended to talk past each other. Apologists for the Polish past have been apt to claim that in the assessment of how people acted, or more importantly failed to act, the perspective of a situation-based ethics is applicable not merely to what took place inside the concentration camps on Polish soil but also to the abnormal circumstances of Poland as a whole during this period and the reign of terror under which it suffered. Those who attacked Błoński along these lines failed to see that though a situation-based ethics can legitimately exonerate individuals from accusations of criminal responsibility, it must at some point break down and cannot assuage the claims of moral shame. As Bauman put it, the 'choice is not between shame and pride. The choice is between the pride of morally purifying shame, and the shame of morally devastating pride.'[53] In the desperate attempts to dress up 'tainted' or shameful memory as proud or apologetic memory, we are made aware of the extent to which the understanding of the conflictual and painful operations of disturbed memory that Langer derives from his study of Holocaust witnesses has applications also to the reckoning of a nation with its past, and that 'disturbed memory' must surely be an essential category through which to attempt to make contemporary Polish society intelligible.

But are these intensely intimate disclosures of the travails of a nation an internal Polish problem? In an obvious respect they certainly are, but we should not only view them in this light for in question here, quite beyond the specific circumstances of Poland itself, is the moral significance of the Holocaust. In his book *Modernity and the Holocaust*, Bauman powerfully criticized the tendency in the West to entrench the Holocaust in 'public consciousness as an exclusively Jewish affair, of little significance to anyone else . . . obliged to live in modern times and be members of modern society'.[54] To return to our earlier discussion, if a sealing has taken place in Poland around 'Oświęcim', so it also has in the West around 'Auschwitz'. In the Polish case, the collapse of the old divisions between East and West has, as we have seen, burst open the insulated self-understanding of 'Oświęcim' and reawakened repressed memories. Yet if we follow Bauman's reasoning, it at once becomes apparent that we cannot stop here and must put also some of the same difficult questions to 'Auschwitz'. Arguably, the divisions of postwar Europe assisted very conveniently in the marginalization, and indeed trivialization, of the Holocaust and permitted the construction of an 'Auschwitz' that was 'over there', as socially and morally distant as it was physically distant. From this point of view, then, the recovery of the moral significance of the Holocaust, not least its implications for the self-understanding of modernity, cannot simply be reduced to the assimilation of 'Oświęcim' to 'Auschwitz'.

And here we are brought to a dimension of Poland's re-emergence from under the dark cloud of Soviet domination that is generally overlooked. For if in one aspect the condition of Poland as 'the next village' is that of an unresolved internal trauma, it is also and just as importantly that of the awakening of Poland as, for the first time, the sovereign and independent guardian of the Holocaust memory. Auschwitz, it has been rightly said, belongs to Poland as 'a warning to humanity entrusted to Polish keeping'.[55] The widely reported controversy over the siting of a Carmelite convent in the old theatre (subsequently a storehouse for the valuables taken from the bodies of the dead) adjacent to the boundary wall of the main camp at Auschwitz, certainly threatened to become, and perhaps did at points, a dispute between competing nationalisms of the victim, between Polish exclusivism and Jewish exclusivism. But as Władysław T. Bartoszewski shows in a sharp, and scrupulously fair, assessment, there were legitimate grounds for grievance on both sides.[56] For many Jews, the attempted eradication of the memory of the Holocaust by the Poles had in any case for long been the cause of a secondary trauma, and until very recently the Jews had no say in how the dead were to be remembered at Auschwitz. More immediately, the location of the convent appeared to augur a Christianization of the Holocaust and demonstrated, at the very least, a gross insensitivity to contrasting traditions in the memorialization of the dead. And what especially lent offence, perhaps, (evident enough to anyone who has visited the site) was less the relatively inconspicuous presence of the nuns themselves than the gigantic cross, symbol of Christian triumphalism, on the plot of land next to the convent. In certain respects the controversy rekindled old disputes and stereotypes, and efforts at dialogue were hindered both by the ignorant and clumsy utterances of some Polish prelates and by the claims of a number of Jewish leaders that the Jewish people had acquired inalienable rights to Auschwitz. Certainly, a vicious politics of remembrance is a familiar accompanist to the traumas of modernity and, far from being a vehicle of historical healing, remembrance may become a potent instrument in the renewal of trauma. Yet we must listen also to the voices of those who are resolved upon the recovery of 'that most beautiful of Polish historical traditions – the tradition of an open, tolerant society, a multinational commonwealth which did not burn its heretics',[57] and out of the convent controversy, and from other initiatives that had already been set in motion alongside it, there are promising signs of a Poland, unused in the immediate past to pluralism, awakening to the recognition that it now has more burdensome but perhaps more significant responsibilities thrust upon it than the preservation of the symbol of 'Oświęcim' fashioned in the immediate postwar years. The Carmelite nuns will vacate the old theatre building by the autumn of 1992, and an ecumenical centre is in process of completion some distance from the Auschwitz camp that will provide a meeting-point for people of different beliefs; and as early as 1989 the Polish government established a commission, with Jewish representation, to consider the future of the Auschwitz State Museum which has remained largely unaltered since the 1950s, and it has, for example, been proposed to change the name to (surely more appropriate) 'Auschwitz: Place of Remembrance'.

For Poland as the guardian of the Holocaust memory the obvious question to emerge from the convent controversy was how to preserve, as Bartoszewski puts it, 'two separate, conflicting, and essential views of history grounded in the same place'.[58] Yet perhaps there is also a lesson that reaches beyond the reconciliation or preservation of different traditions. So, for example, the heated dispute over whether the convent was inside or outside the boundary of the Auschwitz camp was hardly accidental. How one answers this question is irrelevant, what matters is that in the minds of many observers (Christians, Jews and others) the convent ventured too close to the site of the massacre, to the untransfigured reality of what took place there, and threatened to assimilate it into the narrative of a singular ethical tradition. For the guardians of the Holocaust memory, perhaps the real lesson is that the meaning of the Holocaust cannot be absorbed either into 'Oświęcim', into 'Auschwitz' or into any other ethical and historical tradition, and that there is an important sense in which Auschwitz must be left alone and not tampered with. Adam Michnik proposes, for example, that we enter into solidarity with the Jewish fate, not so much in terms of solidarity with Jewish religion or traditions or customs, but as a certain condition, the condition of people who have been reviled and persecuted, for lack of understanding of which our social and ethical life will be lacking in something essential.[59]

Auschwitz represents a rupture in the progressive narrative of modernity and whilst we must surely respect the longings of narrative to commence the story anew, we must also recognize that the actuality of what took place there cannot be transfigured or absorbed, become 'history', or past time. In listening to accounts of Holocaust experience, Langer observed, we wrestle continuously 'with the beginnings of a permanently unfinished tale'.[60] And hence why our modern condition is one in which, though we may be spared the anguish of those who directly witnessed the Holocaust, we cannot put Auschwitz behind us, but must live 'beside' it. The goal of 'mastering the past' is a necessary one, but as a commentator on the German 'Historikerstreit' observed, we deceive ourselves if we think that it can be 'realised only as the past passes into glass cases', and memory is reified 'through corridors of chronology'.[61] And that is also why the Auschwitz museum is more properly viewed as a place of remembrance, for the point about a museum is that it is necessarily fashioned within a particular tradition but Auschwitz just is that place, outside any conceivable ethical tradition, a warning among other things to the devastating consequences of a social system in which rationality acknowledges no limits and is severed from ethical understanding. Freud, in his benighted understanding of identity and historical memory, pondered on the spectacle of the 'impractical Londoner' who paused 'in deep melancholy' before the memorial at Charing Cross to the memory of Queen Eleanor 'instead of going about his business in the hurry that modern working conditions demand'.[62] For Freud, a memorial once established was 'just there' and to be taken for granted as such, but we might judge that if the integrity of our collective business is to be secured we cannot permit ourselves to become forgetful of the deep melancholy of Auschwitz.

Just along the road from the railway station in Oświęcim there is a new school and the last time I was there as I looked at the children I wondered what it must be like to grow up in Oświęcim. The memory of Auschwitz must continue to be a source of shame for all of us, not only for the inhabitants of Oświęcim and the Poles as a nation. But the shameful fact of Auschwitz itself offers no reason why the inhabitants of the next village should be ashamed of their condition and be seen by western observers as contaminated and lurking behind a pseudonym. We should perhaps show more interest than we have tended to in the ethnography of a locality whose inhabitants are fated to be the eternal custodians of a traumatic past, and the people of Oświęcim and the Poles in general surely deserve our respect and support in their awesome task.

Goldsmiths College, University of London

NOTES

 1 Langer (1991).
 2 Langer (1991: 5); Delbo (1985: 13).
 3 Langer (1991: 52).
 4 ibid.: 174–5.
 5 ibid.: 34.
 6 ibid.: 6; Delbo (1985: 13–14).
 7 Langer (1991: 48).
 8 ibid.: 40.
 9 ibid.: 49.
10 See Blanchot (1986).
11 Langer (1991: 80).
12 ibid.: 83.
13 ibid.: 94.
14 ibid.: 96.
15 ibid.: 199.
16 ibid.: 198.
17 Taylor (1989).
18 ibid.: 44–5.
19 ibid.: 47.
20 ibid.: 27.
21 Langer (1991: 201).
22 Langer cannot have read very deeply into Taylor's text. Consider, for example, Taylor's remarks (1989: 480) apropos Thomas Mann's *The Magic Mountain*: 'Human life is irreducibly multilevelled. The epiphanic and the ordinary but real can never be fully aligned and we are condemned to live on more than one level. . . . The recognition that we live on many levels has to be won against the presumptions of the unified self, controlling or expressive.'
23 Langer (1991: 90).
24 Alter (1991).
25 ibid.: 14.
26 ibid.: 19.
27 ibid.: 17.
28 ibid.: 115–16.
29 ibid.: 83.
30 ibid.: 97; Benjamin (1986: 209–10).
31 Fisk (1990: 5).

32 See, e.g., Gutman and Krakowski (1986), Pinkus (1991), Rubinek (1989) but also Tec (1986).
33 Rittner and Roth (1991); see also Dawidowicz (1981).
34 Tanay (1991).
35 Krajewski (1991: 118).
36 Smolar (1987: 31).
37 ibid.: 66.
38 ibid.: 67–8.
39 Tanay (1991: 107).
40 Rubenstein (1991: 40).
41 Mendelsohn (1986).
42 See in particular Abramsky et al. (1986); Bartoszewski and Polonsky (1991).
43 Smolar (1987: 64).
44 Polonsky (1990).
45 Błoński (1990: 40).
46 ibid.: 34.
47 ibid.: 35.
48 ibid.: 46.
49 Conference discussion, quoted in Polonsky (1990: 188).
50 Bryk (1990: 161).
51 Smolar (1987: 31–2).
52 Rymanowski (1990: 155).
53 See introduction to Polonsky (1990: 26–7); also Bauman (1989: 205).
54 Bauman (1989: ix).
55 Modras (1991: 55).
56 Bartoszewski (1990).
57 Michnik (1991).
58 Bartoszewski (1990: 137). The matter here is gravely complicated both by the topography and history of the Auschwitz complex and by the mythology that has developed around it. For the history see in particular Czech (1990), and for distortions in the statistics about Auschwitz that have tended both to exaggerate the overall number of deaths and especially the number of Polish victims see Bauer (1991). It is, however, important to note the contributions of Polish scholars from the Auschwitz Museum to the revision of previous judgements (for example, Piper, 1991). Despite the enormous literature on Auschwitz, the history of the construction of the symbols of 'Oświęcim' and 'Auschwitz', and the selective and sometimes devious uses that have been made of the historical record in support of them, still awaits an adequate treatment.
59 Michnik (1991).
60 Langer (1991: 21).
61 Maier (1988: 139).
62 Freud (1910: 16–17), and for discussion Homans (1989).

BIBLIOGRAPHY

Abramsky, C., Jachimczyk, M. and Polonsky, A., eds (1986) *The Jews in Poland*. Oxford: Blackwell.

Alter, R. (1991) *Necessary Angels: Tradition and Modernity in Kafka, Benjamin and Scholem*. Cambridge, MA: Harvard University Press.

Bartoszewski, W. T. (1990) *The Convent at Auschwitz*. London: Bowerdean Press.

Bartoszewski, W. T. and Polonsky, A., eds (1991) *The Jews in Warsaw*. Oxford: Blackwell.

Bauer, Y. (1991) 'Auschwitz: the Dangers of Distortion', in C. Rittner and J. K. Roth (eds) *Memory Offended: the Auschwitz Convent Controversy*, pp. 251–3. New York: Praeger. (First published in the *Jerusalem Post*, 30 September 1989.)

Bauman, Z. (1989) *Modernity and the Holocaust*. Oxford: Polity.

Benjamin, W. (1986) *Reflections*. New York:

Blanchot, M. (1986) *The Writing of the Disaster*. Lincoln: University of Nebraska Press.

Błoński, J. (1990) 'The Poor Poles Look at the Ghetto', in A. Polonsky (ed.) *'My Brother's Keeper?': Recent Polish Debates on the Holocaust*, pp. 34–52. London: Routledge.

Bryk, A. (1990) 'The Hidden Complex of the Polish Mind: Polish–Jewish Relations during the Holocaust', in A. Polonsky (ed.) *'My Brother's Keeper?': Recent Polish Debates on the Holocaust*, pp. 161–83. London: Routledge.

Czech, D. (1990) *Auschwitz Chronicle*. London: I. B. Tauris.

Dawidowicz, L. (1981) *The Holocaust and the Historian*. Cambridge, MA: Harvard University Press.

Delbo, C. (1985) *La Memoire et les jours*. Paris: Berg International.

Fisk, R. (1990) *Pity the Nation: Lebanon at War*. Oxford: Oxford University Press.

Freud, S. (1910 [1957]) 'Five Lectures on Psychoanalysis', *Standard Edition of the Works of Sigmund Freud*, Vol. II, pp. 9–55. London: Hogarth Press.

Gutman, Y. and Krakowski, S. (1986) *Unequal Victims: Poles and Jews in World War II*. New York: Holocaust Library.

Homans, P. (1989) *The Ability to Mourn: Disillusionment and the Social Origins of Psychoanalysis*. Chicago: University of Chicago Press.

Krajewski, S. (1991) 'The Controversy over Carmel at Auschwitz: a Personal Polish-Jewish Chronology', in C. Rittner and J. K. Roth (eds) *Memory Offended: the Auschwitz Convent Controversy*, pp. 117–34. New York: Praeger.

Langer, L. (1991) *Holocaust Testimonies: the Ruins of Memory*. New Haven, CT: Yale University Press.

Maier, C. (1988) *The Unmasterable Past*. Cambridge, MA: Harvard University Press.

Mendelsohn, E. (1986) 'Interwar Poland: Good for the Jews or Bad for the Jews?', in C. Abramsky, M. Jachimczyk and A. Polonsky (eds) *The Jews in Poland*, pp. 130–9. Oxford: Blackwell.

Michnik, A. (1991) 'Poland and the Jews', *New York Review of Books* 38(10): 11–12.

Modras, R. (1991) 'Jews and Poles; Remembering at a Cemetery', in C. Rittner and J. K. Roth (eds) *Memory Offended: the Auschwitz Convent Controversy*, pp. 53–62. New York: Praeger.

Pinkus, O. (1991) *The House of Ashes*. London: I. B. Tauris.

Piper, F. (1991) 'The Number of Victims in Auschwitz-Birkenau', *Yad Vashem Studies* 21.

Polonsky, A., ed. (1990) *'My Brother's Keeper?': Recent Polish Debates on the Holocaust*. London: Routledge.

Rittner, C. and Roth, J. K., eds (1991) *Memory Offended: the Auschwitz Convent Controversy*. New York: Praeger.

Rubenstein, R. (1991) 'The Convent at Auschwitz and the Imperatives of Pluralism in the Global Electronic Village', in C. Rittner and J. K.Roth (eds) *Memory Offended: the Auschwitz Convent Controversy*. New York: Praeger.

Rubinek, S. (1989) *So Many Miracles*. Harmondsworth, Mx: Penguin.

Rymanowski, W. (1990) 'The Disseminator of Anti-Semitism? A Rejoinder to Jan Blonski', in A. Polonsky (ed.) *'My Brother's Keeper?': Recent Polish Debates on the Holocaust*, pp. 155–60. London: Routledge.

Smolar, A. (1987) 'Jews as a Polish Problem', *Daedalus* 116(2): 31–73.

Tanay, E. (1991) 'Auschwitz and Oświęcim: One Location, Two Memories', in C. Rittner and J. K. Roth (eds) *Memory Offended: the Auschwitz Convent Controversy*, pp. 99–112. New York: Praeger.

Taylor, C. (1989) *Sources of the Self*. Cambridge: Cambridge University Press.

Tec, N. (1986) *When Light Pierced the Darkness: Christian Rescue of Jews in Nazi Occupied Poland*. Oxford: Oxford University Press.

HISTORY OF THE HUMAN SCIENCES   Vol. 5 No. 3

© 1992 SAGE (London, Newbury Park and New Delhi)   pp. 57–63

Philosophy as the mirror of time

ZYGMUNT BAUMAN

Richard Rorty, *Philosophical Papers*. Cambridge: Cambridge University Press, 1991.
Vol. 1, *Objectivity, Relativism, and Truth*, x + 226 pp.
Vol. 2, *Essays on Heidegger and Others*, x + 202 pp.

Alan Malachowski (ed.), *Reading Rorty: Critical Responses to Philosophy and the Mirror of Nature (and Beyond)*. Oxford: Blackwell, 1990. xiv + 384 pp.

The mark of great works of art, literature or philosophy is that they impose their presence on the past as well as on the present: they redraw, simultaneously, the histories and the maps of their respective territories. Great works create their own ancestors, thereby changing the received readings of shared tradition, reshuffling the accepted hierarchies, turning around the logic of past developments and reallocating their visible destinations. The appearance of a great work is recognized by the widely felt urge, and a massive effort, to rewrite history. On the other hand, great works become the poles from which new grids are spun so that other works, extant or about to be conceived, are charted in a novel way. The appearance of a great work is recognized by renegotiating the parameters, themes and rules of the ongoing discourse. Great works, so to speak, short-circuit the past and the present: they define the sense in which the present discourse is the act of reliving the tradition, and the sense in which tradition makes the present meaningful.[1]

By these standards, Richard Rorty's writings have reached the status of the 'great work of philosophy', and they did so in an incredibly short time-span; barely a decade has passed since the *Mirror of Nature* was published. Neither the past of western philosophy nor its current agenda, not even its own understanding of both, look the same as ten years ago. The depth of Rorty's impact on the life of philosophy is truly remarkable. Even more astonishing is the immediacy of impact, the speed with which the force and importance of Rorty's ideas have been recognized far and wide and their reverberations come to be felt throughout the philosophical discourse. That latter circumstance suggests that Rorty's work appeared at a time already ripe for its reception; time already waiting for someone to perform the job Rorty will have done. Thus Rorty's work passes also another test of greatness, one set by Wilhelm Dilthey and elaborated by Lucien Goldmann: that of a cultural creation encompassing and giving expression to the most seminal 'tendency of the epoch'.

Where exactly lies the significance of Rorty's work? An orderly answer to this question is not immediately obvious, as the significance of all revolutionary acts is first lived and felt, sometimes for quite a while, before it may be sensibly theorized about. First sightings are shaped by the questions the viewers – steeped as they are in their 'unreformed' tradition – have been trained to ask in their formative period, when acquiring the skills of their profession. Most philosophical readers of Rorty have been trained to seek the ways to satisfy themselves and to convince their listeners that there are – somewhere, waiting to be found – foolproof ways to set apart the propositions everybody *can* be sure of (and *will* be sure of, if only freed of 'bias' or 'prejudice'), from propositions that do not possess this quality; and that they, philosophers, are in command (perhaps also in sole possession) of the methods which warrant and allow such a setting-apart. Elaborating the tests all knowledge is required to pass under the penalty of disqualification in case of failure, was to most practitioners of philosophical art the unquestioned purpose of philosophical activity. No wonder that the appearance of Rorty's works has been greeted with a mixture of dismay, embarrassment and irritation. Rorty struck at the heart of philosophical enterprise. Not just this or that test was questioned (and whatever had been questioned was questioned not because its efficacy or technical perfection was doubted) – but the sense and need of test-setting itself came under attack, to be in the end dismissed as a pastime both wasteful and damaging. Rorty's work, it was felt, not only made light of the philosophers' current concerns, but invalidated retrospectively the most cherished legacy of hundreds of years of philosophical labour from which the current practitioners of the art drew their confidence of doing the right, and useful, job. In other words, Rorty's work threatened to make the most coveted philosophical skills redundant, while in the bargain depriving their owners of their past glory.

'Knowledge', says Rorty, is not 'a matter of getting reality right' – but, rather, 'a matter of acquiring habits of action for coping with reality' (1:1). This, one would say, amounts to saying that there is no more to what one may name 'getting reality right' than to cope with it; and that – since the lay members of the public are masters supreme of 'coping' – the work assigned professionally to trained philosophers has no edge over the skills of ordinary mortals: both are busy doing basically the same thing, though the uninitiated have the advantage of being free of delusions that haunt those ostensibly better informed. 'Getting reality right' in any other sense – and particularly in the sense favoured by the last three centuries of philosophizing, that of 'getting knowledge to *represent* reality truly' – is neither called for, nor a viable proposition ('There is nothing to be said about either truth or rationality apart from descriptions of the familiar procedures of justification which a given society – *ours* – uses in one or another area of inquiry' [1: 23]). It may be also, and it often was, pretty damaging in its consequences, political and moral ('Dewey' – Rorty notes with approval – 'thinks that muddle, compromise, and blurry syntheses are usually less perilous, politically, than Cartesian clarity' [1: 211]).

True, statements to this effect are not entirely unfamiliar. They have been made before from sites marginal to academic philosophy (remember Simmel, and more recently Schütz, Garfinkel and the massive ethno-methodological practice they spawned; remember as well less boldly articulated, yet consistently 'non-representationalist' activity of most cultural anthropologists). They have been, for some time now, ensconced *in potentia* in the increasingly mainstream currents of philosophy (think of Nietzsche, Heidegger, Foucault; in America, the country of Dewey, James and Peirce, the distance from mainstream was never great). Rorty himself repeatedly quotes Sellars, Quine and Davidson as his most immediate intellectual creditors. But it was left to Rorty to give an unmistakable and uncompromising formulation to intuitions, inclinations and unreflected-upon practices, to forge out of the 'anti-representationalist' stance the programme of philosophy, and to disavow bluntly the crusade against 'anti-realism' and 'relativism' as sacred mission of philosophers. As Alan R. Malachowski observed, 'Rorty should be given credit for putting his own slant on things. The rich sources for some of his main ideas may create the flavouring, but the brew is his own' (RR: 140).

No wonder many a philosopher responded in anger (most notably, philosophers of the analytical philosophy denomination; for a characteristic sample, see 'Auto-da-Fé: Consequences of Pragmatism' by Bernard Williams, in Malachowski's collection). No wonder – as together with the truth hovering above the practices of life off went the elevated status of truth-priesthood. Or so it may have seemed, as long as that status continued to be argued, justified and legitimized by pointing to a privileged, direct hot-line to Platonic ideas and to however articulated practice of censuring and correcting common sense, 'mere opinions', and all and sundry 'local', 'parochial' views, from the standpoint of supra-temporal and supra-communal universality; as long as the cultural centrality of philosophy, and thus of the philosophers, was held to be synonymical with the extra-territorial status, non-partisanship and global reach of the Supreme Court of truth and moral rectitude.

And yet it can be shown that Rorty is not in the business of undermining the importance of the philosopher's job. He only suggests the revision of the job-description. Or is it rather the updating? Bringing it in line with the mood and longings of new times? Making it, if anything, more reliably settled in a world which displays less and less interest in the kind of services the philosophers thus far promised to render? Salvaging the philosophical profession from the debacle threatened by the waning of modern hopes and ambitions?

Rorty denies the existence of 'skyhooks' and derides the philosophers' pining for finding them as well as their pretensions of having found them. He does all this, however, not in the name of a philosophy without a hold (as his most dismayed critics feared), but in the name of a hold more solid and reliable than any thus far discovered or, rather, imagined. Skyhooks are not to be just disposed of: they are to be *replaced* – by 'toeholds'. The metaphors are illuminating. As Lévi-Strauss has admirably shown, in the eternal binary ordering of the universe the sky stands for everything too high and lofty to be reached by ordinary mortals, something meant to be admired but not possessed; while toes tread the lowly ground, which stands for everything 'down here', familiar and homely, not noble perhaps yet instead assuringly accessible, solid, reliable. The hooks philosophers try earnestly, yet in vain, to grasp, are indeed *sky*hooks in as far as they are viewed from the vantage point of the *toe*holds.

Disposing of the skyhooks, Rorty suggests, is called for not because of our disinterest in truth or objectivity, but because unless we are Gods we cannot grasp them, and not being Gods we cannot even imagine what grasping them would feel like. Disposing of the skyhooks is not an act of surrender, but a manifestation of sobriety and good sense. If we know how to cope (or, rather, if we cope without necessarily knowing) it is because we *belong* to a *community*, and we belong there not because of our decision to belong, but before any decision can be made and the decision-making itself appears on our agenda. 'Our acculturation is what makes certain options live, or momentous, or forced, while leaving others dead, or trivial, or optional' (1: 13). Whatever may follow, can only belie, never refute, this plight. The resilience and incorrigibly 'foundational' status of acculturation, of communal determination, was denied in theory by Kantian–Cartesian–Lockean philosophical enterprise, while the nation-states, bent on eradicating locally rooted and thus obstreperous powers in practice and smothering them in the uniformity of legislated rights and duties, had to dress up their own particularity as universality of human rights or human nature. The theory has been discredited, while the practice has been, at least in our part of the world, abandoned. Resistance, nay immunity, of communal roots to the artifice of legislation has been proved and vindicated.

To communal rootedness – an existential situation, not a choice – Rorty gives the name of 'ethnocentrism'. Perhaps, to avoid ambiguity, he should have chosen the name of 'ethnicity' instead. It would be thus clear that what he meant was a *des*cription, not a *pres*cription. But then it may be that the ambiguity has been intended and the choice of the name is deliberate. At any rate, on this point Rorty keeps his readers in the dark, offering abundant evidence for both interpretations. And so we read that 'To be ethnocentric is to divide the human race into the people to whom one must justify one's beliefs and the others. The first group – one's *ethnos* – comprises those who share enough of one's beliefs to make fruitful conversation possible. In this sense, everybody is ethnocentric when engaged in actual debate, no matter how much realist rhetoric about objectivity he produces in his study' (1:30). But we also read that because of that circumstance we should be concerned with questions like 'What are the limits of our community?' and that the question 'What sort of human being do you want to become?' translates then into the query 'With what communities should you identify, of which you should think of yourself as a member?' (1:13).

There is little doubt as to Rorty's own choice. Time and again he spells out the meaning of those 'we' who entail the 'I' of his own: 'Our community – the community of the liberal intellectuals of the secular modern West' (1:29); 'we postmodernist bourgeois liberals' who 'no longer tag our central beliefs as "necessary" or "natural" and our peripheral ones as "contingent" and "cultural"', and who 'are going to have to work out the limits case by case' (1:208). Rorty's confidence that community is not only the inevitability one has to put up with, but also a good thing, a blessing even (particularly if compared with the cold, dehumanized artifice of the promoters of objective truth, where 'institutional backups for beliefs take the form of bureaucrats and policemen' [1:26]) stems ultimately from his unclouded satisfaction with the concrete community to which he assigns himself, one of 'increased tolerance and decreased suffering' (1:213). This very special community is indeed – there is little question about it – a humane, civilized place, pleasant and comfortable to be in, one that mixes the security of the family home with the anonymous freedom of a five-star international hotel and where a drawerful of airline tickets insures the pleasures of homeliness against turning into the agony of parochiality. One may say that Rorty's celebration of communalism is an obverse of Kantian categorical imperative: one would wish to make a universal rule out of the way of life one finds palatable and gratifying for oneself.

For the most, if not all, of its residents, this particular community of Rorty's birth/choice is preferable to any other known or imaginable. For this reason, communalism – known to the residents in the only experiential mode available to them, their own – is a blessing and a privilege. No wonder the boundary between description and prescription is blurred. No wonder either that the question about transcendental, community-free proofs and foundations seems both bizarre and superfluous. With such a nice toehold who needs skyhooks? And for what conceivable benefit? We know this community of ours is good when we look at it. There can be nothing wrong with communal roots as such. All things nasty and contemptible – like pugnacious tribalism, intolerance, cruelty, moral numbness, refusal of humanity to the 'community' round the corner – have nothing to do with communalism, and everything to do with inferiority of other communities when compared to the remarkable qualities of our own. . . .

Rorty's communalism (philosophical code name: 'anti-representationalism') is a defensive policy, in opposition to its universalist adversary bent on offensive. Our task is to protect the precious form of life which by fortunate yet fortuitous coincidence happens to be our own. Intercommunal differences are to be resolved, if at all, by being thrashed out in civilized discussion, instead of through invasions and annexation. Most importantly, our own community no more believes that differences present a challenge and require action. It is up to the others to make the effort. By the way (accidentally?), this change of mood chimes well with the waning of proselytizing ambitions of nation-states – those characteristically modern forms of social power which legitimized their exclusiveness in universalist terms. Peter Drucker's recent slogan – 'no more salvation by society' – fits neatly into a world in which societies (thus far synonyms for nation-states) no more promise or contemplate salvation. This leaves communities free from threat, but also bereaved. They may count on their own resources only. If there is to be an emancipation, it can be done only, Baron Münchhausen-style, by pulling one's own hair. Some hairs need more pulling than others, but this would hardly irritate those whose hair needs no pulling at all.

Rorty's revision of the philosophical agenda is, in other words, made to the measure of our time: *our* time, complete with the chosen and enviable space it has allotted us, the 'postmodern bourgeois intellectuals' (this is why the possessive pronoun 'ours' conveys more than mere chronological technicality). Hence its remarkable success, the truly wildfire-like spread of its popularity and influence. Giving the thus-far fullest and sharpest articulation to the momentum of our communal culture, it has become an instant classic of that culture. 'When tolerance and comfortable togetherness become the watchwords of a society, one should no longer hope for world-historical greatness. If such greatness – radical difference from the past, a dazzlingly unimaginable future – is what one wants, ascetic priests like Plato, Heidegger, and Suslov will fill the bill' (2: 81). Our time, and above all we whom our time pampered, think of the 'radical watersheds' and 'new starts' of the past with incredulity, and those of the future with revulsion. Our time, and above all we as its spokesmen, want rather more of the same. To this mood, itself such a 'radical difference' from the modern spirit, Rorty has given philosophical articulation.

In the light of the above, Rorty's late disavowal of self-definition as a 'postmodern philosopher' comes as a surprise. 'I now wish that I had not' used 'postmodern' to describe myself, says Rorty. 'I have given up on the attempt to find something common to Michael Graves's buildings, Pynchon's and Rushdie's novels, Ashberry's poems, various sorts of popular music, and the writings of Heidegger and Derrida' (2: 1). Well – to be sure, one can hardly imagine a phrase more postmodern than the one quoted above. Rorty is at his 'most postmodern' in his denial of his postmodernity. What is postmodernity about, if not about resolute refusal to see connections in things, and above all about inability to conceive of itself as an entity, and a *historical* entity with that; to think of itself as a product and a correlate of selfsame processes which determined the autonomy it mistakes for indetermination?

University of Leeds

NOTES

1 One cannot avoid the temptation to recall in this context George Orwell's memorable description of the 'inside the whale' complex, to which intellectuals with singed fingers must want to succumb: 'The creature that swallowed Jonah was a fish . . . but children naturally confuse it with a whale, and this fragment of baby-talk is habitually carried into later life. . . . For the fact is that being inside a whale is a very comfortable, cosy, homelike thought. The historical Jonah, if he can be so called, was glad enough to escape, but in imagination, in day-dream, countless people have envied him. It is, of course, quite obvious why. The whale's belly is simply a womb big enough for an adult. There you are, in the dark, cushioned space that exactly fits you, with yards of blubber between yourself and reality, able to keep up an attitude of the completest indifference, no matter *what* happens. A storm that would sink all the battleships in the world would hardly reach you as an echo. Even the whale's own movements would probably be imperceptible to you. . . . Short of being dead, it is the final, unsurpassable stage of irresponsibility' (*Inside The Whale and Other Essays*, Harmondsworth, Mx: Penguin, 1986: pp. 42–3).

HISTORY OF THE HUMAN SCIENCES Vol. 5 No. 3

© 1992 SAGE (London, Newbury Park and New Delhi) pp. 65–70

Thin ice

RONALD BEINER

Leszek Kolakowski, *Modernity on Endless Trial*. Chicago: University of
Chicago Press, 1990. vii + 261 pp.

First come the disclaimers. Leszek Kolakowski professes to have no philosophy
of modernity to offer, and he claims to be at a loss to know even how to define
modernity, let alone being able to define such newfangled constructions as
'postmodernity'. Yet he has a sufficiently definite notion of modernity to be able
to understand very well why modern intellectuals are such a gloomy lot, and he
has enough of a position of his own on the issue of modernity to be able to share
to quite a fair degree this mood of discomfort or unease. And while he would no
doubt be put off by the faddish vocabulary, it might even be reasonable to say
that the essays in this book give evidence of a 'postmodern' sensibility.

  While the diverse pieces collected in the book were written over a period of
thirteen years and for a wide variety of occasions and publications, a set of shared
themes and preoccupations runs through the collection as a whole: the conflict
between science and religion; the disenchanting effects of secularization; the
cultural malaise of modernity; the conceits of intellectuals (as well as their
indispensability); the tendency of theoretical pretensions to turn into ideological
pretensions, which in turn stifle political freedom (modern historicism is one
example of the conversion of theory into ideology); the unattainability of
perfection, the unavoidability of evil; and the irrationality of absolute rationality.
One of the recurrent themes of the book is that whichever way one turns, whether
towards faith or towards secular reason, towards modern science or towards
theology, civilizing tendencies and barbarizing tendencies seem to intersect in
unexpected ways, with the consequence that one is often drawn, willy-nilly, in a
direction directly opposed to one's own best intentions. Yet this is offset by
another of his themes, the persistence of hope and the unreasonableness of despair.

In the title essay, Kolakowski comes close to affirming Nietzsche's judgment on modernity: '"*Without the Christian faith*," Pascal thought, "you, no less than nature and history, will become for yourselves *un monstre et un chaos*." This prophecy we have fulfilled, after the feeble-optimistic eighteenth century had prettified and rationalized man.'[1] Except that Kolakowski adds the necessary qualification of the good liberal, that attempts to enforce a political return to pre-modernity (or to leap out of modernity altogether) produce forms of barbarism at least equal to, and often much greater than, the barbarisms of modernity. In fact, modernity, however much it may be repudiated in word and intention, proves well-nigh irresistible in practice, as Kolakowski shows with the following example (p. 10). The Reformation, seeking to restore Christianity to an older and more authentic experience of faith, paradoxically and contrary to its own intentions, gave further impetus to the inexorable rationalism of modern times. Or again (another of Kolakowski's examples), nationalistic movements in our own century, determined to resist or roll back modernity, have given rise to ghastly regimes that are not only devilish but also hyper-modern. The more one aspires to resist modernity, the more it seems to hit back with a vengeance.

One might describe Kolakowski as an uneasy liberal. He insists that modern Europeans must summon up the self-confidence to celebrate the successes of western civilization in promoting an attitude of scepticism and self-criticism relative to other less open, less tolerant societies. At the same time, he realizes all too clearly the price one must pay for the liberalizing achievements of the West:

> . . . cultural influences act according to their own principles of selection, which are almost impossible to control. The first thing the rest of the world expects from European culture is military technology; civic freedoms, democratic institutions, and intellectual standards come last. Western technological expansion entails the destruction of dozens of small cultural units and languages, a process which really gives no cause for rejoicing. There is nothing uplifting in the fact that a great family of Indo-European languages, the Celtic branch, is dying out before our very eyes, despite all efforts to halt the process of its extinction. (p. 23)

Even worse, what is at stake is not merely the survival of the most vulnerable cultures, but rather, as Kolakowski acknowledges very openly, the possibility of cultural diversity as such in the face of western dynamism: 'If our destiny were to annihilate cultural variety in the world in the name of a planetary civilization . . . human civilization as a whole, not merely particular civilizations, would be in danger of extinction' (p. 23).

Kolakowski's concern here is with what one might call the paradox of openness and abrogation of openness. It is to the enormous credit of European civilization that it has opened vistas, expressed curiosity for other cultures, triumphed over parochialism, scrutinized its own assumptions with scientific detachment, and distinguished itself in relation to the closed societies of other traditions. Modernity represents the consolidation and consummation of this European legacy. Yet it is this same liberalizing civilization that today threatens to sink all the diverse cultures that it has studied and appreciated into a homogeneous cultural void. Modernity seems to have taught us that there are moral limits to universalism. As Kolakowski acutely demonstrates, to be equally open to everything is to be left with nothing in terms of cultural and civilizational resources. If one carries liberalism too far one ends up with no traditions at all, neither one's own nor those of alien cultures, so what was initially an admirable openness to other cultures ends by dissolving or annulling other cultures (or gobbling them up with promises of technological marvels). For all that one celebrates the openness and tolerance of the West, too much openness does not liberate but casts one into the shapeless abyss of nihilism. Starting from a defence of European liberalism, Kolakowski again finds himself drawn into the gravitational field of Nietzschean insights.

Although Kolakowski begins the book by emphasizing his inability to define modernity, it is not long before he does present at least a rough definition (p. 13). To inhabit modernity is to live in a world without taboos (or a world that is moving in the direction of the gradual lifting of all taboos). That is, a modern world is one that has increasing difficulty in conceiving a distinction between good and evil that is independent of human design, and hence, ultimately, in sustaining *any* distinction between good and evil. The supreme philosophical question for Kolakowski is whether the preservation of a moral universe requires appeal to revelation, or whether (as in Kant) secular morality can rescue the good/evil distinction from the taboo-destroying process of modernity. Living in a world without taboos is, expressed in religious terms, living in a world without the distinction between the sacred and profane, and since it is impossible for the latter distinction to be generated out of secularity alone, we are left with the implication that we cannot contend with the challenges of modernity without some recourse to religious categories and religious experience. Hence Kolakowski intimates that without religion, no barriers will be left to the most hubristic impulses of modern humanity.

Kolakowski seeks in the Christian tradition for an antidote to modern hubris. But he understands that Christianity itself has been historically implicated in the process that has generated modern hubris. European modernity has in important respects been shaped by Christianity and Christian forms of consciousness. When Bacon articulated for the first time the aspiration to conquer nature and eliminate unnecessary human misery by establishing 'the empire of man over things',[2] he was writing from within at least one version of the Christian consciousness. As noted above, the Reformation, while it sought to humble human reason, in fact contributed to the process whereby reason was liberated from the authority of tradition (pp. 30, 96, 147). And as Kolakowski also argues, the Enlightenment, which in appearance was an anti-Christian movement, had its roots in western Christianity. In these and other respects, modernity and Christianity stand in a highly complex mutual relationship.

Kolakowski delights in the paradoxicality of the human condition, hence his fascination with tracing how, for instance, liberal cosmopolitanism is metamorphosed into cultural imperialism, the quest for faith promotes the total sovereignty of reason, myths of liberation become ideological pretexts for enslavement; in short, how what is supposed to civilize us often ends by helping to barbarize us. (Conversely, barbarism sometimes contributes to civilization, spurring the creative spirit by, for instance, driving the best minds into exile – the topic of Chapter 5.) Judging from these essays, Kolakowski's intellectual heroes are figures like Erasmus (a religious reformer who refused to join the Reformation), Pascal (a scientist who depreciated scientific reason) and Kant (a philosophical Jacobin who laid the foundations for contemporary liberalism). These are, like himself, thinkers for whom the fabric of human life is rent with self-stymying contradictions. As Kolakowski puts it in one place (p. 80), for every increment of moral progress there is a price to be paid, and it is always uncertain whether the gain outweighs the cost or vice versa. For instance, our modern culture prides itself on having put behind it doctrines of hell, the devil and original sin. Yet for this accomplishment it pays the price of a belief in human perfectibility and the unreality of evil. Kolakowski is close enough to orthodox Christian theology in his judgements about human nature to be unsure of whether this represents a net progress.

Kolakowski is certainly not 'anti-modern', but he is (with good reason) concerned about some of the Promethean aspects of modernity, and he is particularly anxious about how Promethean human beings might be tempted to become in a decisively post-Christian modernity. All of us today must surely applaud the victory of the Enlightenment in liberating us from superstition and intolerance, and yet the legacy of the Enlightenment, in common with every historic human legacy, is a mixed one. Kolakowski's response to all of this is the usual liberal's refrain about the impossibility of utopia, the impossibility of combining all individual hopes and aspirations in the compass of a single individual life, or of combining all communal hopes and aspirations in the compass of a single political community. To this true but tiresome message Alan Ryan supplied a definitive rejoinder when he observed in a *London Times* obituary for *Encounter* magazine (for which several of the essays in Kolakowski's book were originally written): '*Encounter* set out to persuade the thinking classes never again to be tempted by totalitarianism; for 30 years they have not been tempted, and you can't go on for ever asserting what nobody wants to deny.' As Kolakowski himself acknowledges, the millenarian impulse seems to have lost its steam in recent years, certainly among intellectuals, and with the example of post-Gorbachev Russia before its eyes, the West hardly needs to be reminded of the delusions of utopian politics.

In a three-page credo, Kolakowski presents himself as a conservative-liberal-socialist. The essays bear out this credo. It is when he dons his Catholic theologian's cap that Kolakowski's conservatism comes most to the fore. (And who among us can really gainsay the pessimism about human nature that lies at the well-spring of conservative insights?) It is when he reflects on the longing for utopia that his liberalism is most evident. And it is when he thinks about the limits of conservatism and the limits of liberalism that Kolakowski's residual socialism shows itself.

If, according to Kolakowski, theoretical stances of pro-modernity and anti-modernity can be equally productive of species of barbarism, does this perhaps give us some grounds for thinking of him as a 'postmodern' theorist? According to one very influential definition, the postmodern condition signifies the renunciation of the kind of grand 'meta-narratives' by which philosophers have hitherto sought to locate meaning in history.[3] This is why postmodern thinkers tend to prefer Heidegger to Hegel, and prefer Nietzsche to Marx. Put like this, Kolakowski is certainly close to being situated in the postmodern camp. Not that Kolakowski is eager to embrace Heidegger or Nietzsche! But Heidegger and Nietzsche at least preserve the sense of Pascalian *Angst* that Kolakowski associates with the best of the Christian tradition (as opposed to the optimism of the Enlightenment). Combining Lyotard and Kolakowski, one might say that what marks off postmodern from modern theory is that, having witnessed the horrors unleashed by the grand 'meta-narratives' of modern philosophy, henceforth philosophers sufficiently temper the ambitions of their theorizing that they no longer help to spawn ideologies.

Kolakowski writes: 'It would be silly, of course, to be either "for" or "against" modernity *tout court*' (p. 12). This is certainly true. But the symmetry of this 'for' and 'against' is somewhat misleading. For in saying 'yes' to modernity (even with elaborate qualifications) we are saying 'yes' to what we are and whither we are going, while in saying 'no' (again with qualifications) we are questioning ourselves and keeping alive the scepticism and self-doubt that for Kolakowski are the difference between civilization and barbarism. Kolakowski is right to remind us that a facile repudiation of modernity can be just as dangerous as a facile affirmation of it. Indeed, there are no ready 'solutions' for our predicaments, and any intellectual who promises to show us an escape-hatch from the modern condition is a charlatan. Yet the assurance that modernity is for us an irresistible fate can breed complacency, or cowardly submission to its imperatives. This is a complacency that Kolakowski is least of all the sort of intellectual to encourage. For this reason we heirs of modernity are better off hearkening to the foes of the modern age than to its partisans and cheerleaders. Better Nietzsche than Hegel. For Nietzsche never lets us forget that modernity, with all the blessings it brings and all the forms of liberation that it secures, also leaves us in a spiritually precarious position. It is the critics of modernity like Nietzsche, not proponents of modernity like Hegel, who alert us to our lack of secure footing:

> Disintegration characterizes this time, and thus uncertainty: nothing stands firmly on its feet or on a hard faith in itself; one lives for tomorrow, as the day after tomorrow is dubious. Everything on our way is slippery and

dangerous, and the ice that still supports us has become thin: all of us feel the warm, uncanny breath of the thawing wind; where we still walk, soon no one will be able to walk.[4]

University of Toronto

NOTES

1 Friedrich Nietzsche (1968) *The Will to Power*, ed. Walter Kaufmann, trans. W. Kaufmann and R. J. Hollingdale, pp. 51–2 (section 83). New York: Vintage.
2 Francis Bacon (1960) *The New Organon*, ed. Fulton H. Anderson, p. 118. New York: Macmillan.
3 Jean-François Lyotard (1984) *The Postmodern Condition: A Report on Knowledge*, p. xxiv. Minneapolis: University of Minnesota Press. 'I define *postmodern* as incredulity toward metanarratives.'
4 Nietzsche, op. cit. Note 1, p. 40 (section 57).

HISTORY OF THE HUMAN SCIENCES   Vol. 5 No. 3

© 1992 SAGE (London, Newbury Park and New Delhi)   pp. 71–79

Beyond the 'iron cage': Anthony Giddens on modernity and the self

IAN BURKITT

Anthony Giddens, *Modernity and Self-Identity: Self and Society in the Late Modern Age*. Cambridge: Polity Press, 1991. paper £11.95, 256 pp.

For Max Weber, writing in *The Protestant Ethic and the Spirit of Capitalism*, human beings in the modern age have become slaves to the products of the rationalized economic order and bureaucracy. Weber evokes the words of Baxter when he claims that 'the care for external goods should only lie on the shoulders of the "saint like a light cloak, which can be thrown aside at any moment". But fate decreed that the cloak should become an iron cage' (Weber, 1930: 181). In this last sentence, Weber encapsulated so much of the discontent felt by those who live in the era we have come to call 'modernity'. Both for Weber and for Giddens, the age of modernity came into being with the shattering of the traditional social order. In traditional society individuals were bound to a local place in which they lived out their entire lives, to an inherited status within the social strata and to institutions of authority that were rarely questioned. As the traditional order was slowly marginalized by social transformation, new institutions and authorities came to prominence which promised to fulfil hopes of human happiness and security. Rationalized modes of production and bureaucracy were meant to meet human needs, and rational modes of action and thought were to provide stable social structures and give answers to the questions that people asked of the natural and social worlds. The dream was not to last.

By now, in the late twentieth century, we are all familiar with the loss of faith in modern institutions and rationality. They have not delivered on their promises. From Nietzsche through Weber, and in critical theory, psychoanalysis and postmodernism, we can see disillusionment reflected in the loss of belief in 'progress' and the realization of the limits of rationality. What is so refreshing and stimulating about this new book by Anthony Giddens is that he does not accept this analysis at face value. For Giddens, while modern individuals are separated from the institutions of authority that would have guided their actions in the traditional order, they are not re-encapsulated in an iron cage of slavery to modern commodity production or to bureaucratic 'expert' systems. The central theme of the book is that modern institutions are grounded in 'reflexivity', which is to say that they require knowledgeable and skilled social actors to produce and reproduce them and so disseminate a large body of information to the population, along with a variety of life choices. This also means that modern institutions penetrate the very core of the self. Without the guidance of traditional authority, individuals must self-reflexively – knowledgeably – construct their own identities and chart their biographical courses through the mediation of modern institutions.

In taking on this social analysis, from the standpoint of what he refers to as 'high modernity', Giddens has employed familiar themes from his theory of structuration. However, now that this theory is applied to the modern world, it is shorn of many previously abstract features. So the notions of 'time–space distantiation' and 'reflexivity' are given more substance by their application to the institutions and everyday life of modernity. Giddens also employs a dialectical method of analysis which enables him to see the double-edged nature of modern life, and this lifts the work above the one-dimensional understanding of most critical theories of modernity, especially poststructuralism and post-modernism. Because of this Giddens notes how modernity not only tears apart traditional orders and local social relations, but reintegrates them at a new global level. Similarly, with belief systems, morality and public life, modernity does not only fragment these systems, but reconstitutes them through wider systems of mediation.

Indeed, one of the main points that Giddens wishes to make is that 'high' or late modernity is essentially a global order. While this is no longer an original insight, Giddens threads this idea through the whole book and shows how global systems have come to mediate even the most intimate areas of life. So while the dynamism of modern institutions undermines the possibility of establishing settled social traditions and relations, those institutions reorganize the time–space dimensions in which social relations and individual lives are constituted. For example, in pre-modern settings time and space were connected through each individual being situated in a particular place. With the development of more abstract methods for calculating time and charting space – such as clocks, calendars and maps – social activities could be coordinated across broader networks that were not confined to particular places. Because of the creation of international time zones, it is now possible to coordinate travel, business activities and media events across global spans of time and space. Thus the relation between time and space is not disintegrated but recombined in a dialectical fashion 'in ways that coordinate social activities without necessary reference to the particularities of place' (p. 17).

Equally modernity promotes what Giddens calls 'disembedding mechanisms', such as money or systems of technical knowledge, which mediate social relations and are recognized as valid in many different localities. This allows social relations to be 'lifted out' of local contexts and reconstituted across wide vistas of time–space. Again, although these mechanisms decontextualize the medium of social exchange, they dialectically recombine the relations they mediate at a global level. Disembedding mechanisms create further impetus to the move away from traditional, pre-established precepts and practices, towards the reflexive monitoring of action necessitated by the dynamism of modernity.

However, reflexivity itself is at the centre of two dialectical paradoxes that are characteristic of modernity. First, while reflexivity empowers individuals, giving them greater choice within their lives and in the development of self-identity, it also creates powerlessness and deskills agents by the 'sequestration of experience', in which expert systems intervene in times of existential crises. In these instances the experience of madness, sickness, death, criminality, sexuality and nature is often lifted out of everyday routines and dealt with by experts, mainly in specialized institutions. The removal of these troubling phenomena creates a feeling of security in expert systems, but only at the price of the exclusion of existential issues that all human life must sooner or later address and at the cost of deskilling individuals in dealing with such issues.

Second, while reflexivity gives agents power over modern institutions, which they constitute and reconstitute through knowledgeable action, the very fact that such institutions exist in global interdependence gives them a dynamic over which individuals have little control. In the world order, institutions respond to global influences and it is at this level that the main dynamism of change occurs. As Giddens says, for individuals, 'the sheer sense of being caught up in massive waves of global transformation is perturbing' (pp. 183–4), especially when this change involves inter-state tensions and conflicts. Here individuals face some of the potentially disastrous effects of globalization, such as the risks of nuclear war or the rise of totalitarian, militarized states. There are also other global dangers, including the risks of ecological disaster from pollution, or the possibilities of a worldwide economic collapse due to instabilities in international markets. All this leads Giddens to characterize the modern world as a juggernaut going out of control that all present-day men and women must ride. In many ways they have greater power over their lives than those who lived in traditional societies, and yet they face dangers of a global nature over which no one has control.

Giddens therefore sees modernity as an epoch infused with risk, and all who live in it are placed within a culture of risk-taking. Globalization creates a world that is constantly changing, where there are no settled traditions and no authorities to guide the actions people take. Furthermore, reflexivity undermines the Enlightenment belief in rational systems of thought and action that will adequately guide human behaviour in the absence of traditional authorities. The very method of scientific progress rests on the challenging of established paradigms with the aim of the furtherance of knowledge. However, this creates a situation where science is constantly undermining itself, and there exists a choice of expert systems and knowledge. The atmosphere in which modern people live is therefore one of radical doubt where no knowledge, whether technical or constituted by everyday belief, is secure.

To live in such a climate of risk, each individual must establish trust in the world and in others which forms a 'protective cocoon' that screens out many of the potential dangers individuals could face in everyday life. From the earliest years of infancy we must develop a system of tension management that provides a secure basis for self-identity and a protective cocoon against the dangers of living. Unlike Weber, Giddens does not see the development of individual personality as a heroic achievement in the face of an over-rationalized world; but he does see the formation of the basic structures of trust in the personality as the factor which allows for a feeling of security and the ability to maintain a biographical narrative in an age of constant crisis and risk.

This biographical narrative is itself mediated by reflexive institutions and expert systems. As an example of this Giddens chooses self-help psychotherapy manuals which enable individuals to make choices in their lives and to maintain the biographical narrative in times of upheaval. This takes courage and the willingness to grasp opportunities offered by modernity. But it also requires security in self and others because such choices are filled with risk. This mode of activity which opens up a person's life to constant change and risk requires self-reflexivity – a constant monitoring of action and feelings – and the formation of a life-plan which plots an individual's trajectory across the time he or she can expect to live and on the basis of which choices can be made about courses of action – what decisions to take and what life-style to adopt. All of this is coordinated by the biographical narrative and the life-plans which constantly orientate us to the future. Indeed, one of the effects of modernity is what Giddens calls the 'colonization of the future', in which events whose course guides our lives are not seen as our 'fate', but are open to influence so that individuals can, to a degree, control the future.

However, this does not mean that individuals have extensive powers. Authority still exists in the modern world in terms of expert systems and the power they have of the sequestration of experience. In this sequestration Giddens claims that day-to-day life is separated from what he calls 'original nature' and from existential questions that all human life must face. The result is that moral questions are institutionally repressed, and while expert systems and institutions may help us feel secure, they remove from everyday life the moral dilemmas that put meaning into social action. Existential issues are pushed to the fringes of day-to-day routines, making our lives meaningless.

This is where Giddens believes that the emerging politics of modernity plays a role, and he associates this politics with new social movements. The aim of these movements is the collective reappropriation of institutionally repressed areas of life, returning moral-existential questions to the heart of modernity. Giddens thus distinguishes between the 'old' 'emancipatory politics', which was concerned with establishing social equality, and the 'new' 'life politics' which is concerned with self-actualization, the global state of the environment, and the according restructuring of institutions. Life politics is focused upon self-identity and the environment, concentrating on moral questions that modernity has so far pushed to the fringes. Such a politics is, of course, also concerned with questions of human rights and emancipation, but it morally revitalizes these issues.

Again, Giddens is emphasizing the active and reflexive nature of modern life and arguing against those, such as Lasch and Sennett, who see modernity as involved in the destruction of social and political realms and thus essentially narcissistic. Giddens shows how what appears on the surface to be narcissistic concern with the self is in fact connected to the very reflexive nature of modernity and, by that token, is in fact collective mobilization of a new variety. Once more we see Giddens' more sophisticated reading of modernity and his ability to show how modern times are implicating individuals in new forms of social and political activity, not causing them to retreat from it. However, there are areas where I believe Giddens' analysis is fundamentally flawed and these need to be addressed for a more adequate theorization of, not only modern life, but social life more generally.

AN HISTORICAL PERSPECTIVE ON MODERNITY

One of the things lacking from Giddens' theory is an historical perspective in which he could show the development of modern institutions and modes of activity that constitute our everyday lives. This is a point Kilminster (1991) makes against Giddens' sociology, contrasting it with that of Elias who uses a historical and developmental model. Like Giddens, Elias (1991) has also noted the tendency in modern thought towards radical doubt, taking Descartes' model of the isolated ego as symptomatic of this attitude. This was the notion that the existence of everything outside the individual ego could be doubted, including the natural world, other people and even the individual's own body. The only thing that could be said with any certainty to exist was doubt itself and also, therefore, the ability of individuals to think their doubt. Existence could then be seen as residing in individual consciousness.

However, for Elias, this type of thinking is the manifestation of a particular social structure at a certain point in its historical development. State formation and social interdependence have reached a level of complexity at which individuals feel separated, not spatially but emotionally, from the others who make up the social network. This is the source of 'existential' questions where individuals feel anxiety about the security and ontological status of everything that exists 'outside' them. The problem is that Giddens tends to take these existential problems as given: they are not historically created but are ones that are encountered when individuals confront 'original' nature (p. 8). But what does Giddens mean when he talks here of 'original' nature? The phrase implies he has a notion of a purely natural state of existence that is not affected by human action. Indeed, this comes to the fore when he talks about 'socialized' nature being different from the 'old natural environment, which existed separately from human endeavours and formed a relatively unchanging backdrop to them' (p. 137). And Giddens also talks of the modern city as an 'artificial' setting for human activity which becomes 'sequestered from nature' (p. 166).

Thus Giddens fails to see existential problems as a social product of modernity and takes these issues to be an eternal backdrop to all human life. The problem of modernity is that it sequesters these timeless problems – such as the nature of life and death – from everyday existence and subjects them to institutional repression. This creates a fragile security, for beyond the morally empty and meaningless routines of daily life, there lurk 'chaos' and 'dread' (p. 37). Only the ontological security created by day-to-day routines keeps these feelings of anxiety partly at bay. But not only has Giddens dehistoricized the social contexts in which individuals feel existential loneliness and anxiety in the face of such dilemmas, he has naturalized them and thereby desocialized them. That is, Giddens sees existential and moral issues as dealing with the relation between individuals and external, original nature, as if this relation was not mediated by *social relations*. Thus he fails to take account of the theories of Marx or Elias which call into question the idea of an original nature and show how the idea of 'nature' is created in the social relations and activities through which individuals make contact with the natural world. Indeed, Elias has described what he calls 'the three basic coordinates of human life: the shaping and the position of the individual within the social structure, the social structure itself and the relation of social human beings to events in the non-human world' (1991: 97).

The result of ignoring such a position is that Giddens does not analyse moral problems as *social* problems; rather, for him, morality is to do with the way individuals deal with existential issues, those moments when nature permeates the protective cocoon of everyday life. But morality is about the way humans relate to one another and the way they deal with non-human events *within* social relations. As Giddens himself admits, such events cannot be totally excluded from modern institutions as moral questions exist about the way we deal with birth and death in places like hospitals and hospices. Also modern technology and expert systems raise moral issues themselves, such as questions about new reproductive technologies. The extent to which modernity has kept such issues at bay, put them on the fringes of society or repressed them institutionally, is therefore highly questionable.

Furthermore, if Giddens were right about this, and the real substance of human life and the subject of morality are pushed out of modern life for the fear and dread they cause, then the protective cocoon created by everyday routines is highly unstable because it is constituted by unreality. As Giddens observes, the meanings established in everyday interactions, and which 'answer' existential questions, are taken for granted because of the trust we invest in our world: however, these 'answers' might wither away under a sceptical gaze (p. 39). But this leaves Giddens open to the charge that everyday life, trust and ontological security are illusions, and it is more realistic to be paralysed by anxiety and existential dread. The individual who is so afflicted is responding in a more reasonable way than those who carry on with daily life. The problem for Giddens is that the ontological foundation for daily life and for meaning is undermined in his theory. Everyday life may just be an illusion that masks a deeper reality.

However, not only does this call into question Giddens' concept of modern, everyday reality, it also throws doubt upon his theory of self-identity.

FROM THE IRON CAGE TO THE PROTECTIVE COCOON

While Giddens does not picture modern individuals as slaves to the forces of commodity production or bureaucracy, he does, nevertheless, see them as swathed in a protective cocoon that screens out some of the realities that cause anxiety. The protective cocoon is instilled in the self in infancy through the relations of trust the child establishes with its care-takers. This trust acts as an 'emotional inoculation' (p. 39) against existential anxieties – the future risks and dangers that await the child in modernity. The 'inoculation' blocks off negative possibilities and creates a general attitude of hope, where risk and anxiety are screened out. This allows the individual to become a risk-taker, to have a basic sense of security and invulnerability which allows him or her to go about life's business in a creative way without being paralysed by anxiety.

However, the idea that children must be *inoculated* against the possibilities of anxiety suggests once again that uncertainty and dread may be an endemic tendency of humans or the most realistic attitude for them to take. It ignores the fact that it may be a response of children, especially in early infancy, to be fearless and it is the duty of parents, not to inoculate children against fear, but to *teach* them fear in order to protect them (Laplanche, 1989). Do we not have to stop our children from putting their hands in the fire, from running across the road without looking, or from jumping out of an upstairs window like superman?

Fear and anxiety are only *one* of the responses of which humans are capable and, like the others, we *learn* when to be afraid just as we learn how to feel secure.

This leads Giddens to ignore a crucial factor about the learned fears and insecurities of modern-day individuals – the way they are linked to the power structure of the everyday world. Elias (1978; 1982) has shown how the shame and embarrassment people feel when they have breached social rules is linked to the power and status structure of everyday life. People who infringe the rules have shown themselves to be unworthy of high status and have demeaned themselves in their own eyes and in the eyes of others. This mode of acting in accordance with the rules that reflect a particular balance of social power relations, also creates a situation in which individuals are forced to repress certain drives or responses that have been learned in different contexts (Burkitt, 1991). One of the most disappointing aspects of Giddens' book is that he does not explore in detail such themes relating to the formation of personality, and simply *assumes* that individuals have conscious and unconscious levels of psychological functioning. He barely takes this assumption further than in his earlier works (1979; 1984) where the unconscious is taken as operating according to the classical Freudian model. As Livesay (1989) points out, Giddens' conception of the personality within structuration theory would be greatly strengthened by looking at theories of the social formation of the unconscious and conscious mind, as, for example, in Lichtman's (1982) work. Unhappily Giddens has not taken the opportunity to pursue these issues.

On final consideration of this book it has to be said that despite its more thoughtful and sociological treatment of modernity, a major failure is the lack of analysis of power relations within the modern world. Giddens does consider the authority of expert systems in terms of the sequestration of experience, but does this notion exhaust the extent of power relations in our times? I feel a more thorough analysis of power is needed at the global, institutional and day-to-day level, and in terms of how power relations structure the self. Also, the concept of the sequestration of experience takes the moral and existential dilemmas facing individuals to be ones where *natural* events intrude into the socially well-ordered realm of daily life, ignoring the moral and political dilemmas surrounding the everyday interactions *between people* and the wider balances of power that structure them. Thus Giddens understands life politics as the reintroduction of natural events or environmental concerns into the political realm, revitalizing the older, emancipatory social movements. But he does not say how emancipatory politics must affect the realm of life politics, which is primarily about self-actualization. In a world of unequal power balances, some groups and individuals have more time, space and resources than others to actualize themselves to greater degrees, and these privileges will also cushion them to an extent from the privations environmentally informed politics may demand.

Through the concept of reflexivity Giddens has achieved an analysis of modernity in which self-identity is not simply a construction of autonomous signs or discourses that the individual cannot control. Nor is the self simply a cog in the wheel of rationalization, consumerism and bureaucracy. However, what Giddens fails to do is to connect relations of power at a global level to the reflexive institutions of modernity, and therefore show how power is also connected to the self-reflexivity of individuals. Do we, for example, have perfect knowledge of the way that our institutions work and a clear self-reflexive understanding of our own personality, or our needs and desires? For a more adequate conception of modernity Giddens would need to analyse more thoroughly the connections between modern institutions, power relations and the self. Morality is not just about politics that considers a new relation to nature, but one that also considers a new relation between human beings.

University of Bradford

BIBLIOGRAPHY

Burkitt, Ian (1991) *Social Selves: Theories of the Social Formation of Personality*. London: Sage.

Elias, Norbert (1978) *The History of Manners: The Civilizing Process*, Vol. One. Oxford: Blackwell.

Elias, Norbert (1982) *State Formation and Civilization: The Civilizing Process*, Vol. Two. Oxford: Blackwell.

Elias, Norbert (1991) *The Society of Individuals*. Oxford: Blackwell.

Giddens, Anthony (1979) *Central Problems in Social Theory: Action, Structure and Contradiction in Social Analysis*. London: Macmillan.

Giddens, Anthony (1984) *The Constitution of Society*. Cambridge: Polity.

Kilminster, Richard (1991) 'Structuration Theory as a World-view', in C. Bryant and D. Jary (eds) *Giddens' Theory of Structuration: A Critical Appreciation*. London: Routledge.

Laplanche, Jean (1989) *New Foundations for Psychoanalysis*. Oxford: Blackwell.

Lichtman, Richard (1982) *The Production of Desire: The Integration of Psychoanalysis into Marxist Theory*. New York: Free Press.

Livesay, Jeff (1989) 'Structuration Theory and the Unacknowledged Conditions of Action', *Theory, Culture and Society* 6(2): 263–92.

Weber, Max (1930) *The Protestant Ethic and the Spirit of Capitalism*. London: Allen & Unwin.

© 1992 SAGE (London, Newbury Park and New Delhi)   pp. 81–91

Modernity and its Other(s)

DIANA COOLE

Jürgen Habermas, *The Philosophical Discourse of Modernity*, trans. F. G. Lawrence. Cambridge: Polity Press, 1987.

Stephen K. White, *Political Theory and Postmodernism*. Cambridge: Cambridge University Press, 1991.

Alice A. Jardine, *Gynesis. Configurations of Woman and Modernity*. Ithaca, NY and London: Cornell University Press, 1985.

The belief that modernity is in crisis has become increasingly widespread since the Enlightenment, and the three books discussed here are all to be read against this background. Their main interest lies in addressing those discourses which have sprung up in response to modernity's rationalistic closure and here they are especially concerned about the nature of postmodernism, which they disagree about. What is distinctive about its reaction, is that it rejects the Enlightenment language and criteria which earlier critics employed in their attempt to set the emancipatory potential of modernity free. This makes it difficult to associate postmodernism with the radical critiques and political practices developed by (neo)Marxism, democratic political theory and feminism, and it is the relationship between postmodernism and these critical but modern discourses that Habermas, White and Jardine respectively explore. What is at stake here is whether some form of reason yet remains our best hope of escape from modernity's crisis, or whether we should rather appeal beyond reason to its Other. If we take the latter step, might it finally release us from a will to mastery lodged in the very foundations of enlightenment, or does it rather abandon too much and signal the death-knell of all emancipatory hope?

It is Habermas who adopts the most hostile approach towards postmodern-ism, and indeed he is explicit that his motivation for writing *The Philosophical Discourse of Modernity* is precisely to reinvigorate that discourse against its poststructuralist opponents. The overall structure of this collection of twelve lectures is therefore a dichotomous one with polemical intent. The discourse to be defended is a critical one of counter-Enlightenment: a 'venerable tradition' that has accompanied modernity from the outset and recognizes the inadequacy of its Cartesian–Kantian foundations in a philosophy of the contemplative subject. From Hegel and Marx through to Adorno and Horkheimer, and intertwined with an aesthetic discourse evolved by romantics and the avant-garde, this critical thinking recognizes a dialectic of liberation and domination within modern forms of reason, and struggles to develop the former aspect by unfolding a broader and more comprehensive rationality that would enlighten the Enlightenment about its own narrowness. This then marks its distinction from the undialectical post-Enlightenment discourses whose origin Habermas finds in Nietzsche and against which he delivers a series of effective blows.

His distinction is, however, difficult to sustain clearly. First, Habermas seems unsure on what grounds he wishes to indict the postmoderns. He repeatedly asserts the performative contradictions of their position: they no longer possess any normative grounding or basis for validity claims on which to base their assault against reason. But at the same time, he seems not to believe that they really do abandon reason, accusing Nietzsche and his epigones of secretly relying on the same ideals of an undamaged intersubjectivity and aesthetic modernity that had explicitly grounded the dialectical critiques.

Habermas's dichotomy is also made less clear because of the role he accords his own contribution within this narrative. For although he explicitly sides with the critical modernists, he finds them all failing in their attempts to develop an unambiguously emancipatory reason since none finally manages to escape the Enlightenment's subjectivist foundations. This is a failure they allegedly share with the postmodernists, and so despite their different attitudes towards modernity, they are all in the end placed together in their failure, against Habermas's own solution of intersubjective rationality and communicative action. Moreover, all share in a broad agreement as to the nature and source of modernity's central problem, namely its subjectivist foundations. They agree that the disembodied, decontextualized transcendental subject whose reason is the guarantee of knowledge is deeply problematic. It is severed from an external nature it objectifies for purposes of representation and mastery. To achieve this, it must also repress, exclude and objectify its own inner nature – its body, needs, passions, unconscious – if it is to remain transparent to itself. The decisive question is then whether this purposive, instrumental reason is the whole story, or whether reason harbours critical and emancipatory possibilities beyond this particular subject–object relation. Habermas claims it does and that this is to be understood intersubjectively.

Communicative rationality springs, then, from mutual understanding and reciprocity which are open yet orientated towards consensus, thanks to the formal rationality of differentiated spheres of value, each with its own criterion for validity claims. It is in this Kantian differentiation between the cognitive-instrumental, normative and aesthetic, with their respective criteria for establishing propositional truth, normative rightness and aesthetic harmony, that Habermas finds modernity's promises sustained. But he would replace its oppressive subject–object relations with a more dialectical exchange between a consensually based praxis, on the one hand, and a permeable if dense lifeworld, on the other. Habermas has written more extensively about this solution elsewhere, but here I am more interested in the discourses of counter- and post-Enlightenment as he unfolds and criticizes them.

The former finds its origins in Hegel, who is the first to recognize the philosophical problem of modernity: that given its future-orientated sense of time, it must be self-grounding. Kant had already tackled this dilemma by grounding meaning and truth in the formal rationality of the self-conscious subject, whose faculties permit a tripartite division between theoretical and practical reason and aesthetic judgement. But Hegel recognized that Kant's system rested on a series of dualisms – subject/object, truth/justice, under-standing/reason and so on – which rendered it an inadequate basis for the reconciliation modern society required. Habermas then presents both Hegel and Marx as seeing reason's primary task as one of restoring an ethical community: an insight that might have led them to pursue his own communicative solution had they not lacked an adequate model for conceiving it. Thus Hegel's failing is that he cannot see beyond an obsolete *polis*, and ends up instead looking to an absolute reason which is indeed inclusive, but which fails to reconcile the diremption between philosophy and the people. Reason loses its critical potential and consciousness again triumphs over its other. Marx accordingly realizes that reason must be made concrete: instead of individuals knowing the world, the species now labours to change it. But what gave this labour its normative basis, according to Habermas, was an anachronistic aesthetic vision of unalienated handicraft, and this succumbed to the purposive rationality of a goal-directed and self-assertive producing collective. Like Hegel, Marx is therefore driven back into the philosophy of subjectivity whereby the subject dominates its objects and institutes a narrow form of reason predicated on domination.

By the time Horkheimer and Adorno took up the question of reason, its instrumentality seemed all-pervasive. They pose something of a problem for Habermas, because their position comes so close to the postmodern disavowal of reason as such, and Habermas discusses their *Dialectic of Enlightenment* with the express aim of distancing them from it. His own view is that the autonomous logics of validity claims lodged in theoretical science, democratic procedures and the avant-garde, keep alive a critical reason and that when his predecessors find even this rendered instrumental, they are in danger of succumbing to the

Nietzschean performative paradox. They respond by an ungroundable determinate negation of ever deepening critique, yet they do, Habermas insists, hold on to a critical approach motivated by hope of a rational alternative. Nevertheless, this distinction has become a fine one by Adorno's *Negative Dialectics*: if there is still hope, it is apparent only in the non-identical aesthetic experience of avant-garde art. The distance between negative dialectics and deconstruction is clearly less than Habermas would like.

At this point, it is necessary to mention the third, aesthetic component of Kantian reason. It is strange that Habermas barely mentions *The Critique of Judgement*, because Kant intended it as a resolution to the dualisms he already recognized as problematic, and it was this which a romantic tradition took up when it saw art as a reconciling force, looking to the aesthetic for a model of a different, more harmonious, sort of subject–object and intersubjective relationship. But it is here that we find disparities between the dialectical and postmodern positions opening up. In romanticism as Habermas portrays it, there was a gradual purging of the aesthetic from cognitive-instrumental and moral-practical reason although its aim remained one of revitalizing modernity. Nietzsche, however, took this drift further and abandoned its goal, now associating the aesthetic with archaic forces modernity had renounced; an experience of non-discursive excitement and self-oblivion that offered a route to reason's Other. Nietzsche's 'aesthetically inspired anarchism' thus becomes, for Habermas, a surprisingly early threshold of postmodernism. With Nietzsche, what were moments of aesthetic judgement and therefore able to command rational consensus, now become a frenzy outside reason, ecstatic rather than self-conscious. Worse, as far as Habermas is concerned, this aesthetic now overflows its boundaries to impose its particular validity claims on cognitive and moral reason, such that truth and value become matters of taste. It is then this heritage that he traces through Heidegger, Derrida, Bataille and Foucault, finding there (if more ambiguously in Foucault) a Dionysian project of escaping reason. Allegedly, they thus mistakenly reduce reason to its oppressive forms in order to reject it, although they secretly rely, according to Habermas, on a normativity drawn from aesthetic modernity. This is then where a postmodern opposition between reason and its incommensurable Other opens up, no longer inspired by explicit hopes of a dialectical reconciliation. By conflating 'ecstatic sovereignty or forgotten Being . . . bodily reflexes, local resistances, and the involuntary revolts of a deprived subjective nature' (pp. 58, 307), as well as the 'feminine', as simply different names for this Other, however, Habermas surely fails to do justice to what is distinctive about recent poststructuralisms.

He finds Nietzsche's Dionysian messianism again in Heidegger's Being, where reason is a forgetting and Being's truth is reclaimed not by reflection, but (according to Habermas's less than sympathetic reading) by surrender to its authority; by a mystical ecstasy that is condemned as immune to any criterion of validity. The subject–object relation of the Enlightenment then appears as merely reversed, as Being discloses itself to Dasein via a poetic language (a subterfuge that Habermas associates with Nazism). It is then this mysticism of which Habermas goes on to accuse Derrida, insisting that he remains close to the general structure of Heidegger's destruction (deconstruction) of metaphysics. Derrida's contention that all language is rhetorical similarly puts it beyond the type of validity claims Habermas would insist on, while ignoring the ordinary language that coordinates action to deal with the social pathologies Derrida, like Heidegger, is accused of mystifying. Habermas sees in Derrida's archewriting only another name for Being. 'In the metaphor of the archewriting and its trace, we see again the Dionysian motif of the God making his paranoid presence all the more palpable to his sons and daughters of the West by means of his poignant absence' (p. 180 f.). Once this equation is made, Derrida is vulnerable to accusations of closet messianism and inverted foundationalism; of making a mystical appeal to an absent god. Bataille is then added as part of the same camp. For him, it is the heterogeneous and excessive, once expressed in a primordial Sovereignty, which is Other and subversive of modern instrumentality. Again we find an appeal to the archaic, something prior to reason and immune to it yet retrievable through transgressive experiences which would extinguish the rational subject.

Habermas's implication is thus that postmodernism, from Nietzsche on, equates the Other with some prediscursive referent which precedes reason and which might be retrieved, by non-rational strategies, as a way of reinvigorating (post)modernity. It is associated with some unspeakable and amorphous excitement. Unlike the Romantics' aesthetic, this Other is not then a split-off and suppressed part of reason, but is temporally related to something preceding it, something allegedly authentic, archaic, a primordial and mysterious Other. Having established this commonality, Habermas can then write off postmodernism as an appeal to mystical, apolitical and irrational forces which would replace reason and truth with an undifferentiated chaos.

Yet does Habermas do justice to the postmodernists here? For poststructuralist allusions to the Other are surely not typically of this order. What intervenes is a whole theory of linguistics, after which the Other is, to misquote Lacan, structured like a language. This allows reason, with its illusions of presence, transparency and omniscience, to be subverted not by some wild primordial referent, but by the sheer non-coincidence, spacing and motility of language itself. Derrida's appeal to *différance* is not messianic if one finds here the differences and deferrals within the chain of signification, such that its heterogeneity is invoked not to replace sense by nonsense, but to subvert reason's illusion of mastery. The Other then emerges only as a sort of mobile negativity, a disruptive force but not one that might be installed as an ontological alternative to reason, a counter-symbolic. Its irruptions are but strategies for opening spaces through which the unnameable and hence uncolonizable, might be glimpsed/created as a subversion of reason's closures. The Other is not then a new foundation, but a demonstration of the untenability of all foundations. It is Habermas, not postmodernism, who sets up an opposition of reason/non-reason in order to invert it. For the latter deconstructs such oppositions and, in this process, it transgresses, plays along, boundaries, such that the non-rational irrupts into reason only to destabilize, not to replace it. Postmodernism is not then on the side of truth(/untruth) or goodness, but openness, an openness which springs from the structures of meaning itself. Indeed, its subversions are the sort of permanent guarantee against closure that Habermas's communicative participants might themselves rely on if their consensus, too, would not harden into a new closure and in this sense postmodernism is continuous with an earlier critical theory. Its subversion takes over where a necessarily complicitous critique must end, but without positive vision or hope.

It is only in his discussion of Foucault that Habermas acknowledges this resolutely non-emancipatory thrust. Foucault's Other is only the excluded other of constantly shifting discourses, and shares their contingency and mobility. Yet even here, Habermas would reclaim Foucault to a resilient modernity, claiming to discover beneath Foucault's radical historicism 'the passions of aesthetic modernism' (p. 275). It appears after all that postmodernists have always been secretly nurtured by the problem Hegel originally saw at the heart of modernity: of restoring an 'undamaged intersubjectivity'. And so it finally seems impossible, on reading Habermas, that we can fall out of modernity: we are only after all clear or confused about our normative intent.

*   *   *

Political Theory and Postmodernism is about just what its title suggests: an ingenious (if flawed) attempt to integrate two very different discourses. Stephen White is more sympathetic to postmodernism than Habermas and wants to integrate what he calls its 'responsibility to otherness' into a political theory he finds overly concerned with abstract universals and action-coordination. Yet he is also wary of the way postmodernism exercises this responsibility, which he summarizes as 'impertinence', a 'permanent withholding gesture' (pp. 6, 19) – that is, a merely negative strategy for shocking us out of the habitual in order to reveal its contestability and costs of exclusion.

I have already indicated that I think this is precisely the importance of postmodernism, as a permanent refusal of reified and closed meanings or institutions, but White is not happy with this. The central issue for him is 'what theoretical resources are needed for an adequate model of postmodern politics' (p. 33). For him the two discourses need synthesizing, and White attempts this by interpreting their opposition as the postmodern responsibility to otherness, aligned with a 'world-disclosing' function of language, versus a responsibility to act, lined up with the more action-coordinating (more Habermasian) function of language associated with modern political and ethical thought.

By summarizing postmodern and modern approaches in this way, White already of course implies some common ethical ground centred on responsibility. This is the first step in what I find the main problem with his argument: it subtly transposes postmodernism onto the terrain of political and ethical modernity as the book progresses, so that although White is able to conclude with a flourish of reconciliation, this fails to do justice to the sensitivity with which he outlines poststructuralist subversiveness in the opening chapters. In particular, he achieves it by (like Habermas) conflating rather different senses of the Other.

White's argument takes the following course: having described postmodernism's attention to otherness as its defining feature, he finds the stance Heidegger wants us to adopt to Being quite promising. This is captured in the notion of 'nearness', a disposition whose intersubjective implications he develops by reference to feminist discussions of care. With this accomplished, he can move into a discussion of justice and the way this responsibility to otherness, now safely redefined as care, might be integrated into political theory.

The argument is insightful, and White's greatest strength lies in alerting us to problems political theory needs urgently to reconsider in a late modern/postmodern age: in particular, the balance between difference and universality, plurality and constraint. But by the final chapter, we are back on the reassuring ground of liberal pluralism and without very much to show for White's fascinating excursus, beyond perhaps more beautiful souls and a change of mood.

This deradicalizing of poststructuralism is made possible because White subtly shifts his understanding of the 'otherness' to which responsibility is owed. The crucial passage here is the following:

> The Harmony, unity and clarity promised by this [modern cognitive] machinery have, for the postmodern, an inevitable cost; and that cost is couched in the language of an Other that is always engendered, devalued, disciplined, and so on, in the infinite search for a more tractable and ordered world. One might speak here of something like a moral-aesthetic sense of *responsibility to otherness*. Its moral dimension is most clearly evident when the Other attended to is a human being. But how one cultivates and responds to this in general goes beyond traditional moral reasoning in ways that might seem to involve deeply aesthetic qualities. (p. 20)

Here, then, we have a 'responsibility' to an Other that is the excluded, relational Other of poststructuralism rather than the primordial and mystical Other of Habermas's demonology. But it is difficult to see in what sense we could owe it *responsibility* (for example, as *différance*), or how this could be defined as the postmodern attitude. If that attitude is a moral-aesthetic one, this surely makes sense *only* when the other is human. But if postmodernism is redefined as a responsibility to other people, it has already re-entered the familiar discourses of political and ethical theory and the work of integration becomes the rather different one of trying to reconcile two moral systems. It becomes remarkably similar, in fact, to work being done by feminists on the ethics of care, and by assimilating Heideggerian nearness with feminist care, White quietly shifts the postmodern into the register of the modern.

Heidegger's Being now appears more like Derrida's mobile *différance*. Our escape from the willing–wanting–grasping of modernity arises from coming face-to-face with its plurifying, dissolving motility, accomplished by an 'other thinking' that White interprets as a learning process: an attempt to orientate ourselves to finitude and otherness. 'Nearness' manifests a way of experiencing otherness that lets it remain other in its difference while bringing it into presence, in a complex of closeness and distance (p. 67). The moods of this disposition are ambiguous – grieving joy, anxiety and awe, fascination and mourning – as we discover the fragility and finitude of our world and learn to be at home in our homelessness. White is not very successful in discovering this mood among the poststructuralists, although he does think hints might be found in Derrida's interest in friendship, Lyotard's everyday sublime and Foucault's passing linkage of curiosity with care. But in any case, he reminds us that we cannot use Heidegger to develop a politics: the mood elicited still needs translating into intersubjective terms and this is where 'difference feminism' comes in.

It is telling that the feminism whose help White elicits here is the one influenced by Gilligan's pursuit of a 'different voice' in ethics. There is no mention of the poststructuralist feminists who have developed a rich literature associating the feminine with the Other. The debates about care allow White to move definitively away from the Other to others, whose ethical relations focus on connectedness and sensitivity to context. With this move, he leaves behind the ontological-epistemological Other and replaces it with human others in ethical-political relations. The relationships in this new morality more closely resemble the aesthetic ones of Kant's Third Critique than the cognitive-instrumental and moral-practical orientations of the first two. In other words, we are now safely back on the ground of Kant's tripartite reason, and it is only a matter of redressing the balance, of bringing the aesthetic power of harmony back in line with the oppressive rationalism of pure and practical reason.

White claims to find a strong echo of Heideggerian nearness in this feminist ethics, especially in Ruddick's 'maternal thinking', and this allows him to translate responsibility for otherness into 'an attitude of care for the other'. But with this move, all sense of the Other as something *radically* different, incommensurable, disappears. Indeed, what Gilligan et al. most dislike about universalist ethics, is its way of rendering concrete, and often familiar, others, alien and other. And what they value most about *their* ethics, is a certain intimacy and familiarity with others it accommodates. Of course I am not saying this is unimportant for feminists, only that this is their concern and not one that can be mapped on to the postmoderns, who precisely do want to preserve a sense of strangeness and unrecuperable distance. Although White tries to find a balance between intimacy and distance in his 'lightness of care', he acknowledges that even feminists have so far failed to achieve a workable synthesis. This results in a disclaimer that an alternative is anyway the aim, as opposed to 'modes of counterpoint' to dominant modes. Yet this is an odd conclusion in the light both of feminists who pursue just such an alternative, and White's previous insistence that a more affirmative postmodernism is exactly what he seeks. In fact he now retreats from his earlier quest, to argue that it is not the state but the sub-political that concerns him, where the important thing is to open public breathing spaces for abnormal discourse. But is this not precisely why postmodernism has always insisted on the very negative, subversive stance that it was White's aim to transform into a more action-coordinated approach? Moreover, there is no sense of power here, or of the fact that women have been excluded as others, where a willing reciprocity is not the issue.

On broader questions of justice, the orientation to care is now translated into the suggestion that tolerance be supplemented by a fostering, even a celebration, of otherness as difference. White is eager to distinguish this from Mill's toleration of diversity, but his notion of fostering surely gives the game away, for who is to do the fostering but the already privileged, and why? The postmodern and feminist point is that there are already very many others and a multiplicity of differences, which have been designated other and excluded, silenced. They do not require a celebratory engendering or fostering, but an empowering and resourcing. Their purpose is not to enrich the lives of those who might suffer from an undelightful conformity, but to speak their difference in a way that does pose serious difficulties for universalist and foundational political thought. White is probably right to say that postmodernists rely too heavily on a vague idea of correspondence between heterogeneity and radical democracy, and he is right to point political theorists in this direction. But his conclusions show exactly why postmodernism must retain its subversive 'impertinent' stance outside this assimilation to a practical politics. For what White excludes is a militancy by which the others demand a voice by subverting dominant discourses, while insisting on their difference.

White again raises an important question for political theorists when he discusses constraints on difference – are we also to value street gangs or ethnic violence? But again, does postmodernism not answer this: no, because these are hierarchical and exclusive models of closure, to be subverted like any other form exercising a will to mastery. This might remain weak in practical terms, but surely less so than White's urge to self-restraint in recognition that 'the urge to dominate constitutes a refusal to bear witness to one's limits, a refusal to recognize finitude' (p. 137).

Perhaps in recognition that this does not really amount to very much, White closes with an extraordinarily humble footnote, given the rather grand claims with which he began: 'A more independent attention to phenomena of injustice and to the whole issue of fostering are all that I would claim emerge out of a sensitivity to the responsibility to otherness that is greater than that of Habermas's communicative ethics' (p. 141 n.).

*   *   *

I want to mention Jardine's work only briefly. This was a fairly early attempt at bringing French postmodernism to the attention of American feminists, and subsequently that attention has issued in a voluminous literature. Nevertheless, I think two aspects of Jardine's *Gynesis* remain important in the light of my criticisms of Habermas and White. First, she is extremely self-conscious about her own position in bringing together two very different discourses, characterizing American feminism as 'a primarily ethical discourse as prescription for action' and the French poststructuralists as emphasizing linguistic and symbolic structures (p. 43). She would not therefore eliminate or assimilate postmodernism, and indeed offers a sympathetic account which presents a more serious appreciation of its attempt to think through the West's epistemological crisis at its foundations, than White's 'impertinence' allows. Indeed, if anything, her aim is to show how modernist discourses like feminism have been problematized by the deconstruction of those foundations. But at the same time, she is worried about the implications for women and therefore, like Habermas, wants to ask whether postmodernism extends or ends the critical and emancipatory projects of modernity.

Secondly, Jardine explores precisely the association between the Other and the feminine that so much postmodernism has insisted on, and that Habermas had noted as merely a currently popular name for an Other that had previously had many different names. The aim is to find within western discourse a new space for what has eluded them, and this 'other-than-themselves is almost always a "space" of some kind (over which the narrative has lost control), and this space has been coded as feminine, as woman' (p. 25). It is not concerned with real women, but uses woman as a metaphor for what has been left out as unrepresentable. Jardine calls this coding 'gynesis', a mapping of these new spaces where the feminine comes to signify processes disruptive of western symbolisms.

Jardine does not, as we might have expected, explore women poststructuralists like Kristeva and Irigaray here, although she says they remain on the horizons of her work. Instead she offers detailed accounts of three male postmoderns – Lacan, Derrida and Deleuze – to show why they have designated the Other feminine in more than a popular or contingent move. As a feminist, she is deeply interested in their inquiries into cultural codings as these relate to sexual difference. She is sympathetic to the need to invoke a strange new world that requires speaking and writing in new and strange ways, and thus to the cultural impact of the postmodern, especially in the light of feminist designations of dominant discourses as masculine and phallocentric. A differently positioned subject within meaning, where (gendered) identities are produced, thus emerges as a vital aspect of escaping the philosophy of the subject and mastery, although Jardine recognizes the implications of this for feminist projects of retrieving/ inventing a female subject. She also realizes that precisely because the feminine is not about women as such, its relevance for feminists is not self-evident: it might remain a product of male fantasy and risks permanently labelling women as unnameable others.

Nevertheless, Jardine's work is important in its insistence that feminist questions are a central aspect of postmodernism. I think her emphasis also reminds us of the dangers of assimilating postmodern otherness to existing modern discourses. For as women's experience shows, it is possible to be incorporated within the dominant consensus while still being excluded and degraded as other; it is also much easier to participate in liberal pluralism when one speaks its dominant languages, but it is much more difficult to find space for a genuinely different voice there. This, then, is the real question of otherness that political theory and radical discourses must examine, and this requires that we take seriously suggestions that the Other is genuinely other to the dominant discourses of reason.

University of Leeds

HISTORY OF THE HUMAN SCIENCES   Vol. 5 No. 3
© 1992 SAGE (London, Newbury Park and New Delhi)   pp. 93 97

Is postmodern politics politics?

GEOFFREY HAWTHORN

William E. Connolly, *Identity/Difference: Democratic Negotiations of Political Paradox*. Ithaca, NY: Cornell University Press, 1991. $27.50, xii + 244 pp.

Stephen K. White, *Political Theory and Postmodernism*. Cambridge: Cambridge University Press, 1991. £25.00/£9.95, xiv + 153 pp.

Liberal Americans – William Connolly is one, and writes for others – are anxious. They have a sense, as Connolly puts it, of owing their 'life and destiny to world-historical, national and bureaucratic forces' that they can no longer control. They have lost confidence 'in the probable future to which they find themselves contributing'. And from their affluent insulation they sense 'an even more ominous set of future possibilities that weigh upon life in the present'. They are in a state of 'dependent uncertainty' and 'generalized resentment'. They feel trapped in the cages of modernity which construct their identities and constrain their lives, yet sense that this modernity has become 'late modernity', a 'black hole located between the drive of late-modern states for mastery' and 'the world-systemic effects' that are created by that drive. And their lives are ordered by and for a state which cannot admit that it has less and less purchase on the 'contingent globalization' of events. 'The experience of freedom' – the voice here is most distinctively American – 'is drained from the exercise of choice; the experience of choice is wrenched from the requirement to convert life into a project; the assurance of temporal stability is withdrawn from the time covered by a life project'.

Yet the more orthodox political theorists go on as if nothing has changed. Individualists assume 'that civil society is the road to world mastery, that freedom for the individual involves control over personal destiny, and control over personal destiny is perfected to the extent that the impersonal structure of civil society succeeds in subjecting nature to human purposes'. Collectivists – Jürgen Habermas, for instance – agree 'that freedom involves mastery over nature and insists that its highest locus of expression is the collectivity (a state, a people, a class) that establishes a settled plan to achieve it'. Communitarians – Michael Sandel, Charles Taylor, Alasdair MacIntyre – see 'more than indifference in nature' and discern a 'direction in the world to which the self and the community must . . . become attuned'; for them, to be free is to realize 'fulfilment and harmonization' in aligning oneself to a 'higher direction'. In Stephen White's more abstract way of putting it, all three are concerned to suggest a way in which citizens can coordinate their actions, and in so doing, to press solutions. But 'deconstruction' alerts us to the fact that in any such solution, some identities will be pressed against others, and there will always be 'exclusions'.

Connolly accepts this charge. We must, he says, acknowledge 'the paradox of difference' which the deconstructionists insist on, and convert it into 'a politics of the paradoxical, into a conception of the political as the medium through which the interdependent antinomies of identity and difference can be expressed and contested'. White is more circumspect. He invites us to hold 'languages for the coordination of action' at arm's length and, through the thoughts of Heidegger, Derrida, Lyotard, Rorty, 'difference feminism' and Walzer, to explore those that can instead 'disclose' the world. 'The practice of deconstruction', he says, 'always has a politicizing effect.' But his question is also Connolly's: can anything constructive come from this practice?

White himself havers. At its worst, he points out, postmodernism, once it has done its job of exposing, withholds. Consider Heidegger. For him, there was no distinction worth making between existing political arrangements. They were all expressions of the metaphysically grounded, one-dimensional closure of modernity. But Being has withdrawn from the world. We can but wait. In time, we might be redeemed, but there is nothing we can do to hasten *das Kommende*, 'that which will come', the start of *Seinsgeschichte*, the 'history of Being'. This, White continues, is because 'anything that could qualify as a better political world would have to be describable in terms of practices and institutions; and to speak that language is to speak about how actions might be coordinated – how the tensions between claims and wills would be related to structures of normative expectation'; it would be to speak in a way that Heidegger himself ruled out. At its best, White argues, in Reiner Schürmann's extension (in *Heidegger on Being and Acting*) of Heidegger's deconstruction of metaphysical reasons for acting, or in 'difference feminism', postmodernism invites us to listen to the other, and not to corral what she says into a pre-existing frame: actually to care for what she says, that is to say, to accept what Seyla Benhabib and Nancy Fraser think of as the motivating force of an affective orientation, and not just airily to agree that she has a right to say it; to allow what Schürmann calls 'the play of a flux in practice, without stabilisation . . . an incessant fluctuation in institutions [as] an end in itself'; to find some way in which the other, in order to play this game of 'an-*arche*', can be empowered to do so. But unless, like Richard Rorty, we are prepared – because there is no other – to accept our own standpoint and the political direction it suggests, a solution which seems to restate the problem rather than to solve it, postmodernism condemns us to act without a goal. As Lyotard and others have more or less cheerfully agreed, its politics therefore can at best be a series of improvised strategies for survival, none of which can be morally 'privileged' over another.

This is where White resists. 'World-disclosing' is all very well, but we must have some way of discriminating between the depredations of marauding gangs in downtown Los Angeles and more peaceful strategies for recognition and self-help, something with which to guide us through the babel of voices and coordinate our actions towards a defensible end. For White himself, as he has said elsewhere, this could be a version of Habermas's 'communicative ethics'. It is wrong, he insists, to see this as Walzer does, as a model of normative conversation intended 'to press the speakers toward a preconceived harmony'. If there is a harmony to be had through Habermas, it is constructed, not discovered. This is not to say that one has to take his argument as it is. 'Taken within the overall perspective I am offering', White argues, Habermas's 'metanarrative can be seen as telling only one part of a larger story about modernity.' 'It can be interpreted in a more clearly pragmatic way' to identify 'a responsibility to otherness at as deep a philosophical level as the responsibility to act' and accordingly give 'a stronger independence to the moods and attitudes associated with hesitation and listening to the other'. We can thereby have 'a narrative that is recounted to those with whom we radically disagree, with the intention of showing them that they could freely recognize themselves as having a place within it, could find some sense of affirmation within it'. It might even produce the picture that Walzer has sketched (in a paper in *Political Theory* in 1990) of a communitarianism rooted in the liberal values of difference, that is to say, a political community whose solidarity is affirmed, and not denied, by the different ways in which the people within it choose to lead their lives.

This is a bland conclusion, and evasive; and at just the point at which he should, White takes it no further. Like many of those who write political theory – and even more of those who write about it – he barely touches on the reality that the theory might be for. He merely asserts that 'societal rationalisation' is largely the result of what he calls 'corporate capitalism', and that there would be a sufficient opposition to it in 'decentralised, democratically controlled enterprises' which would be more responsive to the communities and environments in which they operate. But he gives no indication of how these enterprises might be financed, what part they would play in the economy, and how, exactly, their 'democracy' would work. In fact, he says nothing at all about political agency, or about the more directly political institutions and the sovereignties within which his diffuse and implausible new solidarity would exist and be worked.

Connolly presses harder. He too has a picture of a politics in which 'the antagonism of identity' is transformed into 'the agonism of difference', a politics 'in which each opposes the other (and the other's presumptive beliefs) while respecting [him] at another level as one whose contingent orientations also rest on shaky epistemic grounds'. 'An antagonism in which each aims initially at conquest or conversion of the other can now (given other supporting conditions) become an agonism in which each treats the other as crucial to itself in the strife and interdependence of identity/difference. A "pathos of distance" (to borrow a phrase from Nietzsche) begins to unfold whereby each maintains a certain respect for the adversary, partly because the relationship exposes contingency in the being of both.' But the 'supporting conditions', Connolly insists, are crucial, and they are not yet given.

Moreover, they are conditions which the new politics – although Connolly does not quite say so – cannot itself produce. There are three. The highest income must not be more than five or six times as large as the lowest and there must be 'general access to economic, educational, and cultural opportunities'. Conventionally competitive party-political democracy, which generates resentments to strengthen the identities that are necessary to incite the fights on which such a democracy depends, must be transcended. And we must reshape the relation between sovereignty and democracy. 'The state, as the legitimate centre of sovereignty, citizen loyalty, and political dissent, must give more ground to other modes of political identification. . . . If democracy is not to become a political ghetto confined to the territorial state, the contemporary globalization of capital, labour, and contingency must be shadowed by a corollary globalization of politics.'

Until these changes take place, we are trapped. 'Either democracy remains confined to the territorial state and becomes increasingly a conduit for converting global pressures into disciplines and burdens for its most vulnerable elements, or the terms of sovereignty itself are extended to supranational institutions that progressively widen the gap between the scope of democracy and the source of policies governing people. Either way, the asymmetry between the late-modern time as an indispensable object of political reflection and the sovereign state as the exclusive site of democracy places the established terms of democratic accountability under tremendous stress.' If the new agonal openness is not to incite a reactive dogmatism, a resurgence of the desire to conquer and convert, or an attempt once again to silence the other, we have, in short, to change all our existing institutional frames. The only move we can make now, Connolly rather desperately concludes, is to a 'non-territorial democratization of global issues' through 'creative intervention by non-state actors'. Pressed further, one concludes, even by its sympathizers, the possibility of a postmodern politics is indefinitely postponed.

It is nonetheless clear why liberal Americans should now be so attracted to it. They inhabit a political society in which the strains of political identity and the connection of identity with rational mastery have always been unusually acute, in which the limits of actually existing democracy are felt with exceptional pain, and in which a new impotence, national and international, is now evident. In the older societies, in Europe and elsewhere, individual and social identity *is* – and has long been – difference, not a strained similarity; technical mastery is a technical matter, on which identities do not so intimately depend; and the shortcomings of democracy, from which much less has always been expected, cause less agony. Here, the political irony that the Americans want to argue for is endemic.

This contrast, of course, is crude. But it runs deep. And it explains why it is that for a European reader, these new American arguments – especially Connolly's, which itself runs more deeply than White's, even if it eventually runs out – seem like nothing so much as a restatement in new language of the old insights of Hume and Adam Smith and – one might add – of Madison too. There is no solution to the questions of politics. That is what makes them the questions of *politics*. There has to be authority, sovereignty – in the state, or in some state-like agency – for security and law. There will at the same time be protesting and contesting claims for liberty. There will of course always be those who dream of resolving the two. To the 18th-century sceptics, these were the civic republicans; that dream reappeared in Rousseau's reassertion of republicanism, in Kant's abstraction of Rousseau, and in Hegel and Marx's historicist reformulation of that abstraction; it continues in the constructions of latter-day collectivists and communitarians and of sentimental liberals like Walzer and White. But however seductive these visions may be – and however malleable one may try to make them, as White tries to make Habermas's – they are in the end evasive, and necessarily so. The fact of authority is inescapable; and as the inescapable fact it is, will invite, even incite, opposition. There is a circle. It is, it is true, the contribution of the late 20th century, the contribution of the self-described 'postmodernists' and others, to insist that this circle is not always drawn in the same way: that new identities will be constructed in new circumstances, and that new interests will be formed for them. It is also true that at the end of this century, the post-Westphalian state, the frame within which all modern democracies have been constructed and in which identities and interests have been contested, is starting to lose its efficacy. But the circle remains. In 'social movements', in states, in super-states, or in some dreamed-of universal state, there is nowhere to go – except to an impossible 'an-*arche*' or an unacceptably unchecked authority – outside it.

Cambridge University

POSTMODERNITY USA
The Crisis of Modernism in Postwar America

Anthony Woodiwiss *University of Essex*

In this coherent and challenging analysis of American postmodernity, Anthony Woodiwiss re-examines the political, economic and social life of the United States over the past 60 years. Exploring the rise and fall of modernism as a social ideology, he offers a distinctive and original interpretation of the unique experience of American modernity and the arrival of the postmodern world. The result is both a novel history of postwar America and a significant contribution to the idea of postmodernism as a social and cultural form. **Postmodernity USA** also carries lessons for the understanding of class, culture and politics in late industrial societies in general. Offering an innovative synthesis of postmodernist and Marxist approaches it will be essential reading for scholars and students as a key interdisciplinary text.

Published in association with Theory, Culture & Society
March 1993 • 192 pages
Cloth (8039-8788-9) / Paper (8039-8789-7)

SAGE Publications Ltd
6 Bonhill Street
London EC2A 4PU
England

SAGE Publications Inc
2455 Teller Road
Newbury Park
CA 91320 USA

HISTORY OF THE HUMAN SCIENCES   Vol. 5 No. 3
© 1992 SAGE (London, Newbury Park and New Delhi)   pp. 99–103

The idea of the political

PETER LASSMAN

Tracy B. Strong, *The Idea of Political Theory: Reflections on the Self in Political Time and Space.* Notre Dame, IN: University of Notre Dame Press, 1990.

The question of the nature of political theory presupposes a concept of the political. This has been a central concern for much 20th-century thought, from Weber and Schmitt to Arendt and Oakeshott, in its attempt to make sense of the nature of the modern world. Strong's book is representative of several trends in contemporary theorizing but, partly because it is based upon a series of lectures, it leaves more unsaid than said. The overall structure of the argument is hard to follow while much of what is presented, such as a brief history of postwar political theory, will be familiar to most of his readers.

The basic premiss of Strong's book is that 'the mode of dealing with human relations that is politics has a particular validity, and that this validity is challenged by much that is characteristic of modernity'. This entails that we must consider the boundaries between politics and other human practices. It is even more crucial to explain what is meant by the term 'politics'. Strong's definition quoted in full is:

> I take *politics* to be that form of human activity which constitutes the most general response to the simultaneous asking of the two questions, 'who am I?' and 'who are we?' In this politics overlaps the other modes of discourse that make up the complexities of life. Among these other questions we might note: 'what should I do?' which I take to be the energizing question of morality; 'how do I get what I want?' – that of economics; 'what do I want?' – one of the questions of psychology; 'why do I suffer?' – the

question of religion. Politics is an activity not unrelated to the answers to these other questions, but never identical to them. (p. 3)

According to Strong's account there are three temptations to leave 'the space and time of politics' and these correspond to different dimensions of the self. The first is a 'theatrical' temptation. It is an attempt to substitute the perfection of a completed performance represented by drama for the world of politics. The second refers to the project of treating politics as a proper object for scientific understanding. The third temptation is to look for a rigorous theoretical truth that obscures the essentially historical and particular character of political activity. These three 'temptations' are modes of discourse which are in constant tension with the political realm. 'It is the glory of the political that it keeps each of these temptations constantly present to us, all the while showing us what we would lose (and gain) were we to yield to them.' The particular threat that seems to be embedded within modernity is that 'we will cast off politics as useless and, so as to live unbounded, succumb to one or another of the temptations'. The basic idea here (the phrase is borrowed from Kuhn) is that the *tension* between politics and the three temptations is an *essential* one for the preservation of any living or open society. Presumably, it is part of Strong's definition of modernity that it contains within itself a particularly powerful and self-destructive threat to these productive and creative tensions.

Much of what Strong has to say is familiar although his way of expressing his ideas is not always easy to follow. However, I want to concentrate on the key issue of the idea of politics and of the political that is implied here. What are we to understand by it? What is this form of political theory about? Strong presents a description of what he calls the 'crisis' of post-1945 Anglo-American political theory. This crisis originally was concerned with the so-called 'death of political theory' after its supposed demolition by logical positivism. (This is itself not so self-evidently correct an account of what actually happened as Strong assumes.) Three responses to the argument for the 'death of political theory' are described. The first is that of Leo Strauss and his followers who argue that modern thought has taken the wrong path in its rejection of natural law. The second response is represented by those such as Weldon who proposed to make peace with logical positivism and redirect political theory in the direction of conceptual analysis. The third response is that of 'Berkeley metaphysics' represented by such figures as Wolin and Schaar who proposed that we repossess the neglected great 'tradition' of western political thought.

Strong sees merit in all of these styles of work and he owes much, it seems to me, to theorists such as Wolin. Nevertheless he is also a victim of some specifically 'postmodern' anxieties. Taking his cue from Connolly's populariz-ation of the thesis of the 'essential contestability' of political concepts, Strong argues that all of the above accounts suffered from an essential weakness. They all failed to see that the central notion of the self was itself problematic and contestable. Why does this matter? According to Strong the account put forward by Connolly made constant reference to 'our' politics, 'our' understanding and 'our' political practices. Now what this seems to mean is that the use of the word 'our' implies a 'we' which implies a necessary reference to the value of community. Strong's thesis is that the claim being made here is that the political theorist is making an appeal to a community of discourse and that that is also a claim to authority. Political theory, according to Strong, is primarily an attempt to make explicit an answer to the question 'Who are we?'

Strong does not engage in an analysis of the concept of authority. Nevertheless the approval given to a communitarian position is clear enough. Strong does not have much to say about those liberal thinkers, such as Rawls and Berlin, whose writings are, at least, just as relevant to an understanding of the political predicament of modernity as are those of the communitarians and deconstructionists. In fact, Strong is dismissive of their ideas in a way that does not do them justice. After all, many of these writers have argued that the fundamental problems of modern politics and ethics arise precisely from the fact that we do not possess anything like a shared community of discourse. Furthermore, even if we did possess such a community of discourse that would not make it right. The claims of community are expressed by Strong in the following way:

> I am thus claiming for politics and the vision of the political person something that will not always sit easily: that to be a member of a free community, one has to accept as true for oneself the proposition that at certain times in fact and always in principle, someone may know better than one does oneself just how it is with oneself. (p. 160)

'Always in principle'? Strong himself raises the obvious problem here of the acceptability of the 'we'. What if the 'we' is Nazi Germany? As far as I can understand his account of this issue it seems to me that Strong, as with most communitarian theorists, cannot provide a coherent answer without undermining his own idea of politics. The basic question for Strong must be one of the meaning of the 'we'. Political theory, it is argued, must be parochial. It always belongs to a particular 'we', a particular community. This parochialism is reinforced by Strong's radical separation of politics from morality which he understands in terms of Kantian universalizability. He argues that the possibility of politics presupposes the impossibility of a universalizable morality. But Strong does not consider that it does not follow that human beings can be said not to have absolute ethical conceptions. Furthermore, it can just as easily be argued that if we are true to such conceptions then it is politics that is morally impossible.

Strong states that 'the political – the acknowledgement of a specific historical other – is thus necessarily parochial, and ultimately, though not necessarily, in conflict with the demands of morality'. In fact, he asserts a thesis of the 'priority of politics' over morality. Using the example of abortion Strong argues that we cannot rationally debate the moral issue until we have resolved the issue of the place of this particular abortion in this particular community and that this is a political question. If Strong is arguing against the presumption of theory in ethics then it could be argued that the same argument holds against the possibility of political theory. Strong asserts, hoping to clarify this view, that

> . . . the vision of what should be is unattainable and that I accept it as our vision and in doing so find myself wanting that which generates the free community.

There are obvious problems with this statement. Most glaring of all is probably the question of the rationality of accepting an unattainable vision which, presumably, you also know to be unattainable. Or, we might ask, what is a 'free community' meant to mean here? Surely not a community enslaved to a false (unattainable?) vision? These criticisms are possibly unfair. It could be argued that Strong has not set out to write a tight analytical book but, rather, to draw our attention to some central and troubling questions. Strong fears that modern men and women will come to accept that there are good reasons for believing that the modern world has no need for politics. Here Strong is in the company of many other distinguished thinkers. Writers such as Arendt, Wolin, Lefort and Oakeshott have all been notable, although in different ways, for their defence of the value of politics and of the political domain. In order to make this clearer one has to see, as does Strong, that the practice of politics is distinct from rule or government. Government in one form or another has existed in most societies but politics has not. The fear here is that the modern state makes politics unnecessary rather than impossible. If there is no need for politics then a valuable and necessary source of human community has been undermined. It follows that if politics as a human practice withers away then political theory does too.

This kind of pessimistic thinking, which has its roots in the 19th century, is falsified by books such as this. On Strong's own account a fundamental task of political theory is to argue against and to prevent the reduction of the political sphere. His own critique of functionalist and structuralist social science points out very clearly the absurdity of that kind of discourse with its claims that the political 'function' could be replaced by some other 'function'. Strong himself is cautiously optimistic in that he implies that the 'crisis' in political theory and in politics may be no more than a transitional phase between periods of 'normal' politics. This, again, is a view reminiscent of many late 19th-century thinkers.

What authority do the statements of the political theorist possess? Strong argues that political theorizing cannot be usefully discussed in terms of its truth or falsity. This was the basic error of the positivists and behaviouralists in political science. We make much better sense if we consider the texts of the tradition of political theory not as being true or false but as being either truthful or untruthful. There are no clear criteria of truthfulness and each case is a matter of judgement. I take it that Strong's argument leads to the view that political theory is descriptive. Its task is to describe the complexity of political judgement and of political practice within particular contexts and traditions. Strong presents this as a way of looking at political theory and I think that it is a merit of his book that we can read it in these terms.

University of Birmingham

HISTORY OF THE HUMAN SCIENCES   Vol. 5 No. 3

© 1992 SAGE (London, Newbury Park and New Delhi)   pp. 105–119

Tradition and modernity

CHARLES MARTINDALE

Alasdair MacIntyre, *After Virtue* (1981), *Whose Justice? Whose Rationality?* (1988) and *Three Rival Versions of Moral Enquiry* (1990).
London: Duckworth.

Three Rival Versions of Moral Enquiry (hereafter *TV*) (1990) is a further stage in
the grand project initiated in *After Virtue* (hereafter *AV*) (1981; second edition
with postscript, 1985) and continued in *Whose Justice? Which Rationality?*
(hereafter *WJ*) (1988). I shall not attempt to summarize, in its entirety, the
argument of the new book. In his introduction MacIntyre suggests convincing
reasons why, in the sense in which these things are usually understood, such a
summary could be undesirable and even impossible, a consequence of the nature
of reception. Any contribution to discourse becomes an intervention in a
conversation – or rather many conversations – which are always already taking
place, and is assimilated to, appropriated for, those different conversations (cf.
p. 196); even a direct quotation is already an act of (re)contextualization, of
(re)interpretation. Instead I shall respond to aspects of what, from my
perspective, I take to be MacIntyre's position, in six specific areas, in the spirit of
'conversation' as defended by Oakeshott or of dialogism, whether of a
Bakhtinian or a Gadamerian type.

1 POSITIONALITY

Most 'theorists' position themselves, or are positioned by others, 'on the left'.
MacIntyre has thus become that, comparatively, *rara avis*, a major right-wing
theorist (though we must always beware of essentializing these political
categories). His own trajectory has carried him from Catholicism, via a distinctly
Trotskyite version of Marxism, to his current Thomism. Those whose

master-code is provided by psychology may conclude that, by temperament, MacIntyre is someone who likes to be outside the tent pissing in. In his current guise he should not, however, be too readily associated with educational ideologues of the Right, nor should his somewhat mandarin, 'conservative' prose be allowed to disguise the 'radical' implications of many of his positions. Significantly he pours scorn on the Great Books proposals of conservatives like Allan Bloom or E. D. Hirsch, standard-bearer for 'valid' – that is, determinate – interpretation:

> If one fails to recognize that what this provides is not and cannot be a reintroduction to the culture of past traditions but is a tour through what is in effect a museum of texts, each rendered contextless and therefore other than its original by being placed on a cultural pedestal, then it is natural enough to suppose that, were we to achieve consensus as to a set of such texts, the reading of them would reintegrate modern students into what is thought of as *our* tradition, that unfortunate fictitious amalgam sometimes known as 'the Judeo-Christian tradition' and sometimes as 'Western values'. The writings of self-proclaimed contemporary conservatives, such as William J. Bennett, turn out in fact to be one more stage in modernity's cultural deformation of our relationship to the past. (*WJ*, p. 386)

This argument looks attractive, but objections are possible. Is there such a thing as a 'contextless' text? Rather, are not texts continually *re*contextualized, a function of what Derrida calls their 'iterability'? Likewise canons are constantly being *re*negotiated, and there is no reason why what from one perspective can be represented as a fairly random set of texts should not, in time and institutional setting, generate productive and novel filiations: indeed one can argue that, almost inevitably, it will do so. MacIntyre's restatement of this argument in *Three Rival Versions* is altogether less bullish and rather more supple:

> It is not of course that such texts are not important reading for anyone with pretensions to education. It is rather that there are systematically different and incompatible ways of reading and appropriating such texts and that until the problems of how they are to be read have received an answer, such lists do not rise to the status of a concrete proposal. Or to make the same point in another way: proponents of this type of Great Books curriculum often defend it as a way of restoring to us and to our students what they speak of as *our* cultural tradition; but we are in fact the inheritors, if that is the right word, of a number of rival and incompatible traditions and there is no way of either selecting a list of books to be read or advancing a determinate account of how they are to be read, interpreted, and elucidated which does not involve taking a partisan stand in the conflict of traditions. (p. 228)

Here we see how MacIntyre shares with self-styled 'radicals' a recognition of the necessary interestedness of all discourse seen as perspectival and rhetorical all the way down.

2 NARRATIVE

In MacIntyre's writings we see a yet further instance of a return of grand narrative. This is something to be welcomed, since human beings define themselves by the stories they tell as well as by the company they keep. Virtually all discourse could be given a narrative form. MacIntyre himself writes: 'In moral enquiry we are always concerned with the question: what *type* of enacted narrative would be the embodiment ... of this particular theory?' (p. 80). Of course any narrative of past events such as MacIntyre supplies in support of his case is open to the response that it is teleological, that it erases all kinds of other meanings, and that it emplots itself as a story of a particular type. MacIntyre is well aware of this, and his response is that *all* history is, and must be, of such a kind (p. 150 f.; cf. *AV*, p. 3). MacIntyre has thereby succeeded in offending both historians, who dispute his historical claims, and analytic philosophers, who argue that the coherence of propositions is not dependent on an historical analysis (*AV*, postscript p. 265 ff.) It is precisely this latter claim for a decontextualized rationality (involving the separation of history and philosophy) which MacIntyre aims to unmask: 'there are *no* grounds for belief in universal necessary principles ... except relative to some set of assumptions' (*AV*, p. 266; cf. *TV*, p. 173), assumptions which always have a 'history'. A different objection would be, not so much to the historical form of MacIntyre's project, but to the mode of historical writing he employs; an account, distinctly positivistic in character, of philosophers' views is hardly the most effective type of historical narrative to embody the idea of tradition-constituted inquiry. MacIntyre's history is not over-emplotted, rather it is not artistically emplotted enough: the style is not fully adequate to the thesis.

In his new book MacIntyre distinguishes three principal modes of inquiry, which he starts by tracing to particular founding texts: first, the methods of Enlightenment rationality which he finds fully embodied in the ninth edition of the *Encyclopaedia Britannica*, with its commitment to a progressively refined movement from 'facts', by methods which reveal their intelligibility, to general 'laws'; secondly, the approach of the anti-foundationalists, or, as MacIntyre prefers to call them, the genealogists, after Nietzsche's seminal *Genealogy of Morals* (1887); and thirdly, a revived Thomism promoted in Pope Leo XIII's encyclical letter *Aeterni Patris*, issued in 1879, which provides MacIntyre with his preferred model of tradition-based inquiry. On his own admission MacIntyre's account of the first two modes is given from the perspective of the third, since there is no disinterested, non-perspectival account available. We can look briefly at each of these in turn (the first two can be seen as yet another instance of that quarrel of the ancients and the moderns which belongs to the realm of the always already).

(i) Enlightenment

Here we are, perhaps, at or near the heart of MacIntyre's project, the insistence that Rationality is always relative to, and embodied in, a tradition. Many liberals, children of Enlightenment, are guilty of reifying Reason, detaching it from the discursive contexts through and in which alone it can have meaning, thereby simultaneously securing their own hegemony and betraying their principles. Liberalism, on this view, always becomes illiberal in practice whenever it confronts a rationality different from its own; its vaunted pluralism is offered only to those who accept its premises. (Its contradictions, one may add, have recently been painfully exposed to view in the Salman Rushdie affair.) Any theoretical inquiry has one or more theoretical presuppositions already inscribed within it as a prerequisite for that inquiry. The scientific-liberal view of 'objectivity' is, in that sense, just one among a number of possible modes of inquiry, not necessarily a uniquely authoritative one as its adherents usually assume, and certainly not one free from prior belief. It follows that (say) a theological mode of inquiry cannot be regarded as 'prejudiced' in a way that other modes of inquiry are not (cf. p. 179). Liberalism, however, remains arrogantly secure in its own superiority; of the encyclopaedists MacIntyre writes: 'their minds were closed to the possibility that, for example, a Polynesian view of Europeans might be rationally superior to a European view of Europeans' (p. 182). This point strikes at the heart of some of the most cherished liberal presuppositions of the 20th-century university, with its commitment to a single, 'secular' rational method. Against these presuppositions MacIntyre invokes the authority of Thomas Kuhn's *Structure of Scientific Revolutions*, to maintain that 'there is no way of identifying, characterizing, or classifying' data 'in a way relevant to the purposes of theoretical enquiry except in terms of some prior theoretical or doctrinal commitment' (p. 17).

(ii) Genealogy

MacIntyre is much more sympathetic to the genealogists' position, part of which he appropriates for his own critique of Enlightenment as a form of emotivism masking itself as rationality. His observations on both Nietzsche and Foucault evince an excited engagement. The genealogist exposes to view the fetishization of morality and rationality and 'common sense' used to occlude a will to power. But the genealogist is also necessarily implicated in, even parasitic upon, the views of Rationality which she rejects, and from that bind neither Foucault nor Nietzsche can offer us any escape: 'can genealogy, as a systematic project, be made intelligible to the genealogist, as well as others, without some at least tacit recognition being accorded to just those standards and allegiances which it is its avowed aim to disrupt and subvert?' (p. 55).

(iii) Thomism

I lack the competence to assess MacIntyre's account of the significance of the thought of Aquinas to which he devotes four chapters. His principal claim is that Aquinas was able to reconcile Aristotelianism and Augustinianism in a synthesis which surpasses the virtues of either system in its ability to solve the internal problems of both of them. The notion of the coherence of the pre-modern Tradition looks, however, like a nostalgic myth, a historicized version of the Fall, with the decisive rupture put by MacIntyre in the period immediately following Aquinas. Given MacIntyre's belief that modes of rationality cannot be separated from the historical configurations within which they emerge, it is odd that he has nothing to say about the 'drawbacks', from some 20th-century perspectives, of medieval social structures; so too in *After Virtue* the account of Aristotelianism-in-its-Greek-context somewhat downplays such institutions as slavery and patriarchy and the extent of their instantiation in embodied tradition (cf. Isaac, 1989: 666, 669). Nevertheless, however much idealized, MacIntyre's account of Thomism affords a model of what a tradition-based inquiry, at its best, might look like. MacIntyre describes a productive rationality which is, precisely, *interested*. It entails membership of a community in which one participates in 'a history of dialectical encounters' (p. 202), and which provides 'narratives of the moral life' (p. 78), a community, however, from which – ominously – 'fundamental dissent has to be excluded' (p. 60). Perhaps any community is based on exclusions. But here one must ask what dissent is to count as 'fundamental' and who is to decide. (Within Thomism, of course, there 'is' an Authority beyond the discussion.) On this model rationality becomes a sort of 'virtue-guided craft' (p. 63), with a 'rational teaching authority' to which one submits oneself in trust:

> To share in the rationality of a craft requires sharing in the contingencies of its history, understanding its story as one's own, and finding a place for oneself as a character in the enacted dramatic narrative which is that story so far. The participant in a craft is rational *qua* participant insofar as he or she conforms to the best standards of reason discovered so far, and the rationality in which he or she thus shares is always, therefore, unlike the rationality of the encyclopaedic mode, understood as a historically situated rationality, even if one which aims at a timeless formulation of its own standards which would be their final and perfected form through a series of successive reformulations, past and yet to come. (p. 65)

The procedure conforms to a divinely created order, in which the world is a text and objects intelligible in themselves. This certainly solves – if at a price – the mind/body dilemma which has haunted western philosophy, and removes the lingering traces of idealism which one finds even in the writings of Derrida: 'we cannot . . . first characterize the mind and then ask epistemological questions about what it can know, for it is only in the actuality of empirical knowledge that the mind exists in its completeness, and that is to say that the mind essentially, and not only accidentally, requires the body for its operations' (p. 153). However, if we grant that something like the 'Thomism' portrayed by MacIntyre constitutes a coherent tradition with a coherent conceptualization, it would seem easier to be born within such a tradition than to enter it from outside. Could some such tradition-based inquiry resolve the dilemmas of modernism? And does it not occlude those self-interested operations of power which are always everywhere, diagnosed by Foucault, hiding them behind a Transcendental Signified? And is a secularized version of such an inquiry even on the agenda?

3 TRADITION

A central concern of MacIntyre's is to recuperate the idea of Tradition and to find a means of reconciling Tradition to some conception of progressive intellectual inquiry. We all help to instantiate a tradition insofar as we all have social identities as (for example) daughters, mothers, fathers, sons, colleagues, etc. (Bernstein, 1986: 132), social identities which both enable and constrain. As we have seen, to MacIntyre a living Tradition is an 'historically extended, socially embodied argument' (*AV*, p. 222). This is an attractive conception, but a number of difficulties arise. One is raised by Julia Annas who, in a review of *Whose Justice?*, points to some slippage in MacIntyre's use there of the term tradition. At some points he seems to be working with a 'strong' notion, which Annas calls one of 'essential location' (1989: 394), according to which a tradition is situated in a specific and historically contingent setting whose needs it sustains; tradition is thus related to 'a particular social configuration', with whose fate it is intricately connected. MacIntyre needs this strong version, first to argue that the culture leading up to the Scottish Enlightenment constituted a distinct tradition product of specific, non-repeatable historical conditions to which Hume's 'Anglicizing' contribution was foreign, and secondly to deny the status of a tradition to contemporary liberalism which is represented as composed of incoherent fragments of earlier traditions. But elsewhere MacIntyre employs a weaker conception, which Annas calls one of 'historical understanding' (1989: 394, 401). According to this version a reason has force only within a whole *structure* of thought, which in turn has a history. MacIntyre needs this weaker version to solve the problems of rational inquiry today. We are all, to an extent, products of a decentred Modernity; but we can identify, and rationally choose between, rival traditions. Clearly the notion of a culture and its institutional expressions is much weaker on this second model. On the other hand, on the first model, it is difficult to see how we could be anything other than excluded from past traditions, even if we could identify them in the first place. In his new book MacIntyre is perhaps defter, if more evasive: Tradition is seen as one mode of inquiry, different in its structure and operations from other rival modes.

Again, it can be asked whether liberalism itself should not be described as a tradition. To MacIntyre, as we have seen, it is rather a mere patchwork, but any tradition will contain numerous traces of prior elements. To MacIntyre liberalism has no coherence save a vacuous and ultimately unsustainable commitment to 'pluralism', and depends on 'a tradition-independent, universal conception of rationality' (Wallace, 1989: 343). But is this so? It could be argued, as does one reviewer of the earlier books, that liberalism can be redefined as 'a political conception, designed to frame terms of social cooperation for historically-situated individuals who precisely differ in their comprehensive views about the good' (Wallace, 1989: 343). But MacIntyre could reply, first, that since for the system to work there would have to be constraints and limits either negotiated or imposed, in what sense is such a political order best described as 'liberal', and secondly, that even if such a system could provide the conditions for a workable polity, it hardly solves the question of how to attain coherent solutions to problems in rational, cooperative intellectual inquiry – little more could be achieved than an agreement to differ. So we are back with the original problem, the incoherence of our educational procedures. One further related weakness in MacIntyre is that he sometimes himself implies universal claims of a kind he elsewhere excoriates as liberal 'universalization'. For example, there appears to be, in his account, a universal human right to choose to adhere to such a tradition-based inquiry as he describes (so Bernstein, 1986: 138).

There is a third, more deconstructionist objection. How do we identify *a* Tradition without gross reification? How do we decide where one tradition begins, and another ends? Whether to stress continuity within change, or breaks with continuity? Should Thomism be seen as a logical continuation of Aristotelianism, or as constituting a fresh start, another tradition? This is where we encounter the ideology of periodization/categorization. Different descriptions of sets of data/events are always possible. Differences that, from one perspective, seem fundamental, from another can be represented as unimportant. Any talk of tradition negotiates the discursive space generated within the poles of 'continuity' and 'change' in a way which is always and never arbitrary. If we retain the notion of tradition as a useful one but reconstrue it as plural and changing, then conceptions of what is rational will change *within* the same tradition as well as between different traditions. In sum, the notion of tradition – because of the differences within the term – can easily be destabilized, and can only be sustained, like all other such descriptions, by a Nietzschean act of will. Nonetheless we may decide to retain the notion, on pragmatic grounds, because of its empowering character. What matters will then be not whether a tradition really exists, but whether people are able to position themselves within what they see as commensurable structures of rationality. Tradition, in other words, becomes not a thing but a way of conceiving the character of an intellectual inquiry (or a body of texts, or whatever). The title of MacIntyre's book suggests that he has himself moved some way along this road since his earlier works. We cannot go back behind Modernity and Enlightenment, only beyond them.

4 METAPHYSICS

We have heard much from Marxizing theorists about the 'political unconscious'. MacIntyre's book reminds us, valuably, in the context of an Anglo-American academic philosophical tradition which has often favoured the erasure of ontology and metaphysics, that there is also such a thing as a 'theological unconscious' (Moore, 1989: 36). For example, Derrida's obsession with the impossibility of full 'presence' could be read as suggesting a frustrated religious drive, which could be traced back to his Jewish upbringing in Algeria. Indeed it is one of Derrida's own insights that, however much we may try to drive out metaphysical presumptions, they are always lurking there to catch us out. (The thought can usefully be related to one of Nietzsche's: 'I fear we are not getting rid of God because we still believe in grammar', cunningly glossed by MacIntyre, p. 98.) If we take, for example, the question of how the anti-foundationalist is to present her case, we can defend her communication as 'utterance on the move' (p. 44), but something has to be held still, if only momentarily and if only as an enabling fiction: 'it is . . . necessarily presupposed by the act of writing for a particular reader or readers that the ego of writer and that of reader have enough fixity and continuity to enter into those relationships constitutive of the acts of reading-as-one-who-has-been-written-for and of writing-as-one-who-is-to-be-read' (p. 46). In that sense genealogy can never escape being implicated in the metaphysical systems it is contesting ('The function of genealogy as emancipatory from deception and self-deception thus requires the identity and continuity of the self that was deceived and the self that is and is to be': p. 214). Deconstruction tries to resolve this conceptual problem by repeated deconstructions and reconstructions, repeated demystifications and remystifications, repeated reminders that the ground under our feet is never stable or that we are always about to fall into an abyss of infinite regress, a spiral of non-meaning or superfetation of meaning, and so forth. These figural reminders indeed become themselves yet another trope, yet another comforting metaphor, themselves requiring further destabilization. And so on, ad infinitum. Deconstruction, in other words, hopes not to be, but is always becoming, a praxis.

Examples of a 'theological unconscious' are easily adduced. For example, with Foucault power becomes reified as a (strangely diabolic) 'metaphysical entity', rather than as a way of analysing social interactions, as that is a concept itself discursively generated. Metaphysics is often an occluded presence within interpretative paradigm-changes; various Romanticisms, for instance, can be seen as attempts to bring back a supposedly unified, unfallen world (Moore,

1989: 35). The similarity between Deconstruction and 'negative theology' is evident in a sentence like this from Derrida's *Positions* (trans. A. Bass, Chicago: University of Chicago Press, 1981, p. 26): 'Nothing . . . is anywhere simply present or absent. There are only, everywhere, differences and traces of traces.' MacIntyre's determination to foreground these hidden metaphysical vestiges is to be welcomed.

5 TRANSLATION

> The conclusion to which the argument so far has led is not only that it is out of the debates, conflicts, and enquiry of socially embodied, historically contingent traditions that contentions regarding practical rationality and justice are advanced, modified, abandoned, or replaced, but that there is no other way to engage in the formulation, elaboration, rational justification, and criticism of accounts of practical rationality and justice except from within some one particular tradition in conversation, cooperation, and conflict with those who inhabit the same tradition. There is no standing ground, no place for enquiry, no way to engage in the practices of advancing, evaluating, accepting, and rejecting reasoned argument apart from that which is provided by some particular tradition or other. (*WJ*, p. 350)

One problem with so strong a conception of Tradition as this is that it opens the gates to a potentially inert and vacuous relativism, in which it becomes impossible for one Tradition usefully to interrogate or criticize another. (MacIntyre cites Nietzsche's neat aphorism: 'Man does *not* pursue happiness; only the Englishman does that', p. 190; but of course he cites it *in English*.) In many people's eyes the disadvantage of any extreme relativism is that it provides a weak basis for action or choice, for living a life found useful in specific historical conditions. Let us restate MacIntyre's initial aporia. Without some rational unity of inquiry discussion becomes feebly undirectional and perhaps impossible. Philosophers – because they have been working with incommensurable paradigms of what constitutes rationality – have been unable to resolve the problems whose solutions the discipline exists to tackle. Richard Rorty concludes that philosophy should cease to pursue these lofty designs and should redescribe itself as a pragmatic discipline concerned with immediate social negotiations, more like (say) literary criticism. MacIntyre argues instead that some means should be sought for adjudicating between these rival rationalities. In this way he distinguishes his position from that of the cultural relativist. Relativism, he argues, is thus not entailed by a commitment to tradition. In this way Tradition, reception, culturalism and progress can be reconciled in an empowering synthesis, a heady brew indeed. What eventuates is not some tradition-free, non-contextual Truth, but the-'best'-account-so-far-currently-available-in-the-present-context.

How, though, to proceed? In his review of *Whose Rationality?* Bernard Williams asks how any understanding of other people or cultures could be possible except on the assumption of some shared 'standards of rationality', what he calls 'a common human capacity to reason practically' (1989: 6). MacIntyre, of course, can have no truck with this liberal *petitio principii*. There are no neutral, non-perspectival grounds for deciding such questions of rationality, no position from outside-tradition, or outside-discourse, from which to argue. One can only criticize one conception of Rationality from within another. MacIntyre's position here is very close to that of another pragmatist, the theorist and literary critic Stanley Fish, except that Fish talks about 'interpretative communities' and 'institutions' rather than about 'traditions' or 'modes of enquiry'. It follows that one tradition cannot simply be translated into the terms of another, since this would presuppose a universal context-free model of meaning and translatability. As Martha Nussbaum has it, 'Traditions are embodied in languages and conceptual schemes which cannot easily be translated into one another' (1989: 36) (though one could ask how she knows this). To try to translate the accounts of your rivals wholly into your own language could be to refuse to allow those accounts any independent existence at all: is it, in short, to refuse dialogue of any kind? By imposing a universalist conception of rationality on all 'legitimate' debate the liberal is thus engaging in an act of covert cultural imperialism, akin to neo-colonialism in the political sphere.

But how can one learn an alien idiom? To answer this question MacIntyre employs a model of translation in the light of *untranslatability*. When someone learns a new language, she starts by learning supposed equivalences, and then, as she becomes more inward with the language, she learns what is untranslatable. When fully inward with the new language, she can return to instruct members of her original language community about it. As with language, so with culture or tradition: one can, as a sort of anthropologist, learn to inhabit rival conceptual schemes, gradually recognizing those cultural elements which are not translatable. MacIntyre cites an instance of an ideologically highly charged, divergently encoded, case of naming:

> Consider as an example the two rival place names 'Doire Columcille' in Irish and 'Londonderry' in English.

> 'Doire Columcille' embodies the intention of a particular and historically continuous Irish and Catholic community to name a place which has had a continuous identity ever since it became St Columba's oak grove in 564 – 'Doire Columcille' is the description 'St Columba's oak grove' turned into a name – while 'Londonderry' embodies the intention of a particular and historically continuous English-speaking and Protestant community to

name a settlement made in the seventeenth century, information about whose commercial origin in London, England, is conveyed as effectively by its name as the corresponding religious information is conveyed by 'Doire Columcille'. To use either name is to deny the legitimacy of the other. Consequently there is no way to translate 'Doire Columcille' into English, except by using 'Doire Columcille' and appending an explanation. 'Londonderry' does not translate 'Doire Columcille': nor does 'St Columba's oak grove', for in English there is no such name. (*WJ*, p. 378)

MacIntyre's argument here proves rather too much. For what is true in this strong case of a contestation of names would be true in other weaker cases. Thus 'Roma' would not translate adequately as 'Rome', because the linguistic differences, with their various traces, within the two signifiers are not identical. Indeed no two users of the *same* language use names, or words in general, identically, since the penumbra of signification will vary in either case. In that sense we are 'translating' words all the time (or failing to do so). MacIntyre – in this like those who have welcomed Bakhtin's concept of *heteroglossia* – here shirks the more 'subversive' implications of *différance*, the key term in Derridean deconstruction. Yet it is *différance* which best accounts for that 'iterability', that capacity for continued and transhistorical survival, of texts, and which can thus provide (paradoxically?) the traditionalist with one of her potentially strongest cards. It is those who resist the mobility of the sign who are most likely to freeze the texts of the past in that past, rendering them less available for that appropriative dialogue which alone can ensure their survival. The attempt by 'New Historicists' to rehistoricize canonical texts within what they claim to be the dominant discourses and discursive con-texts of the time, to show the network of power negotiations they mediate, has served only to perpetuate the centrality of the traditional canon, though the attempt to stabilize ('political') interpretation around such (contingently privileged) discourses would, if successful, eventually impede the iterability of the texts. But, of course, it is highly unlikely that the attempt will succeed in the long term. Traditionalist fears and radical claims for the immanent collapse of the canon seem somewhat exaggerated. History – by which I mean the traces produced by *différance* present in all textuality – is not so easily defeated, something for which some of us, at least, may be grateful.

MacIntyre adduces a number of criteria by which one Tradition could be judged rationally superior to another. First, *coherence*; we can ask if a particular account is coherent within its own paradigms of rationality. However, it is doubtful whether any such account lacks some elements of vulnerability which constitute its specific problematic. Moreover such a judgement could only be made from *within* the tradition, which raises again the problem of translatability. Do we become inward with a different tradition, or do we rather appropriate it? And what would we do with a tradition which denied the criterion of consistency itself? And who is to decide who has won? Secondly, there is *superior-usefulness-in-context*. If a particular paradigm or tradition generates problems which it cannot solve, but a rival tradition/paradigm can both solve those problems and explain why the first tradition/paradigm cannot solve them, then there are rational grounds for preferring the second tradition/paradigm. The 'victory' of Newtonian physics and its eventual 'defeat' by Relativity would constitute two such cases. But all such preferences make sense only in specific historical contexts. Similarly one might be able to offer a convincing anatomy of the ideological blindness of a rival mode of inquiry. The third criterion is *comprehensiveness*. If you can tell a story which can incorporate your rivals' stories, whereas they cannot tell one to incorporate yours, then your own story can justly be said to prevail. As an example of such incorporability MacIntyre gives Dante's *Comedy* (pp. 81, 142 ff.). Dante, within the structure of his own master-narrative, can incorporate numerous alternative versions of experience in a series of mini-narratives. The empathetic telling of these rival but ultimately inferior narratives has often been put down to Dante's secret but unacknowledged attraction towards much that he rejects. On MacIntyre's reading the work constitutes rather a *locus classicus* of rational adjudication between rival paradigms and rival rationalities. Dante concedes to his opponents their positions, in their strongest form and 'in their own words', and *yet* is able to subordinate them to a more encompassing and more widely explanatory scheme of rationality.

An objection to MacIntyre's brilliant attempt to resolve this problem is that it retains a degree of latent and unacknowledged positivism. The mobility of linguistic signs, the presence within them of more meaning than can ever be grasped by any particular user, and the various strategies of accommodation, of appropriation, which result from this, mean that language is and is not translatable, always and never. Can there, on this view, be any constructive dialogue between rival traditions and rival rationalities? One answer would be that, if such dialogue is possible, it is possible because of that iterability which is an effect of *différance*, which in combination allows the appropriation by one person of another person's position which, however, never, or virtually never, achieves a complete identity. This, it seems to me, is how almost all dialogue can be said to work, and it means that, while exchange and interchange are possible, we never know as we are known, at least not in this world, or, if in this world, only in contexts which could be characterized as 'mystical' and thus part of one of those great mystifications, as most would see them, the discourses of religion, of art and of eros, in which such self-transcendence, or self-negation, might, just, be possible.

6 ACADEMY

In his final chapter MacIntyre offers his prescription for what he calls the 'post-liberal' university. In the 1980s an ideologically increasingly self-confident conservative administration launched what could be described, according to one's point of view, as a series of unprovoked attacks against all 'humane learning', or as an attempt (however crude) to force innovation on a self-regulating, self-congratulatory, consensual system marked by excessive collegiality – there may even be virtue in both descriptions. But, whatever one's view of that, it will probably be agreed that public rejoinders by the universities were signally lacking in intellectual authority, indeed little more than an unconvincing reiteration of past cliches. Why was this? MacIntyre's view is that the failure of universities to mount a coherent defence of their practices sprang from one central cause: the unified secular vision of knowledge and its uses which was the project of the Enlightenment and embodied in the ninth edition of the *Encyclopaedia Britannica* was now dead, but remained a sort of 'present absence' (p. 217), a ghost which still requires exorcizing, so that a new project and a new sustaining ideology for universities can be worked out. The project of the ninth edition had, partially unnoticed, lost its hold, amid increasing specialization, the absence of any general empowering scheme of belief, and the (to MacIntyre) fatal exclusion of moral and theological – or anti-theological – questions. In consequence the universities could offer no coherent response to the question: 'In current circumstances what sort of a moral good is a university?', a question which society as paymaster had a right to see put and answered. This, in turn, reflected de facto 'liberal' exclusivity (cf. p. 222). Also at issue, in MacIntyre's view, is the appropriate mode of instruction. There is, he argues, a potential contradiction in the position of the genealogist who gives a lecture, a contradiction acknowledged by Nietzsche when he resigned from the academy. One answer would be to make the lecture into 'a theatre of the intelligence' (p. 233), one subversive of any claim to authority, not excluding the lecturer's. For the Thomist, by contrast, a lecture is a commentary preliminary to public argument, as in 13th-century Paris.

MacIntyre's solution to this general dilemma (as he diagnoses it) is as bold as it is simple. The postliberal university has to become 'a place of constrained disagreement, of imposed participation in conflict' (p. 231):

> In such a university those engaged in teaching and enquiry would each have to play a double role. For, on the one hand, each of us would be participating in conflict as the protagonist of a particular point of view, engaged thereby in two distinct but related tasks. The first of these would be to advance enquiry from within that particular point of view, preserving and transforming the initial agreements with those who share that point of view and so articulating through moral and theological enquiry a framework within which the parts of the curriculum might once again become parts of a whole. The second task would be to enter into controversy with other rival standpoints, doing so *both* in order to exhibit what is mistaken in that rival standpoint in the light of the understanding

afforded by one's own point of view *and* in order to test and retest the central theses advanced from one's own point of view against the strongest possible objections to them to be derived from one's opponents. So systematically conducted controversy would itself contribute to systematically conducted moral and theological enquiry, and both would inform that teaching in which students were initiated into both enquiry and controversy.

Is there a hidden liberal premiss in espousing such dialogism? Not necessarily: MacIntyre could argue that, in the long term, Thomism (or some other version of tradition) could emerge triumphant, and a Thomistic tradition could then be established throughout the system. But, on pragmatic grounds, if universities are to be preserved at all, a system must for the moment be found to regulate and make coherent existing disagreements. Is such a system utopian? Again not necessarily, if two engagements were regarded as a sine qua non for future appointees to the academy, first that they should be committed to intellectual inquiry, and secondly that they should be willing to take part in dialogue and disputation. Dialogue, even when it involves considerable cut-and-thrust, has to be a partly cooperative activity, involving a willingness to let other voices be heard, and the recognition of an Other as well as a Self. Whatever their virtues, the previously dominant modes of learning seem to have outlived their usefulness. If there is any defensible future for the universities in the medium term, it may well lie in a recognition of arguability, and a commitment to dialogism, from which, in due course, a new consensus may – or may not – emerge.

*   *   *

Belief seems once more to be in vogue. So I shall conclude with an expression of a belief which, to some extent, I share with MacIntyre. Or rather it is a prediction, which could, of course, be redescribed as a sort of performative utterance or as an 'intervention'. It is that, far from living 'at the end of history', we are living at the end of history only as defined, positivistically, by classical Enlightenment liberalism. We are seeing not only the return of ideology but perhaps too the return of metaphysics as an available master-term. And thus the whirligig of time brings in his revenges. In a world where rival rationalities can no longer be put in any simple hierarchy of virtue, we shall see, not indeed a flight from Reason, but a flight from that hegemony which, in our academies, is so often reified as Reason. Instead we may discover something worth calling our humanity – a Montaignean provisionality in the face of the multiplicity of possible redescriptions both of what we call ourselves and what we call the world, redescriptions which may at last include those of a whole sex previously marginalized, together with a willingness to make pragmatic accommodations with the discourses which, however contestable and arguable, necessarily contain us as available modes of experience, modes for which the model should be, not the natural sciences as defined by the encyclopaedists, but something more like a religion as a self-sufficient discourse inhabitable only from within in a (hopefully) non-exclusive communality with others – and here I think of a 'language-game' as well as of a 'tradition'. A God's-eye view can never be ours. But – abandoning what MacIntyre (invoking Foucault) calls 'a rancorous will to knowledge' (p. 50) – we could settle instead for the limited but distinct advantages of accepting, as human subjects, our inevitable situatedness and our necessary contingency, in short our time and our place, as constituted within a textuality of traces, where, as T. S. Eliot has it in *Little Gidding*, 'History is now and England'. Never and always. . . .

University of Bristol

NOTES

A version of this paper was given to the Critical Theory Seminar of the University of Bristol. I am grateful to Dr C. H. Edwards for affording me an opportunity to collect some thoughts on MacIntyre, and to her, Dr D. F. Kennedy and Professor C. J. Rowe for insights of various kinds.

BIBLIOGRAPHY

Annas, Julia (1989) 'MacIntyre on Traditions', *Philosophy and Public Affairs* 18: 388–408.
Bernstein, Richard J. (1986) 'Nietzsche or Aristotle? Reflections on Alasdair MacIntyre's *After Virtue*', in *Philosophical Profiles*, pp. 115–40. Oxford: Polity.
Isaac, Jeffrey C. (1989) *Political Theory* 17: 663–72.
MacIntyre, Alasdair (1981) *After Virtue*. London: Duckworth.
MacIntyre, Alasdair (1988) *Whose Justice? Which Rationality?* London: Duckworth.
MacIntyre, Alasdair (1990) *Three Rival Versions of Moral Enquiry*. London: Duckworth.
Moore, Stephen D. (1989) *Literary Criticism and the Gospels: The Theoretical Challenge*, New Haven, CT and London: Yale University Press.
Nussbaum, Martha (1989) 'Recoiling from Reason', *New York Review of Books*, 7 December, pp. 36–41.
Wallace, R. J. (1989) review essay, *History and Theory* 28: 326–48.
Williams, Bernard (1989) 'Modernity', *London Review of Books*, 5 January, pp. 5–6.

HISTORY OF THE HUMAN SCIENCES   Vol. 5 No. 3

© 1992 SAGE (London, Newbury Park and New Delhi)   pp. 121–135

The judgement of Nietzsche: philosophy, politics, modernity

DAVID OWEN

Keith Ansell-Pearson (ed.), *Nietzsche and Modern German Thought.* London: Routledge, 1991. £40.00, 314 pp.

Keith Ansell-Pearson, *Nietzsche contra Rousseau.* Cambridge: Cambridge University Press, 1991. £35.00, xvii + 284 pp.

When in 1892 an advertisement appeared for a new book on Nietzsche, it played on the idea that 'the whole cultural world is stirred' by his importance. 'Naturally Nietzsche was discussed', someone remarked about a meeting of a cultural society which he had just attended, for where 'would one not now be talking about Nietzsche?'[1]

It is a measure of Nietzsche's significance to contemporary culture that were a printing error to add a hundred years to the date cited in this report it would retain its validity (this despite the damage to Nietzsche's reputation occasioned by the Nazi appropriation of his name). Today it would scarcely be overstating the case to suggest that Nietzsche has assumed a pre-eminent position in the philosophical *agon* (although Hegel, as ever, remains owl-eyed on the edges of the arena). Certainly, Nietzsche's thought seems to demand confrontation and contemporary cultural critics have all too readily obliged, locating it as a moment in the internal unfolding of modernity's crisis-consciousness (Strauss, MacIntyre), as an irrationalist rupture with the incomplete project of modernity (Habermas), as a postmodern space within which thinking can begin anew (Lyotard, Foucault), and as an ironic and playful deconstruction of metaphysics

(Rorty, Derrida), to name but a few. The question of Nietzsche's relationship to the tradition of modern thought, it seems, poses as many problems as the question of modernity itself; problems, moreover, which exhibit a certain isomorphic relationship in that the topic of Nietzsche's continuation of, or rupture with, modern thought parallels that of modernity as continuing, or breaking with, the Judeo-Christian tradition. In this context, the claims made with respect to Nietzsche's thought are inevitably also claims concerning the character of modernity and the legitimacy of modernity's consciousness of itself; to try to get clear about Nietzsche's position is always already to try to clarify our own modern or postmodern location. Both *Nietzsche and Modern German Thought* and *Nietzsche contra Rousseau* take up this quest of self-clarification attending to the philosophical and political dimensions of this task respectively.

NIETZSCHE, KANT AND MODERN PHILOSOPHY

If it is Descartes' project of radical doubt which initiates the modern turn in philosophy, it is, perhaps, Kant's 'Copernican Revolution' which represents the triumphal moment of a self-assured sensibility fully conscious of its own modernity. The heart of this self-conscious modernity lies in Kant's claim to ground reason in itself, that is, to eschew any reliance on external supports such as nature, theology or metaphysics. In seeking to establish what one can know, what one should do, and what one can hope for, by reference to a self-determining subject, Kant rejects the authority of religion and tradition in favour of the reflexive authority of reason. Modernity as enlightenment, as maturity, proclaims itself in Kant's work as both a completion of the philosophical tradition and a rupture with this tradition in that it fulfils the theoretical tasks of reason (enlightenment) and, thereby, creates the space within which the practical realization of these tasks (maturity) becomes possible. Indeed, in this respect, Kant may be presented as initiating the paradigmatic genre of modern thought, namely, the end of philosophy thesis. It is, however, precisely in this moment of self-assurance that consciousness of our modernity also becomes characterized by the motif of 'crisis'.

The development of this crisis-consciousness may be located in the starting point of Kant's critical philosophy itself, namely, the antinomy of causality;[2] here Kant sets out two arguments concerning causality which appear to be equally grounded in reason. The thesis involves the contention that, in accordance with the principle of sufficient determination, the idea of causality itself requires the existence of a free causality (a first or final cause). The antithesis, however, embodies the claim that, in accordance with the principle of non-contradiction, the idea of a free causality undermines the idea of causality itself in which all causes are themselves already effects. The mutually exclusive positions expressed in this antinomy arise, for Kant, out of the tendency of theoretical reason to transgress its limits, the boundaries of experience within which it holds sway. Kant's resolution of this dilemma involves the positing of two isomorphic realms of reason: the realm of theoretical reason defined as a phenomenal realm of appearances determined by the scientific laws of nature and the realm of practical reason identified as the noumenal realm of things-in-themselves governed by the moral law of freedom. But does this resolution really work? As one commentator has noted:

> Kant solves the antinomy by demonstrating that the contradiction is not in the real world but in consciousness. But does this not make consciousness itself contradictory? The suspicion arises that Kant's solution is in fact only a deeper and more trenchant problem. He seems to have saved science and morality only by sacrificing man, to have preserved the unity of the world by giving up the unity of consciousness.[3]

This suspicion receives its confirmation when we consider what has been termed Kant's *historical antinomy*. The difficulty identified here is that while Kant's system requires the idea of a history of reason (and, indeed, gains its authority from a claim to complete this history), it also rules out the idea of a history of reason:

> For reason to be a historical principle, it must be embodied in actual time. Yet time, according to Kant's Transcendental Esthetics is merely a 'form of intuition' that cannot apply to reason at all, only to empirical data categorized by the forms of understanding. Yet both theories are equally necessary to Kant's philosophy. They both stem from Kant's presuppositions, the denial of which would incur an intolerable price.[4]

Ironically, it appears that Kant's attempt to resolve the antinomy of causality ends by reproducing a formally isomorphic antinomy in which the principle of sufficient determination requires that reason have a history, while the principle of non-contradiction rules out such a history. The significance of this antinomy is not simply that it cannot be overcome by reference to a transcendental postulate, but also that it provides the impetus for Nietzsche's and Hegel's transformation of Kant's antinomy of causality into an *agonism* of freedom and determination and a *dialectic* of freedom and determination respectively. In both cases, the problem of the crisis of consciousness becomes a problem of historical consciousness, that is, a question of time in which Kantian dualism is transformed into philosophical monisms structured around the Nietzschean metaphor of *will to power* and the Hegelian metaphor of *Geist*.

One consequence of this transformation of the tasks of philosophy is simply this: post-Kantian thought must be capable of accounting for its own historical conditions of possibility. To put this more prosaically, Nietzsche and Hegel must specify the nature of their relationships to the philosophical tradition as an immanent task of their philosophical thoughts. In this context, to judge

Nietzsche's philosophy is at least in part to interrogate the coherence of his account of the tradition and his relationship to it.

It is this topic which John Walker addresses, through the staging of a confrontation between Nietzsche and Hegel, in his essay 'Nietzsche, Christianity, and the Legitimacy of Tradition'. The argument Walker develops operates a double-focus: on the one hand, he attempts to suggest that Nietzsche's own conceptualization of his relationship to the Christian tradition is profoundly flawed and, on the other hand, his question concerns how one should read Nietzsche's relationship to modern thought. The spur to arms which animates this argument is an underlying unhappiness with recent (and influential) French readings of Nietzsche which locate his texts as resisting 'dialectical integration into the history of philosophy'.[5] These readings, on Walker's account, find their legitimation in the rhetoric of rupture which pervades Nietzsche's texts; a rhetoric which proclaims the creation of a new philosophy, which is perhaps also a philosophy of the new. Yet, Walker claims, Nietzsche's attempt to overcome metaphysics – 'a form of thought divided against life'[6] – can only be understood in terms of the tradition of metaphysics, that is, the logic of Nietzsche's argument denies its rhetoric. To develop this claim, Walker attempts to illustrate, first, that Nietzsche mistakenly reads Kant's epistemological arguments as existential arguments and, second, that this misreading stems 'from a central contradiction in Nietzsche's very idea of what "metaphysics" means':

> By metaphysics Nietzsche means both a body of philosophical doctrines and a mode of being: an existential attitude which we can choose to adopt or not to adopt in relation to our experience as a whole. Nietzsche's critique of all hitherto existing philosophy relies for its rhetorical force upon an attack on metaphysics in the second sense. But it relies for many of its arguments on Kant's critique of metaphysics in the first sense. The problem is that Nietzsche's arguments are at odds with his rhetoric, and his rhetoric is at odds with his argument.[7]

It is, moreover, precisely because 'Nietzsche's epistemological arguments against metaphysical doctrines . . . are utterly different in character from the existential arguments which he directs against the metaphysical conception of the activity of philosophy itself'[8] that a related problem emerges in the context of Nietzsche's understanding of the significance of Christianity for his own thought. In contrast to Hegel, whose arguments are both epistemological and existential on Walker's account, Nietzsche's thought cannot hold to the claim that it inaugurates a postmetaphysical philosophy and also say that the truth this philosophy expounds is disclosed by the history of Christianity without an immanent principle which would unify the epistemological and existential; this, however, is exactly what Nietzsche's philosophy lacks. It is, in the end, this incoherence in Nietzsche's argument which leads Walker to suggest that it is only by reading

Nietzsche *not* as breaking with the philosophical tradition but as initiating a crisis *within* this tradition that we can reclaim the pertinence of Nietzsche's critique of modernity while eschewing its antinomies.

The force of Walker's case, however, depends crucially on the claim that Nietzsche's philosophy does not possess an immanent principle capable of playing the role of uniting the epistemological and the existential in the way that reason understood as 'the immanent form of experience itself'[9] does in Hegel's thought. This is, however, by no means transparently the case as the essay by George Stack illustrates. In 'Kant, Lange, Nietzsche: Critique of Knowledge', Stack presents a scholarly case for reading Nietzsche's critical relationship to Kant as mediated by Lange's *History of Materialism* in which a conventionalist account of knowledge is linked to the 'physico-psychological organisation' of the organic individual. Stack presents this argument as illustrating a path on the route to the idea of will-to-power and its correlate in a perspectival theory of affects. The implication of this reading, which locates Nietzsche's thought as a radicalization of the project of epistemology (and also, perhaps, as a closure of this project), is to suggest that the epistemological question concerning the conditions of possibility of knowledge is always already an existential question. For if Nietzsche, creatively completing Lange's argument, comes to regard Kant's constitutive ideas of reason as simply regulative principles, it follows that the epistemological question 'How are synthetic a priori judgements possible?' is necessarily transposed into the existential question 'Why are synthetic a priori judgements necessary?' This existential dimension is, moreover, inevitably the location of a historical philosophy insofar as the question must always be one of why (and how) it is that we have come to hold *these* (e.g. Kant's) synthetic a priori judgements.

This movement towards the suggestion that Nietzsche's philosophical arguments are both existential and epistemological receives further impetus through Nicholas Davey's 'Hermeneutics and Nietzsche's Early Thought'. In this essay, Davey convincingly locates Nietzsche's thought within the context of the hermeneutic tradition as concerned with the practical understanding of ourselves to be gained through an interpretative engagement with the past. Central to Davey's argument is a siting of Nietzsche's concept of *Lebenshorizonten* as the a priori judgements of a culture, that is, the structures of recognition through which understanding is articulated, and an acknowledgement that the cognitive frameworks which attend these structures are necessarily incommensurable with the actuality of Becoming. The implication of these two claims is that Nietzsche's position entails both the historical specificity of its own understanding and yet also recognizes that the incommensurability of the language of Being and the actuality of Becoming entails that 'the epistemological fracture between sense and reason and the accompanying existential dread it provokes is an *imminent possibility for all individuals regardless of culture or historical location*'.[10] The significance of this Schopenhauerian insight for

Nietzsche, on Davey's account, is that although 'two cultures may operate within different cognitive schemata with mutually exclusive presuppositions, both may share approximate forms of that existential anxiety which results from the realization that reality as conceived within either schema is not congruent with the actual'.[11] As Davey goes on to point out, it is on this foundation of a universal existential predicament that Nietzsche's hermeneutics, and in particular his overcoming of the problem of historical distance, rests. Again, however, we may note that this argument also entails the coincidence of the epistemological and the existential within Nietzsche's accounts insofar as it is the impossibility of the epistemological project of a universal and ahistorical understanding which defines our common existential predicament. Further, it is this existential position which informs us why synthetic a priori judgements are necessary in that it is these judgements which constitute the *Lebenshorizonten* within which existence is possible without existential dread. The historical question, thus, once again becomes 'Why *these* synthetic a priori judgements?'; it is in identifying, and accounting for, these judgements that Nietzsche's relationship to the tradition, and the adequacy of his thinking of this relationship, exhibits itself.

In analysing the development of Nietzsche's thought both Stack and Davey present a figure on the way to the idea of will-to-power as an immanent principle of critique, that is, as the principle through which Nietzsche's genealogical investigations are articulated. The character of this idea and the relationship to the tradition it engenders are exhibited in Keith Ansell-Pearson's essay 'Nietzsche and the Problem of the Will in Modernity' and Ian Forbes's 'Marx and Nietzsche: the Individual in History'. For both Ansell-Pearson and Forbes, the idea of will-to-power denotes a drive for freedom, that is, the ability to realize oneself as an autonomous agent in the world, which provides a mode of accounting for how we have become what we are without reference to a metaphysical notion of the subject. As Ansell-Pearson puts it:

> By positing the unity of 'will' and 'power' in the formulation 'will-to-power' Nietzsche attempts to overcome the notion of the will found in the philosophical tradition in which the will is conceived metaphysically as a noumenal substratum lying behind all action, and which posits a metaphysical doer behind every deed.[12]

It is through this principle that Nietzsche attempts to generate an account of how it is that Kant's synthetic a priori judgements become thinkable. Consider first the mode of accounting Nietzsche is able to generate:

> In *On the Genealogy of Morals* Nietzsche employs the will to power as a principle of 'historical method' in order to disclose the misrecognised will to power of the weak and oppressed. Under certain historical circumstances the will to power assumes the form of a will to dominate, not on account of the largely instinctual and pre-reflective actions of the 'masters',

but via the slave revolt in morality which internalises the will to power. It is at this point in the social evolution of the human animal that intentions are ascribed to action and man develops a 'soul'.[13]

This internalization of the will-to-power is based, for Nietzsche, on the 'ressentiment' of the slave; that is, unable to realize themselves as autonomous agents in the world, the slaves engage in an imaginary revenge against the nobles through an inversion of the 'natural' order of values and to ground this revenge invent the idea of the subject to facilitate the ascription of guilt to the nobles and of merit to themselves.[14] The slave-revolt in morals, in other words, is the primary historical condition of possibility of Kant's epistemological project and, further, Kant's moral philosophy remains, for Nietzsche, complicit with this spirit of revenge against life. As this implies, existential and epistemological questions are unified under the principle of will-to-power. What then of Nietzsche's relationship to the tradition of modern thought?

Two interrelated points may be drawn from the discussion as bearing on this question. First, it is apparent that Nietzsche may be read as exhibiting a certain scepticism towards modern thought's consciousness of itself as a radical break with the Judeo-Christian tradition. Modern philosophy from Descartes to Kant is fundamentally structured as an epistemological project which derives its legitimacy from the Christian idea of the soul. At the same time, as Forbes notes,[15] Nietzsche does operate with an epochal concept of modernity as a rupture with this tradition, where modernity is presented as that uncanniest of all guests – nihilism. In other words, it is the death of God which defines the modern condition, that is, the collapse of the idea of the subject and of any foundations for values. Modernity's consciousness of itself, for Nietzsche, is not marked by the self-assured Kantian concepts of enlightenment and maturity, but by a radical dis-ease which undermines all grounds of assurance. The second point follows on from this insofar as Nietzsche's thought, while it can only be understood in relation to the tradition which makes it possible, seems to mark a break with 'modern' thought in abandoning the idea of the subject in terms of which he defines the tradition. Is Nietzsche then a 'postmodern' figure? We will return to this topic in the concluding section of this article; for the moment, however, we can approach this question of Nietzsche's relation to 'modern' thought via an alternative route, namely, his relation to modern political thought.

NIETZSCHE, ROUSSEAU, AND MODERN POLITICAL THOUGHT

The question of Nietzsche's relationship to modern political thought is the central issue of *Nietzsche contra Rousseau*. In this passionate work, Keith Ansell-Pearson attempts to read Nietzsche's relation to politics and modernity through the staging of a confrontation between Nietzsche and Rousseau. The appositeness of this strategy lies not merely in the fact that Nietzsche consciously opposes his thought to that expressed by Rousseau, but also in the argument that it is in Rousseau's texts that the antinomies of modern political thought find their clearest expression. If, as Ansell-Pearson argues in a scholarly opening chapter, 'Nietzsche is compelled to exaggerate and distort certain aspects of Rousseau's moral and political thought in order to highlight, in a rhetorical manner, his challenge to the Christian-moral tradition and its secular successors',[16] a more nuanced reading of their relationship may reveal insights into both the character of Nietzsche's political thought and its relationship to the tradition of modern political thought.

Nietzsche and Rousseau, Ansell-Pearson argues, may be read both as addressing the problem of civilization – its costs and quandaries – through the idea of history and as attempting to resolve this problem through the elaboration of a transfigurative politics. The readings of history they develop and the type of politics they present, however, are radically distinct. Rousseau is 'the political philosopher who "discovers" history to be the central problem of the modern experience of existence',[17] yet Rousseau's *moral* reading of history exhibits a 'terrible ambiguity':

> Only in this world, the world that is the product of historical development, can man attain moral freedom, for such freedom requires a sense of rationality and self-discipline which is the result of the historical evolution of the social animal. And yet this same process of historical development leads to the destruction of man's simple, transparent, self-sufficient happiness.[18]

For Rousseau, time manifests itself as the enemy of harmony and happiness in that the impossibility of going back to an age of innocence entails that our only hope of redemption lies in a future which historical development suggests can only further erode this hope: 'Rousseau thus confronts us with an antinomy, that of nature on the one hand, and of civil society, morality, reason, and history on the other.'[19] In contrast, Nietzsche's *extra-moral* reading of history, while it recognizes the costs of modern man's historical consciousness, poses the problem of civilization as a problem of time, of man's relationship with the past, which requires the overcoming of the *weight* of our historical consciousness (exhibited in Rousseau's all-too-human 'ressentiment' towards time) through a creative future willing which affirms time's 'it was'.

To explore this contrast further we can begin by focusing on Ansell-Pearson's reading of Rousseau's *Discourse on the Origin and Foundation of the Inequality of Mankind* and *Social Contract* as illuminating the antinomies of modern political thought. For Ansell-Pearson, the problem posed by Rousseau's secular account of the corruption of man is simply this:

> History is only meaningful to the extent that it leads to a moral end: namely, man as an ethical, self-legislating and autonomous agent. But if

one loses one's faith in history, as Rousseau did, then one's construal of the problem of civilisation must culminate either in a paralysis of the will, or in an attempt to transcend the problem of history altogether.[20]

While Rousseau exhibits both these responses, the impossibility of returning to a state of natural goodness leads him towards the articulation of a conception of civic virtue elaborated in a politics which transcends the problem of history. In other words, Rousseau's 'ressentiment' towards time exhibits itself in the construal of a notion of the general will as beyond the vagaries of social and historical life.

We may note to begin with that while the idea of the general will represents a brilliant attempt to transcend the antinomies of modern political thought through a speculative reconciliation of individual and collective autonomy, the key question becomes that of how the individual is to be educated to the level of the general will. Rousseau's response is that it is through the law that this process occurs, but as he himself recognizes this does not resolve the difficulty:

> The paradox can be enumerated as follows: If the law provides the means by which the individual elevates itself to the level of the general will – and by which it becomes *moral* – how is it possible for the will of every member to be brought into conformity with the general will? Would individuals not have *to be* moral before they *become* moral?[21]

Rousseau's resolution of this paradox lies in the figure of the legislator who 'must persuade without convincing and constrain without force'.[22] But is this not simply to displace the antinomies of political reason onto another level? Moreover, the impossible figure of the legislator, like the social contract which requires him, is located in an abstract normative space outside of historical time. As Ansell-Pearson argues, the *Social Contract* elides the problem of the movement from an unjust society to a just one by siting itself in an imaginary time in which 'Rousseau moves straight from the state of nature to the decision which establishes the primacy of the general will'.[23] While the strength of Rousseau's idea of the general will lies in illustrating that any adequate response to the modern problem of legitimation must involve a theory of democratic participation, its weakness lies in its avoidance of the problem of history. To put this starkly, having constructed the problem of modern man's existence as a problem of history, Rousseau's political solution to this problem is no solution at all but, rather, a denial of the problem of time facilitated through the construction of the idea of the general will within the space of an atemporal imaginary politics. The central antinomy of Rousseau's thought, on this account, concerns the relationship between time and morality, between history and politics, an antinomy which remains unresolved in his work. The question which arises out of this concerns the relationship of Nietzsche's thought to the problem of history and to the antinomies of political thought which Rousseau attempts to overcome.

Nietzsche's reading of history in *On the Genealogy of Morals* may be seen, at least in part, as inverting the reading offered in Rousseau's second discourse, for while Nietzsche is similarly concerned with presenting a teaching on how to live one's life in accordance with nature, 'nature' itself is presented not as moral but as extra-moral. In this context, Rousseau's ideas of 'natural' morality and natural law exhibit, for Nietzsche, the 'ressentiment' of slave-morality against life. That Rousseau's thought is finally trapped within the problem of time simply manifests the frustration and eventual impotence of this spirit of revenge. By contrast, for Nietzsche, history does not depend for its meaning on the achievement of a moral end, rather, time's 'it was' is redeemed through a creative future willing which is 'beyond good and evil'. In this respect, *On the Genealogy of Morals* plays a double role in Nietzsche's thought being both an account of how we have become what we are, namely, beings for whom the value of values has been called into question, and an exemplification of the redemption of history.

In the first essay of the *Genealogy*, Nietzsche attempts to illustrate how man becomes moralized through an account of the slave-revolt in morals. The genius of this revolt is expressed in the phenomenon of 'ressentiment' as the creative negation of that which exists outside of it: 'the slave morality is totally dependent on a hostile external world for its identity'.[24] What is involved here, for Nietzsche, is an anti-natural devaluation of the world of experience through the construction of an imaginary transcendent realm. Yet insofar as this revolt is itself a manifestation of nature as will-to-power, this anti-natural morality is itself natural, that is, it represents the paradoxical phenomenon of nature contra nature. Nietzsche accounts for this by describing morality as the means by which degenerating life preserves itself. Morality makes suffering meaningful and, thereby, provides a reason for living. However, as Ansell-Pearson notes, Nietzsche's thought confronts a dilemma here: 'If individuals have been taught to be "good" through a process of moralization, how can they now be taught to be "beyond good and evil"?'[25] To put this in the context of modernity as nihilism, we might say that while the death of God destroys grounds of morality, this does not abolish the desire to tell ourselves metaphysical lies, it only makes it impossible for us to believe in these lies, although it is precisely these lies which made life endurable. Here we can see the double role of the *Genealogy*: on the one hand, Nietzsche presents a critique of slave-morality as a denial of life which engenders the desire to believe in metaphysics, while, on the other hand, Nietzsche affirms the slave-morality as producing that capacity for intellectual honesty which finally makes it impossible for us to believe in metaphysics and, thus, opens up the possibility of a new thinking which affirms life.

This possibility, however, still requires that Nietzsche elaborate a teaching in terms of which man as Overman overcomes his 'ressentiment' towards the ever-changing world of experience, towards time's 'it was'. Ansell-Pearson examines this topic through a close analysis of *Thus Spoke Zarathustra* in which the central issue raised is the possibility of teaching the Overman who can affirm time's 'it was'. On the account offered, Nietzsche rapidly runs into a problem which appears isomorphic with that of Rousseau's problem concerning the teaching of the general will:

> As Zarathustra begins to learn the meaning of his *Untergang* he learns what Rousseau had identified as the chief problem of all lawgivers (the political genius who must also be a great artist or architect): that in trying to teach individuals through speaking the language of the over-human it is impossible that they will make themselves either heard or understood. But to speak the language of the human, all too human is to speak a language which has only served to cripple and constrain them.[26]

In the first two books of *Thus Spoke Zarathustra*, Zarathustra attempts and fails to teach the Overman directly; his pedagogy being caught in precisely that aporia encountered by Rousseau's legislator. It is Nietzsche's recognition of this aporia that leads him to articulate the teaching of eternal recurrence as the experience which will transfigure man into Overman and to present Zarathustra's journey towards the affirmation of this thought as an exemplary prefiguration of the self-overcoming of humanity. What then is the nature of this thought of the eternal recurrence of the same? On Ansell-Pearson's account, this idea represents an imaginative thought experiment in which we are confronted with the 'abysmal thought' that to affirm one's life or, indeed, a single moment is to affirm all of time:

> The affirmation of the moment leads to the affirmation of time itself, for no single moment is self-sufficient but is connected to all the other moments of one's life. This is why, for Nietzsche, affirming one single moment entails affirming all of existence, one's own included: we recognise that it took the eternity which we are to produce the one event, and thus in a single moment all eternity is redeemed, affirmed, and called 'good'.[27]

How does this experience transfigure Zarathustra? Fundamentally, this thought teaches a new will which does not simply will itself but also wills its own temporality:

> It teaches the individual to creatively will that existence which hitherto it has willed only blindly and unknowingly. The only manner in which existence can be redeemed is through the recognition and test of its totality, which takes place through the eternity of the moment; hence the testing question of eternal return: does the will have the courage and strength to repeat its existence again and again in its entirety?[28]

Whereas Rousseau conceives of (moral) autonomy as the will willing the general will, Nietzsche presents (extra-moral) autonomy as the will willing the eternal recurrence of the will. However, at this moment in which Nietzsche's thought presents an overcoming of the problem of history which fatally flawed Rousseau's political philosophy, the problem of the legislator re-emerges as the problem of how to get people to subject themselves to the thought of eternal recurrence, particularly given Nietzsche's suggestion that this thought will either transfigure or crush us. This problem remains open at the end of *Thus Spoke Zarathustra* in that this text closes just as Zarathustra prepares once more to go down amongst men; however, this question is central to the topic of Nietzsche's politics.

How can we create human beings capable of willingly and successfully subjecting themselves to the thought of eternal recurrence? For Ansell-Pearson, this is the question Nietzsche poses in his directly political writings (and, it must be said, there is a great deal of textual evidence to this effect). Nietzsche's answer to this question, on Ansell-Pearson's account, is that we can breed this type of human being through an aristocratic politics which is prepared to reduce untold human beings to the order of instruments in order that they may serve as a foundation upon which a higher human type may emerge. Nietzsche's great politics, which is characterized by the rule of artist-tyrants, philosopher-legislators, is a matter of force and violence. The echoes of the figure of Machiavelli's Prince are all too apparent, while the question of legitimacy and right which characterizes Rousseau's thinking on politics is dismissed as the language of the impotent. Here, however, Nietzsche's thought displays its own 'ressentiment' towards history:

> For it too does not allow becoming to become, but seeks to take control of the gruesome accident, which constitutes history, in order to bend the bow of history and shoot it in another direction. . . . In his thinking on the political, Nietzsche shares the delusion which has served to inspire the politics of the modern age, namely, the belief that it is possible to gain control of the historical process and to subject it to the mastery of the human will.[29]

In this thinking of politics, Nietzsche undermines his resolution of the problem of history, just as Rousseau's thinking of history undermined his resolution of the problem of politics.

What are the implications of this close textual reading for the question of Nietzsche's relationship to the tradition of modern political thought? Perplexing, I think. On the one hand, Nietzsche may be read as addressing the central modern theme of autonomy. On the other hand, he abandons the modern relation of autonomy and morality by presenting the Overman as extra-moral. Again, Nietzsche's politics exhibits the modern desire to control time, while his ethical teaching in *Thus Spoke Zarathustra* eschews any such desire. One may add to this Nietzsche's dismissal of the modern political language of legitimacy and rights in favour of a conception of politics as force and violence. While Ansell-Pearson does not rule out the possibility of generating a Nietzschean politics which avoids the dilemmas he locates in Nietzsche's own political writings (perhaps through a mediation with Rousseau), it is one of the merits of the approach taken in this book that it renders visible the tensions within Nietzsche's thought. What then of Nietzsche's relation to modern thought? Is it perhaps that Nietzsche combines a postmodern conception of philosophy with a pre-modern conception of politics? To take up these questions and to raise the question of this mode of questioning, we can conclude this article by staging a confrontation between two distinct styles of reading Nietzsche and by examining the relationship of modernism and postmodernism to the idea of tradition.

NIETZSCHE – MODERNIST OR POSTMODERNIST?

The two essays to be considered here are Jay Bernstein's 'Autonomy and Solitude' which presents a reading of Nietzsche's thinking of autonomy as representative of the aporetic character of modern thought and Howard Caygill's 'Affirmation and Eternal Return in the Free-Spirit Trilogy' which locates Nietzsche's thought of eternal return as beyond the metaphysics of judgement. In the former of these pieces, Bernstein presents a tightly argued case for reading the relationship of will-to-power and eternal recurrence as isomorphic with the relationship of freedom (*Willkür*) and the moral law (*Wille*) in Kant's thinking of autonomy. Nietzsche's thought of eternal return exhibits the aporia of autonomy in which modernity attains its limit and refutation, Bernstein argues, simply because while Nietzsche correctly recognizes that the death of God entails the abandonment of a conception of autonomy as the universality of the will that wills itself, his thinking of autonomy through the doctrine of eternal return as an extra-moral autonomy, thereby, takes the formal character of the idea of autonomy beyond even Kant's position. This empty ideal, as a perpetual refusal of community and mediation, 'terminates in the worldless, death-in-life solitude of the philosopher-legislator'.[30] By contrast, Caygill reads the thought of eternal return against the thought of will-to-power in the context of the crisis of judgement engendered by the death of God. Whereas the principle of will-to-power presents itself as a measure of life, as a judgement of the ascending or descending character of life, the doctrine of eternal return is both a penance for and a liberation from judgement. This emerges, on Caygill's account, when we consider the following:

> [The thought of eternal return] becomes overwhelming, able to transform and destroy, when it is made into a question: 'Do you desire this once more again and innumerable times more?' or, in other words, 'Do you want to judge?'. The question is itself a judgement on whoever is asked it, since it

shows that the yes and no of wanting *this* rests on a yes and amen before every yes and no. To want this yes is to want a singularity which cannot be generalised, cannot be named, and which exceeds the limits of judgement.[31]

For Caygill, it appears, while the idea of will-to-power remains within the domain of metaphysical opposition, the thought of eternal return exceeds metaphysics.

Now it is not my concern to judge the merits of these two essays, rather, I want to raise, in slightly exaggerated fashion, the question of the strategies of reading they deploy. We can begin by noting that both Bernstein and Caygill present Nietzsche as an aporetic thinker; however, while Bernstein presents the aporia of autonomy in Nietzsche's thought of eternal return as a *closure* of philosophical space, Caygill presents Nietzsche's thinking of eternal return as presenting the aporia of judgement as an *opening* of philosophical space. Attending this difference is a further distinction, namely, that Bernstein's presents an *epochal* reading of Nietzsche in terms of the idea of modernity and the idea of the tradition of modern thought, while Caygill offers a reading of Nietzsche which both eludes an epochal thinking of modernity and in locating Nietzsche's thought as both within and without of the tradition of modern thought puts into question the idea of tradition. We can conclude this article by briefly exploring the implications of these strategies of reading as representative of modernist and postmodernist styles of thinking respectively.

Modernism, I suggest, is structured as an epochal thinking in which the spectre of modernity haunts modern thought. It is precisely because modernism thinks modernity as a epochal concept that the idea of tradition is paradoxically central to modern thought, for it is through their constructions of the metaphysical tradition that modernist thinkers have been able to legitimate both the idea of modernity as an epochal concept and their thinking as a completion of, and rupture with, the tradition. This strategy of legitimation defines the genre of modernism as that of the end of philosophy thesis. It is, thus, perhaps unsurprising that the idea of crisis manifests itself as the central motif of this form of thought. By contrast, postmodernism (as its paradoxical name suggests) may be seen as a critique of epochal thinking in which modernity is taken not as an epoch but as an *ethos*,[32] a certain way of thinking our relationship to ourselves and time. Within this mode of thought, the very idea of tradition is located as a strategy of legitimation, of mastery. What then of Nietzsche – modernist or postmodernist? On the one hand, Nietzsche's thinking appears to exhibit an epochal style. On the other hand, though, Nietzsche's perspectival account of knowledge would appear to undercut the legitimation which modernist thought affords itself. Perhaps, in the end and in the beginning, we are simply left with the difficulty of Nietzsche's identity – and our own.

University of London

NOTES

1 R. Hinton Thomas (1983) *Nietzsche in Modern German Politics and Society 1890–1918*, p. 2. Manchester: Manchester University Press.

2 Kant locates the antinomy of causality as his impetus towards philosophy in a letter to Garve cited in M. A. Gillespie (1984) *Hegel, Heidegger and the Ground of History*, pp. 30 and 183, fn. 14. Chicago: Chicago University Press.

3 ibid., p. 33.

4 Y. Yovel (1980) *Kant and the Philosophy of History*, pp. 21–2. Oxford: Princeton University Press.

5 Walker is referring specifically to the readings offered by Deleuze, Foucault and Derrida, *Nietzsche and Modern German Thought*, p. 11. For examples of these 'French' approaches, see the Deleuzian essay 'Art as Insurrection: the Question of Aesthetics in Kant, Schopenhauer, and Nietzsche' by Nick Land and the Derrida-inspired piece 'Reading the Future of Genealogy: Kant, Nietzsche, Plato' by Michael Newman, both in this collection.

6 ibid., p. 12.

7 ibid., p. 17.

8 ibid., p. 23.

9 ibid.

10 ibid., p. 104.

11 ibid., p. 106.

12 ibid., p. 179.

13 ibid., p. 175.

14 cf. Nietzsche's comments in section 13 of the first essay of *On the Genealogy of Morals*.

15 *Nietzsche and Modern German Thought*, p. 155.

16 *Nietzsche contra Rousseau*, p. 49.

17 ibid., p. 4.

18 ibid., p. 5.

19 ibid., p. 6.

20 ibid., p. 77.

21 ibid., p. 96.

22 ibid., p. 98.

23 ibid., p. 99.

24 ibid., p. 129.

25 ibid., pp. 147–8.

26 ibid., p. 156.

27 ibid., p. 179.

28 ibid., p. 184.

29 ibid., pp. 222–3.

30 *Nietzsche and Modern German Thought*, pp. 213–14.

31 ibid., p. 236.

32 Foucault comments on thinking modernity as ethos in his essay 'What Is Enlightenment?' in P. Rabinow, ed. (1984) *The Foucault Reader*, pp. 32–50. Harmondsworth, Mx: Penguin.

RISK SOCIETY
Towards a New Modernity

Ulrich Beck *University of Munich*
Translated by **Mark Ritter**
with an introduction by **Scott Lash** and
Brian Wynne

'This is a book of central political and social importance; it is vital that it triggers off and animates public discussion in this country as it did in Germany. After all, the greatest of risks our risk-infested society carries is the indifference to the risk aspects of our individual, sectional and global actions' - Times Higher Education Supplement

Ulrich Beck's panoramic analysis of the condition of Western societies has already been hailed as a classic. This first English edition will take its place as a core text of contemporary sociology alongside earlier typifications of society as postindustrial and current debates about the social dimensions of the postmodern.

Western industrial society is widely seen to be going through a decisive transitional period into a form defined variously as 'post-Enlightenment', 'post-Fordist' or 'postmodern'. Arguing that we are instead facing a different modernity typified by *reflexivity,* Beck goes beyond these descriptions to provide a coherent picture of the direction of global serial change.

Underpinning the analysis is the notion of the 'risk society'. The changing nature of society's relation to production and distribution is related to the environmental impact, as a totalizing, globalizing economy based on scientific and technical knowledge becomes more central to social organization and social conflict. Within this framework, Beck develops an overview of other key elements of current social development; the centrality of the political economy of knowledge; the changing roles of class and gender in a new work environment; and the politics (both personal and public) of the risk society.

Published in association with Theory, Culture & Society
1992 · 304 pages · Cloth (8039-8345-X) / Paper (8039-8346-8)

SAGE Publications Ltd
6 Bonhill Street
London EC2A 4PU
England

SAGE Publications Inc
2455 Teller Road
Newbury Park
CA 91320 USA

HISTORY OF THE HUMAN SCIENCES   Vol. 5 No. 3
© 1992 SAGE (London, Newbury Park and New Delhi)   pp. 137–144

Political theory without foundations

RAYMOND PLANT

Richard Rorty, *Contingency, Irony and Solidarity*. Cambridge, Cambridge University Press, 1989.

Richard Rorty, *Philosophical Papers*, Vols 1 and 2. Cambridge, Cambridge University Press, 1991.

Richard Bernstein, *The New Constellation*. Cambridge, Polity Press, 1991.

In Psalm 11 the Psalmist asks: 'If the foundations be destroyed, what can the righteous do?' In these two books Richard Rorty indicates what he believes to be the answer to the question, but he is emphatic that the answer does not lie in trying to uncover new foundations for political morality and, in particular, foundations for a liberal social and political order.

It has certainly seemed to be characteristic of western political thought that it has sought to build an account of the nature of politics upon some sort of philosophical or theological foundations. These foundations have been sought in an account of the nature of God and his will for men both individually and collectively; in an account of the nature of human life and institutions within a broader framework drawing from some account of the nature of the cosmos and man's place within it; in Natural Law theories; sometimes in an account of the meaning and development of human history; at others in universal claims about human nature and what this means for an account of human flourishing and for the nature of the institutions which would facilitate this.

In modern times these claimed foundations have become much thinner, partly as a result of a more sceptical view about the capacity of philosophy to establish universal theories, particularly of a sort that would ground a rich conception of human flourishing and the normative content and implications of that; and partly as a result of the moral pluralism of contemporary society which makes it difficult to see how some very substantive theory of the human good, even if philosophers could provide it, would not seem authoritative in a pluralistic culture. So typically rather thin moral conceptions such as Rawls' list of primary goods or Gewirth's generic goods of agency have come to provide some kind of minimal foundational set of goods which could provide in a morally neutral way a set of conceptions over which philosophical thinking could range. Similarly, many modern political philosophers have concentrated on the idea of moral agency as a basis for political theorizing: that behind the diversity of first order moral goods nevertheless lies this basic moral capacity, and that political theory should be about an account of the goods which realizing this basic underlying capacity would require. Many utilitarians too have beat a retreat from the idea that utility should be given some reasonably determinate content in terms of happiness or pleasure, or some sort of pursuit of an ideal (for ideal utilitarians) in favour of defining utility or welfare as some kind of place keeper for whatever an individual may happen to want, with the greatest happiness principle being interpreted, as A. J. Ayer suggested, as giving as many people as possible as much as possible of whatever it is they happen to want.

The idea of foundations has not been entirely abandoned, but what is regarded as being a set of possible foundations has become more and more exiguous or, in the language of political theory, has come to replace thick theories of the good or thick theories of human nature with thinner theories of the sorts indicated. These are to use a useful phrase of Richard Wollheim's 'bleached theories', and as I have said there have been two pressures leading to this view within the analytical tradition: one, the view that philosophy is in no position to provide a foundational basis for thick normative conceptions; second, that moral pluralism, the recognition of which has been central to a good deal of liberal theorizing over the past twenty years, makes such a pursuit of a foundational basis for a specific theory of the good and of human nature and human flourishing seem like a pipe-dream. Nevertheless, despite this retreat from thick theories, the aspiration for moral foundations has not been given up, rather the basis is now seen much more in terms of the moral capacities which have to be in place before conceptions of the good, however diverse, can be pursued at all together with that set of primary goods, generic goods or basic needs which are seen as necessary conditions for the pursuit of any good, whatever it might turn out to be. Along with such thin theories, dealing with rather abstract conceptions, has gone a growth in the use of formal mathematical techniques in political philosophy which attempt to determine rational behaviour and choice in relation to these rather thin conceptions. These have concerned ideas like contract, bargaining theories, prisoner's dilemma types of approaches, and so forth.

One can see immediately why many political philosophers have assumed that political philosophy would be rather bereft without at least some foundational supports whether these are sought in thin conceptions of the good and human nature or whether they are to be found in rather formalistic conceptions of rationality and rational choice. It is not clear what would be left to political philosophy without some such foundational claims. It might be thought that to give up such claims would lead us straight back to the position where political philosophy was in the immediate aftermath of positivism in which normative judgements were thought incapable of being rationally grounded, partly because normative judgements merely reveal the value preferences of individuals, partly because of the is/ought dichotomy. If normative judgements could not be supported by empirical claims and record only preferences, then it is not at all clear how normative political philosophy could constitute a discipline. These might be of interest to and could be studied by those interested in the psychology of moral and political preferences, but there could be no scope for a discipline which sought to provide a foundation for normative judgements.

The compulsion to adopt a foundationalist approach is, however, not just a matter of trying to preserve a tradition which has been central to western intellectual endeavour, but is, in the view of many, absolutely vital to some of the most basic issues of political morality for today. Take just three examples, the first two of which are discussed in passing by Rorty: conceptions of human rights, the nature of community and the nature of social justice. If we believe that there are universal human rights which are supposed to limit what can be done to persons, then these rights by definition, as human rights, will transcend the boundaries of cultures, religious beliefs, nationalities and so forth. If they are seen to depend only on preferences at the end of the day, that these are the values by which I stand, as Margaret MacDonald once argued, then this makes universal rights look very vulnerable. If, however, they have to be grounded on something to be morally compelling, then what they would be grounded on, it might be thought, would be some universal conception of what human beings have in common, despite the first order differences of religion, culture, nationality and ethnic origin and because such a common feature or features would have to be the basis of human dignity and the rights based upon that conception this common element would have to be of moral relevance. No wonder that rights theorists have often appealed to a rather bleached and thin theory of what rights are based on because it has to be both universal and morally relevant. Hence philosophers such as Alan Gewirth have focussed on ideas such as rational agency and generic goods. Nevertheless, these foundations, however thin they might be, have been thought to be vital if rights are to have any general purchase in a morally pluralistic world.

Take too the idea of community and solidarity. It might be thought that without some conception of what human beings share in common there is little purchase in the idea that we have some kind of obligation to meet the needs of others, whether they be the poor within one's own society or the more dire needs of those in other third world societies. Without some conception of what human beings have in common the basis of human community and a sense of common obligation will again look just as though it depends on whatever may be the ultimately unsupported preferences of individuals.

Finally, it has been assumed, particularly by socialists and social democrats, that there must be some rational basis for ideas like social justice as a basis for correcting market outcomes. Unless it is possible to provide a rational basis for social or distributive justice, so it is argued, the buck will be passed to the neo-liberal who assumes that because it is not in fact possible to provide any moral foundation for distributive justice then market outcomes have to be accepted, as Fred Hirsch argues, as being 'in principle unprincipled'. Without some kind of moral foundation for distributive justice then the procedural approach to market economics of the liberal has to be accepted: namely that so long as individual acts of free exchange are uncoerced then the aggregate outcome of all those acts of free exchange has to be accepted as fair and legitimate, since there is no standpoint outside the preferences of individuals in terms of which market results can be criticized.

Hence a concern with rational foundations, however thin and bleached, seems to many to be a necessary condition of political philosophy, and to particularly radical or progressive political action. If as Lyotard argues a concern with social justice is 'just gaming', the play of different preferences and language games, then it seems that such a view will tend to sanction the growth of a market society since a market economy, unconstrained by a concern for end states such as social justice, is seen as institutional embodiment of moral subjectivism and the free play of preferences. This is certainly an inference which many postmodernist French philosophers have drawn from the writings of anti-foundationalists such as Lyotard.

Rorty shows in the books under review that he is equally hostile to the search for foundations whether in its thick or in its thin or bleached forms. He rejects the thick forms because they embody metanarratives (following Lyotard in *The Post Modern Condition*) which cannot be philosophically grounded. The metanarratives of theology, ontology, the philosophy of history and human nature are all rejected as a foundation for a rational politics and of course, as we have seen, many analytical political philosophers would sympathize with many of the assumptions that go into Rorty's and Lyotard's critique of metanarratives since they seem to overreach human finitude and make assumptions about the possibilities of metaphysics which cannot be sustained. They also make assumptions about the nature of reason and rationality which see it as capable of grounding thick and universal conceptions. The influence of the later Wittgenstein lies heavily on this type of critique and of course many political philosophers in the analytical tradition would also reject these assumptions. However, Rorty wants to go much further and to criticize the thinner approaches that I have mentioned earlier because he does not believe that such philosophers who cling to a kind of residual foundationalism and universalism have in fact been consistent in applying the same sorts of arguments that apply to grand narratives of the sort they reject, since these arguments apply equally well to their own residual universalism. What both views have in common is that there is some kind of antecedent order which our moral concepts and vocabulary should track and which provides a foundation for the legitimacy of political principles and the institutions which embody them.

A good deal of Part 1 of *Objectivism, Relativism and Truth* is concerned with explaining why foundationism in its various manifestations – in science as much as in moral and political thought – is misconceived. Most of the central themes here will be familiar, and a good deal of the argument or exploration of these issues turns on Rorty's view of truth which is pursued in this volume as well as in *Contingency, Irony and Solidarity*. He rejects the representational theory of truth. In Rorty's view truth, as he puts it, 'cannot be out there'; it cannot exist independently of the human mind since truth is a property of sentences. Only descriptions of the world can be true or false, whereas 'The world on its own – unaided by the describing activities of human beings – cannot'.

Rorty links this part of his approach to that of Wittgenstein in *Contingency, Irony and Solidarity* when he argues as follows:

> To drop the idea of languages as representations, and to be thoroughly Wittgensteinian in our approach to language, would be to de-divinise the world . . . since truth is a property of sentences, since sentences are dependent for their existence on vocabularies, and since vocabularies are made by human beings, so are truths.

We have to drop the idea that the aim of philosophy or science is to track some antecedent reality, whether that reality described is as it appears in contemporary science or whether we believe that there is an antecedent moral reality, however thick or thin, which it is the task of moral and political philosophy to track and describe. In terms of political philosophy it therefore becomes misconceived to think, for example as Sandel does, that the concept of the self that underpins deontological liberalism as found in the work of Rawls and Dworkin, for example, is defective and that some other more plausible theory of the self has to be deployed by political philosophers. Such an approach assumes that there is a theory of the self which maps the 'real' nature of the self more adequately than the rather thin and unencumbered theories of the self deployed by Dworkin and Rawls.

Against such a representational theory of the truth, Rorty wants to counterpose the alternative that he poses in *Objectivism, Relativism and Truth* in the essay 'Solidarity or Objectivity?'. Rorty defends the solidarity view of truth in which members of a community sharing a set of practices, stories and ways of living do not seek to compare what they do with some kind of non-human truth that stands outside the community, its practices and vocabulary. The objectivist, on the contrary, wants some kind of standpoint outside all particular communities, what Thomas Nagel calls 'the view from nowhere', so that the 'truth' as understood from this standpoint is outside all particular communities and is taken to map some non-human reality. However, given the point made earlier about the relationship between truth, sentences, vocabulary and how these are made by people in particular communities, solidarities and forms of life, this standpoint just goes beyond human finitude for Rorty and has to be eschewed.

Insofar as there might for example be room for a theory of the self in political philosophy for Rorty, it is not at all foundational. It is rather a matter of creating a conception of the self that coheres with the self of practices of a particular form of human community and the vocabulary that goes with that. The attempt to do this is misconceived if we believe that we are, so to speak, developing a 'true' theory of the self that can underpin political institutions. It is rather a case of drawing out the conception of the self implied in a set of social practices. Against the idea that this might appear to be a rather conservative view, with philosophy having no kind of critical purchase on society, Rorty wants to argue that the philosopher, and for that matter the poet, the dramatist, etc., can suggest new ways of looking at the world and new vocabularies, a point that is well put in *Contingency, Irony and Solidarity* when he says:

> The method is to redescribe lots and lots of things in new ways, until you have created a pattern of non-linguistic behaviour which will tempt the rising generation to adopt it, thereby causing them to look for appropriate new forms of non-linguistic behaviour, for example the adoption of new scientific equipment or new social institutions. . . . It says things like 'try thinking of it in this way' – or more specifically 'try to ignore the apparently futile traditional questions by substituting the following new and possibly interesting questions'. It does not pretend to have a better candidate for doing the same old things which we did when we spoke in the old way. Rather it suggests that we may want to stop doing those things and do something else. But it does not argue for this suggestion on the basis of antecedent criteria common to the old and new language games.

The criteria to be used are not some kind of common criteria of truth, but rather helpfulness, pragmatism, existential concern and aesthetic satisfaction. The force of these criteria rather than criteria relating to the concept of truth arises from exposing the contingencies of language, community, self, and so on.

Two important questions arise from this approach for political philosophy (in fact as Rorty makes clear in the books under review he regards the work of the later Rawls, for example in *Political Philosophy: Political Not Metaphysical*, as coming close to his ideal of how political philosophy should be carried on – namely as speaking to the issues embedded in a contingent political order – in Rawls' case, liberal democratic societies). The first is what does Rorty see as the relationship between the nature of philosophy and liberal society, and does he think there is a close connexion? Second, is his characterization of liberalism plausible and in particular is his view that the problems of liberalism are political and not philosophical a cogent view?

I take this latter point first. As Bernstein argues in the chapters on Rorty in his excellent *The New Constellation*, Rorty has a rather simplistic and undifferentiated view of the liberal society which he invokes. It is rather undifferentiated because he does not attend to some of the deep controversies embedded in those societies concerning, for example, the nature and scope of individual rights (for example whether they should include social and welfare rights); disputes about the nature of liberty and coercion (for example whether liberty should be construed in negative or positive ways, whether the lack of economic resources is coercive or not). Different views about the scope of the market and about the role of government are embedded in these disputes. For Rorty presumably these are essentially political disputes, to be solved by what he calls instrumental reasoning, in an attempt to accommodate individual differences of view, against a background of other shared values within the community. However, it still remains true that a good deal of the discussion, for example in relation to positive and negative liberty about whether and how freedom and ability are related, is carried on in what might be called a philosophical genre, and this is reflected at the political level as well as in abstract theorizing. In Rorty's view, based on the points made earlier, this is a misconceived account of what they are doing. So those liberals such as Green and Haldane in the last two decades of the 19th century who were developing a theory of positive liberty as a means of criticizing the laissez-faire assumptions of classical liberalism misconstrued their task if they thought they were providing some 'truer' account of the nature of freedom. Rather they were developing a new vocabulary to enable them to cope with changing social concerns. The judgement about the nature of freedom is not to be made on the basis of truth and falsity, that, as Green and Haldane argued, positive freedom in some sense tracked the real nature of the self and its place in the scheme of things better than that of the classical liberal's view of negative liberty, but rather in terms of coping with new social developments. Disputes of this sort are political and cannot be resolved at the level of some kind of philosophical tribunal.

It is very unclear how one would actually go about undertaking the same sort of task as Green and Haldane did if one were self-consciously to follow Rorty's advice here. While the language of the poet, the novelist and the dramatist is fitted to evaluation in terms of aesthetic and existential criteria, the mode of argument of the philosopher is not, and despite Rorty's general view of the role of philosophy, it is not clear how, if at all, it can be decanted into Rorty's suggested new understanding of what the philosopher is about.

Given Rorty's view about philosophy and the lack of any deep foundations for moral and political thought, resulting in this aesthetic and pragmatic search for and invention of new vocabularies, he sees a close relationship between this and liberal society. The contingency of community, of language and of the self as a decentred network coheres with the traditions of liberal society (in, as I have said, the rather undifferentiated form in which Rorty invokes this idea). These ideas do not provide a foundation for liberalism, they rather provide points of view which cohere best with the practices of liberal society. However, if in some sense liberal society is a way of recognizing and coping with these contingencies, then it is on rather weak ground in dealing with those groups within it who do not construe their beliefs in this way.

This has come out very clearly in some of the Islamic responses to Rushdie's *The Satanic Verses*. Muslims see liberalism as a kind of fundamentalism of doubt, committed to the idea that truth claims cannot be finally grounded, and because of this understanding of liberalism, they reject the view that they the Muslims are the only fundamentalists. They do not see why only one form of fundamentalism should underpin the structures of society. Rorty's response to this sort of approach is to adapt Rawls' view of the overlapping consensus as defining the public realm, and what does not fall within that consensus has to be treated as falling within the sphere of private beliefs and private ideals. However, this assumes that those with these sorts of beliefs are already in a sense liberals, willing to construe this privatization of beliefs. Nevertheless, it may be true that from the perspective of those beliefs some kind of public way of life is called for. If liberal society is to withstand this sort of claim then it is not clear that seeing it as in some sense salient for a world of contingency will do, because it is precisely the contingency of belief that Muslims are attacking. Despite Rorty's philosophical virtuosity it is not clear that a defence of liberal society which can depend on seeing it as giving us a set of institutions to cope with contingency, as opposed to providing us with positive principles which we believe to be right, is going to be a compelling basis for arguing with those who live within liberal society but reject the contingency which in Rorty's view lies at its heart.

University of Southampton

HISTORY OF THE HUMAN SCIENCES   Vol. 5 No. 3
© 1992 SAGE (London, Newbury Park and New Delhi)   pp. 145–155

Therapy for an imaginary invalid: Charles Taylor and the malaise of modernity

JEREMY RAYNER

With the publication of *Sources of the Self* (1989) and its popular companion volume *The Malaise of Modernity* (1991), Charles Taylor returns to one of the central themes of his published work, the consequences of the great social transformation that we call 'modernity'. In some respects, both books are a surprise, for Taylor has long been a trenchant cultural critic of modernity, well known for his attacks on 'atomistic' individualism and the resulting 'flattening and narrowing' of human life, on the perils of 'instrumental reason' and its associated technologies, and the consequences of both for political liberty. All of these themes are still much in evidence but, more clearly than ever before, these two new works remind us that Taylor is no pessimist. In his view, the malaise of modernity is, in large part, caused by a failure of imagination and what has been lost in this way can always be retrieved. Both works are part of a project of retrieval.

Much of the groundwork will thus be familiar from Taylor's earlier work. Moderns, he argues, characteristically endow human agency with a strong sense of self. We are comfortable talking about 'the self' as the subject of agency in a way inconceivable to many pre-modern cultures. In Taylor's view, however, we have come to be deeply confused about this most basic feature of our own self-understanding. Beguiled by scientific models, we have come to think of having a self as like having an arm or, more dangerously yet, having a brain, something that exists independently of the concepts we use to describe it. But this, he argues, is not so. A self exists in a space bounded by moral horizons towards which it is continually testing its orientation, how it measures up against what is worth doing or being. Following Heidegger, a thinker whose 'transcendentalism' seems to have become ever more congenial to Taylor over the years, a self is something whose being is always in question (1988: 298–301; 1989: 111–14).

Now, however, the stress is on the extent to which the 'covering over' or 'forgetting' of our deepest aspirations has reached the point where we can no longer see our way past the tensions and contradictions that so complex a development as modernity inevitably entails. On one level, these tensions find their way into our practices, making them increasingly unsatisfactory. At another, they feed into a modish celebration of loss of meaning, the whole debate about postmodernity against which Taylor has so resolutely set his face. On both counts, *Sources* and *Malaise* are deeply unpopular works, arguing that modernity does have genuine 'moral sources' which are both distinct from their pre-modern or traditional competitors and remain available for us today.

For Taylor, then, modernity is the ensemble of more or less familiar practices that sustains and promotes a distinctive self-identity amongst those who live it. *Sources* is described as:

> . . . an attempt to write a history of the modern identity. With this term, I want to designate the ensemble of the (largely unarticulated) understand-ings of what it is to be a human agent: the senses of inwardness, freedom, individuality, and being embedded in nature which are at home in the modern West. (1989: ix)

Malaise is the story of how this identity systematically disables us from coming to grips with the challenges of modernity in a satisfactory way. In Taylor's view, our misguided belief that there is nothing much to be said here (or the equally misguided naturalistic variant that what is to be said amounts to explaining such ideas away as so many illusions) has made the current debate over the meaning of modernity deeply unsatisfactory. While we remain mesmerized by 'the momentous transformations of our culture and society over the last three or four centuries' (ibid.), simple-minded optimism or pessimism are both equally mistaken. They fail to capture the full complexity, the 'grandeur et misère' of the modern experience that Taylor sets out to retrieve.

But the project of presenting a fully restored portrait of the modern identity, ambitious enough, also has a therapeutic dimension. To see ourselves as we really are will be liberating: '(t)he retrieval of suppressed goods is not only valuable on the Socratic grounds that if we are going to live by the modern identity, it had better be by an examined version of it. It is also a way in which we can live this identity more fully' (1989: 504). Now, the claim that 'it', presumably the act of retrieval itself, enables us to live the modern identity more fully is, at first sight, a puzzling one and later I shall suggest that it harbours a crucial ambiguity that runs right through Taylor's account of modernity. For the moment, however, it is only necessary to underline that Taylor means what he says here. Justifying this kind of claim in 1979, he argued that there is a valid form of transcendental argument that demonstrates the boundary conditions which must hold in virtue of the fact that our experience has a particular character (1978/9). To conclude such an argument successfully will lead to a deeper and more satisfactory understanding of the experience in question. This is much more than the familiar Wittgensteinian concern to dissolve confusion. The experience in question is none other than modernity itself and there is a recognizably Hegelian aspiration to bring us back home by allowing us to understand, for the first time, where we have been all along.

In fact, *Sources* picks up many themes which Taylor last treated at length in *Hegel and Modern Society* (1979), themes which he has been working out in essays and papers for more than twenty years. His paradoxical assessment of Hegel's work as combining an enduring philosophical relevance with a thoroughly implausible metaphysical foundation is central to understanding the whole project of which *Sources* is just one part. In that earlier work (and in its larger companion volume, *Hegel* [1975]), Taylor famously presented Hegel as an 'expressivist' thinker, someone whose problems were set by the homesick Romantic generation and their longing for expressive unity with nature. As he points out, there is an influential narrative which sees Romanticism as a temporary protest against the rougher edges of modernity, a roughness that was eventually overcome by one of the great constitutive compromises that now defines the modern identity, the displacement of the Romantic demands into private life aided by the material compensations provided by an increasingly instrumental, objectifying attitude to both nature and society. But, on Taylor's account, this cannot be the end of the story. The 'modern mixture of private Romanticism and public utilitarianism' (1979: 136) has had the practical consequence of creating a public world in which we fail to identify with anything larger than our own instrumental satisfactions, thereby destroying the possibility of a reconciliation. There is no rose in the cross of this particular present and a Hegelian demand to seek reason in the history of the 20th century, knowing it is there to be found, can only strike us as deeply implausible. As Taylor remarks in a phrase that is going to become something of a trademark, '(t)here remains since the Romantic period a malaise around the modern identity' (1979: 137). Expressivist protest against the philistinism, stultifying conformity, mediocrity and egoism of modern societies continues unabated, uniting an otherwise oddly assorted collection of critics on both the right and the left of the conventional ideological spectrum.

The continuing relevance of Hegel's philosophy, however, lies in its trenchant critique of tendencies within the expressivism of the late 18th century, tendencies that, in Taylor's view, have become even more marked in response to the deepening malaise surrounding the modern, unreconciled identity. He is referring to the 'inward turn' taken by modern expressivism, in which the drive to freedom understood as being true to oneself recognizes no legitimate limits on an agent's self-determining choice. On Taylor's account there is simply no better guide than Hegel for showing that this subjective expressivism is ultimately empty or without content. By dispensing with all the background features that define the human situation as so many impediments to liberation, nothing is left to explain why the content of the choice – the decision to choose *this* rather than *that* – has any value.

Taylor's sympathetic recovery of the Romantic expressivist context has had the paradoxical result that he is himself often characterized as an expressivist thinker. Nothing could be further from the truth. On his account, the expressivist yearning to find meaning in nature and society is simply one strand in the modern identity that has to be accommodated. As *Sources* argues, an unexamined expressivism poses a real danger because of its congruence with the two other sources of the modern identity, the tendency to think of the self as something 'inside' and the retreat from ideas of an ethical hierarchy of modes of existence into 'the affirmation of ordinary life'. Although expressivism may take the form of a protest against both the disengagement from nature and feeling that is associated with the inward turn and the stifling of exceptional creative expression that may result from the validation of ordinary life, it can just as easily appeal to both in a slide into radical subjectivism, the denial that there are any moral sources outside the unproblematic, inarticulate self. Hegel's value lies in his reminder that only a situated freedom, one which accepts some set of boundaries or limits as ours and hence as capable of giving meaning to our choices, can actually satisfy such a demand. To understand both *Sources* and *Malaise*, it is necessary to see that, for Taylor, subjective expressivism is part of the problem. The solution lies in becoming more 'clairvoyant' (to use a Taylor term of art) about what is driving us to the denial of limits and it is just such a clairvoyance that his later work sets out to provide.

This central idea of modernity as an era unable to come to grips with or even systematically denying the constitutive tensions and ambiguities of its own identity has been worked out in a series of articles in which the key theme is the denial of limits. Early examples include contributions to the New Left critique of traditional socialism (1971) and to the limits to growth debate (1977/8). These occasional pieces were reworked into two ambitious articles which introduced the idea of 'hypertrophy', the threat to modernity posed by the unlimited pursuit of what are, within limits, recognizable goods (1985a; 1985c). But, rather than joining the debate about whether we have too much or too little of these goods, Taylor argued that the real need was to understand more clearly what is at stake and to determine what it would mean 'to realize these goods in their authentic form'.

> Our agenda will then no longer be defined as limiting or slowing down the progress of modern values, but rather as finding a way to rescue them in their integrity, as against the distortions and perversions that have developed in modern history. (1985c: 186)

Finally, he developed an account of how to overcome our forgetting through an interpretative approach to the past. We need to uncover the sources of these goods before they are rendered inarticulate by their general acceptance and incorporation into contemporary practices, to catch them at the moment when their adherents were forced to defend and promote them against very different orthodoxies. In a paper published at about the same time, Taylor argued that this made philosophy – whether epistemology or political philosophy – an 'inescapably historical' exercise:

> Instead of just living in [our practices] and taking their implicit construal of things as the way things are, we have to understand how they have come to be, how they came to embed a certain view of things. In other words, in order to undo the forgetting, we have to articulate for ourselves how it happened, to become aware of the way a picture slid from the status of discovery to that of inarticulate assumption, a fact too obvious to mention. (1984: 21)

In *Sources*, the polemical thrust of the argument tends to be hidden in dense discussion of the sources themselves. In *Malaise*, however, Taylor gives a clear polemical example of his approach by taking issue with Alan Bloom's (1987) rejection of the contemporary vogue for soft relativism – I have my values and you have yours and nothing more can be said. On Taylor's account, to condemn this as merely a hypocritical gloss on self-indulgence, a convenient way of making my 'life-style' immune to serious criticism, is to miss the real moral source at work here, none other than the expressivist ideal of authentic self-development. But because this ideal is itself largely inarticulate it is easy enough to miss it. Taylor neatly characterizes the debate between Bloom and his adversaries as a kind of shadow-boxing in which Bloom assaults authenticity in the name of a pre-modern ideal of alignment with a rational moral order, but no one can be found to take him on because of a failure to acknowledge authenticity as a moral source at all, or, on a more sophisticated variant, because of a feeling that the very idea of a moral source no longer makes sense.

In contrast to this dialogue of the deaf (in the engaging colloquies of *Malaise*, between the boosters and the knockers of modernity), Taylor feels that his finer discrimination allows him to end both his works on a note of cautious optimism. Modernity is powered by ideals that, once articulated, cannot but have a powerful hold over us because they are embodied in the familiar practices that have made us who we are. The danger is neither the crushing burden that such ideals might lay upon us if clearly articulated, nor the purely contingent fact that damage and suffering have resulted from the over-enthusiastic or confused pursuit of them, but the damage we do to ourselves by denying who we really are. If we are inescapably situated in a distinctively modern moral space and continually testing our 'selves' against measures of what we could or should be, both the denial of this predicament ('spiritual lobotomy') and the artificial narrowing and flattening of the space by a failure to articulate the horizons are forms of mutilation. Both, on Taylor's view, represent a failure of the imagination that a revitalized moral debate can overcome: 'the dilemma of mutilation is in a sense our greatest spiritual challenge, not an iron fate' (1989: 521).

In the space remaining, I want to tackle three related issues that arise from Taylor's picture of modernity and its various malaises. The first is his confrontation with what he recognizes as an important and often sophisticated alternative interpretation of modernity, the various 'neo-Nietzschean' versions of a postmodern era that not only decisively reject any recovery of modern moral horizons but positively celebrate our liberation from them. On the one hand, Taylor can be brutally dismissive of this whole tendency – he once referred to the 'fog emanating from Paris on the disappearance of the subject' and he has maintained a kind of intertextual sniping operation against Richard Rorty via a series of tart comments on unnamed American admirers of Derrida (most recently in 1991: 68–9). On the other, he has been much more respectful towards Foucault (and even towards his American admirers), welcoming the argument that moral imperatives, by the very fact that they are imperatives, place structured demands upon us which we may not fully understand, including the creation of patterns of exclusion which may contradict the imperatives themselves. All this is grist for his interpretative mill since it will require some careful articulation of the imperatives and their sources to disentangle these contradictions.

However, he is concerned to point out what he sees as a sleight of hand in some of these accounts. While it is true enough that imperatives can cause tragic dilemmas, it is quite false to blame the very existence of moral demands for all the pain and suffering committed in their name. We would not be better off if we were 'liberated' from them, not least because we would then lack the background against which we could condemn pain and suffering or indeed anything at all: 'it is a form of self-delusion to think that we do not speak from a moral orientation that we take to be right. This is a condition of being a functioning self, not a metaphysical view which we can switch on and off' (1989: 99). The practical consequence of the intellectual confusion lurking behind fashionable ideas like 'difference' or 'the aesthetic of the self' has been to intensify the slide to subjectivism, especially among the impressionable young.

Taylor's failure to be impressed by accounts of postmodernity needs more careful examination than can be given here. To be fair, we need to follow the distinction that he makes in *Sources* between two kinds of inquiry. Many of those who claim to be disappointed by *Sources* are looking for an answer to the question of how the modern identity came about. It is this 'very ambitious' question that Taylor specifically disavows. His interpretative aim is much less ambitious, to give an account of the appeal that this modern identity has, identifying the '*idées-forces*' it contains (*Sources*: 202–3). Obviously, as he agrees, these two questions are very closely related and it is, in his view, the disabling fault of the various Marxist and structuralist accounts of modernity that they fail to grasp this relation. But while the kind of balanced explanation that Taylor describes, with a gesture in the direction of Weber's dictum about sociological explanation being 'adequate as to meaning', is an admirable goal, it is notoriously difficult to achieve in practice. And Taylor himself makes no effort to do so, claiming that the purely interpretative account, though suffering from 'unavoidable incompleteness', will at least make sense even though it must not be mistaken for a full historical explanation. Apart from a few gnomic remarks about the causal properties of *idées-forces* and the reciprocal causation of ideas and practices there is is no attempt to justify this large claim (1989: 202–3). At best, what we get is the purely rhetorical justification that an alternative account such as Harvey (1989) is unhelpful because it promotes inarticulacy with respect to moral ideals (1991: 21). There is much more to be said about causal accounts of modernity especially if Taylor's ambition is to make a practical intervention.

The second question about Taylor's thesis is closely related to the first. Once recovered, the sources of the modern identity do reveal a picture variously described as 'secular humanist' or 'neo-Lucretian' that has at least the merit of internal consistency, even if it is damned with the very faintest of praise by Taylor himself. Arising out of the High-Enlightenment aspiration to recover nature and more particularly human nature from the alleged calumnies of Augustinian Christianity, and fuelled in the 19th century by a powerful sense that religious belief has become a cowardly exercise in self-deception, this picture puts us under a positive obligation to accept ourselves as we are and learn to live with humanity as we find it. Taylor argues that we find something like it in Hume, in an interpretation of Nietzsche's 'yea-saying', in some features of Wittgenstein's stress on the arbitrariness of forms of life, and in Heidegger's notion of 'clearing' (1989: 340–7).

Taylor's concern here is whether this picture can bear the weight that modernity puts upon it, particularly the need to justify our drive for universal justice and benevolence. The picture might be promoting otherwise desirable practices that we will find difficult to defend if we have only these sources to fall back on. The Nietzschean debacle looms large, not just Nietzsche's own personal tragedy, but his claim that it is, in fact, benevolence itself that stands in the way of the full acceptance of this picture and all its implications. And, of course, there is the constant danger of a slide into subjectivism, the dissolution of the moral force of the picture, exemplified in the (mis)interpretation of Nietzsche discussed above. Although, once again, his argument is somewhat elusive at this point, it appears that Taylor doubts whether we can detach the ideals of benevolence and justice from an external foundation (such as reason or nature) and treat them as arising in a purely immanent way from undistorted self-interpretation. In the face of this doubt Taylor takes a fateful step, arguing that some kind of theistic foundation is necessary to bear the weight of modern moral demands and, moreover, that this 'necessity' is a question of fact. But what can this mean? As Bernard Williams has argued (1990: 47), about the only inescapable fact here is that many men and women have lived perfectly clairvoyant lives without seeing any need for a transcendental foundation for their moral goods, let alone a theistic one.

The whole argument reveals a deep ambiguity in the central concept of an *idée-force*. To say that, once acknowledged, a moral good has force for me seems perfectly reasonable. This is what acknowledging a moral good amounts to. But Taylor seems to want to take the further step: that I will just *have* to acknowledge the force of some ideas, that failure to do so is a criterion of confusion or lack of clairvoyance about who I really am. As Taylor concluded in his earlier discussion of transcendental arguments, this must always remain an open question – the best he can do is challenge us to deny the force of the picture he has retrieved. I cannot decline the challenge, but my reflective failure to recognize myself in his portrait constitutes prima facie evidence that the picture is wrong.

The same question about the force of Taylor's own argument arises even more clearly in connection with the final issue that I want to consider, Taylor's political philosophy. Here he wants to link the slide to subjectivism to a familiar theme of his earlier writings, the growing 'fragmentation' of modern liberal-democratic states. It has long been his fear (despite being presented as the fear of some unnamed or generalized other) that we may be experiencing a modern version of Tocqueville's soft despotism 'when people come to see themselves more and more atomistically, otherwise put, less and less bound to their fellow citizens in common projects and allegiances' (1991: 112–13). In these circumstances, a society may be 'full of activity and challenges to authority' but only from individuals or partial groupings who, for this reason, lose the ability to undertake genuine collective projects supported by a majority of the citizen body. As Taylor has argued repeatedly, the United States presents an example of this kind of politics.

Again, we are reminded of Taylor's continuing sympathy for Hegel's notion of 'Sittlichkeit', the complex of customs and practices which simultaneously educates and enables, checking the slide to subjectivism by providing appropriate institutions within which freedom can be situated without being experienced as imposing limits. But, having voluntarily renounced Hegel's strong notion of conceptual necessity – that a particular Sittlichkeit is 'adequate to the concept' of situated freedom, to use a Hegelianism – it is difficult to see how many of Taylor's programmatic remarks can be substantiated. There is a drift here, analogous to the one Williams identified in connection with Taylor's theism. In this case, there is a familiar chain of conceptual claims: that what we mean by a 'person' necessarily involves some kind of dialogicality, a dialectic of interrogation and recognition; hence that personality requires a linguistic community in which this dialogue can be carried on; and hence, following Wittgenstein, shared 'forms of life'. But there is also an argument that sometimes runs parallel to but is at other times presented as a further corollary of the conceptual argument just cited, that some 'forms of life' perform this function better than others, namely those where the dialogue includes a place for collective projects.

When it is presented as another conceptual claim, the argument is usually a negative one, deployed against the 'atomist' understanding of human agents as morally autonomous bearers of rights. Taylor sets out to show, in a now familiar way, that the atomist (though often seeking refuge in inarticulacy) values a particular conception of human agency which presupposes a social setting in which the capacity for autonomous choice can develop and be valued. So far, so true, as Taylor might say. But the move to a very different kind of claim is neatly illustrated in this passage:

> The connection I want to establish here can be made following the earlier discussion of the background of rights. If we cannot ascribe natural rights without affirming the worth of certain human capacities, and if this affirmation has other normative consequences (i.e. that we should foster and nurture these capacities in ourselves and others), then any proof that these capacities can only develop in society *or in a society of a certain kind* is proof that we ought to belong to or sustain society or this kind of society. (1985b: 197; emphasis added)

In other words, there is a jump from the unexceptional conceptual claim that social capacities are developed in society to the much more controversial one that valuable human capacities are only developed in particular kinds of societies which we ought, therefore, to belong to or sustain.

There is more mileage in this move than there might seem at first glance for, even if the intelligent atomist has grasped the conceptual point, he can then be pressed to explain how the particular social arrangements he favours do, in fact, sustain the values he is promoting. Will a rights-based society actually produce people who are inclined to treat each other with equal concern and respect? Eventually, however, this same move rebounds upon its originator. Taylor must justify both his oft-expressed scepticism about the stability and desirability of rights-based societies and his preference for what he has called the participatory model. And here, once again, the argument is the elusive Taylor mix of the conceptual and the empirical. Because we are the kinds of people that *Sources* argues that we are, committed to freedom, equality and benevolence, we just will, on his view, find the drift of modern states towards a rights-based model ultimately unsatisfactory.

But, again, what if we welcome such development instead? To the familiar arguments that freedom simply means exercising some control over the society in which we live (means to me? means to you? means to Charles Taylor?), are now added quasi-empirical claims about the stability of societies which fail to accommodate this understanding of freedom through institutions of common decision-making. In *Malaise*, the whole comes together into an almost apocalyptic vision. A fragmented society of atomistic individuals gradually becomes incapable of responding to crises that require a common project since they are inclined to see politics as the sphere in which isolated individuals fight for their rights whatever the cost to the collectivity. This, in Taylor's view, has been the fate of the environmental movement and, closer to home, has contributed to the seeming intractability of the Quebec problem in Canada. In the latter case, once a Charter of Rights on the American model had become a central feature of the Canadian identity, the demand to recognize the distinctive-ness of Quebec within a united Canada could be seen only as an illegitimate claim to special status that undermines equality of rights. The original pressure for the Charter is a consequence of atomism, namely the desire of individuals for political efficacy in the absence of meaningful forms of collective actions. But its adoption powerfully reinforces these very tendencies by making it more difficult to address issues 'that require a wide democratic consensus around measures that will also involve some sacrifice and difficulty' (1991: 116). There is a vicious circle at work here which is making it less and less possible to deal with the problems of modernity, the alienation from communities, the dehumanizing technologies associated with our drive for instrumental control of nature, and the rest. The self-induced malaise becomes a self-fulfilling slide to catastrophe.

Indeed, when set against this picture of politics and modernity, Taylor's suggestion that a 're-enframing' needs to takes place, one that promotes 'democratic empowerment' and feeds on the success of collective projects at the level of 'schools and hospitals', has a curiously dated air about it, as if a youthful contribution to the *Universities and Left Quarterly* had accidentally got mixed up with a later manuscript. This is a pity, for Taylor is posing an important question: what kind of political practice will help articulate the tensions and contradictions of modernity in a productive way? But this is precisely where an institutional account of modernity and the questions of causations that it would raise can no longer be deferred. Set Taylor's account against Giddens's in *Modernity and Self-Identity* (1991) and the difference is clear. Where Taylor is reduced to recycling his preference for 'democratic will formation', Giddens presents evidence that the very fragmentation that Taylor deplores does, in fact, lead to new forms of political practice which help to articulate those unresolved tensions that modernity has so far managed to displace out of politics. In doing so, it suggests that there is something more than just an unavoidable incom-pleteness about an interpretative account of the modern identity.

To end here, however, would be churlish. What Taylor delivers on is his basic promise to restore a picture of the modern identity, providing us with an unparalleled map of the moral space in which that identity is constituted together with a powerful argument why, even though the topography may change, the space itself can never burst free of some bounding horizons. His claims about the consequences of the picture he has drawn must remain, on his own account, contestable and, as I have indicated, there are times at which he has a somewhat eccentric view of the form such a contestation will have to take. But to have reached this point is already to have been drawn into dialogue with a master interlocuter.

Malaspina College, British Columbia

BIBLIOGRAPHY

Bloom, A. (1987) *The Closing of the American Mind*. New York: Simon & Schuster.

Giddens, A. (1991) *Modernity and Self-Identity*. Stanford, CA: Stanford University Press.

Harvey, D. (1989) *The Condition of Postmodernity*. Oxford: Blackwell.

Taylor, C. (1971) 'The Agony of Economic Man', in Laurier LaPierre (ed.) *Essays on the Left*, pp. 221–35. Toronto: McClelland & Stewart.

Taylor, C. (1975) *Hegel*. Cambridge: Cambridge University Press.

Taylor, C. (1977/8) 'The Politics of the "Steady State"', *New Universities Quarterly* 32: 157–84.

Taylor, C. (1978/9) 'The Validity of Transcendental Arguments', *Proceedings of the Aristotelian Society* 79: 151–65.

Taylor, C. (1979) *Hegel and Modern Society*. Cambridge: Cambridge University Press.

Taylor, C. (1984) 'Philosophy and Its History', in Richard Rorty, J. B. Scheewind and Quentin Skinner (eds) *Philosophy in History*. Cambridge: Cambridge University Press.

Taylor, C. (1985a) 'Legitimation Crisis?', in C. Taylor, *Philosophy and the Human Sciences: Philosophical Papers 2*, pp. 248–88. Cambridge: Cambridge University Press.

Taylor, C. (1985b) 'Atomism', in C. Taylor, *Philosophy and the Human Sciences: Philosophical Papers 2*, pp. 187–210. Cambridge: Cambridge University Press.

Taylor, C. (1985c) 'Alternative Futures: Legitimacy, Identity and Alienation in Late Twentieth Century Canada', in Alan Cairns and Cynthia Williams (eds), *Constitutionalism, Citizenship and Society in Canada*, pp. 183–229. Toronto: University of Toronto Press.

Taylor, C. (1988) 'The Moral Topography of the Self' in Stanley Messer, Louis Sass and Robert Woolfolk (eds) *Hermeneutics and Psychological Theory*, pp. 298–319. New Brunswick, NJ: Rutgers University Press.

Taylor, C. (1989) *Sources of the Self: The Making of the Modern Identity*. Cambridge, MA: Harvard University Press.

Taylor, C. (1991) *The Malaise of Modernity*, CBC Massey Lecture Series. Toronto: Anansi.

Williams, B. (1990) ' "Republican and Galilean", rev. of Charles Taylor, *Sources of the Self*', *New York Review of Books*, 8 November: 45–8.

HISTORY OF THE HUMAN SCIENCES   Vol. 5 No. 3

© 1992 SAGE (London, Newbury Park and New Delhi)   pp. 157–173

Is Bhaskar's critical realism only a theoretical realism?

JOHN SHOTTER

Roy Bhaskar, *Philosophy and the Idea of Freedom*. Oxford: Blackwell, 1991. xii + 202 pp.

> The crucial questions in philosophy are not whether to be a realist or anti-realist, but *what sort* of realist to be . . . (PIF,[1] p. 25)

What is the difference between (i) the conditions of possibility necessary for an individual to think and to talk about something, monologically, in a way intelligible to others, and (ii) the conditions necessary for a group, who may all disagree amongst themselves about how a topic may best be characterized, to agree, dialogically, that at least they are all discussing the same topic? Or, to put it another way: (i) do speakers link their utterances primarily to the objects in their surroundings, or (ii) do they link them to their 'roots' in ongoing contextualized social action, i.e. is it representation that makes communication possible, or communication representation? In short, is it primarily through something like theories, or is it in our social activities and practices, that we 'hook up' with reality (Shotter, 1991)? It is in the context of this issue that I would like to discuss this new book of Roy Bhaskar's in which he is critical of many of Richard Rorty's recent claims, particularly in how they relate to political freedom and emancipation.

BHASKAR AGAINST RORTY

Bhaskar divides the first and main section of his book – which he calls 'Anti-Rorty' – into four parts of two chapters each, examining four topics:

knowledge; agency; politics; and (what he calls Rorty's) 'kibitzing'. The second and shorter section contains three texts: a ninth chapter situating his 'critical realism' in relation to the current philosophical tradition, and two appendices. The first appendix clarifies the relation in critical realism between fact and value, theory and practice, and explanation and emancipation; while the second is a synoptic digest of the tradition of Marxist philosophy – a trailer for the volumes to come.[2]

Rorty's 'Kibitzing'

Rather than treating each of Bhaskar's topics in turn, it will be worth trying first to grasp the general tenor of his project, by turning to what he has to say about Rorty's 'kibitzing': In *Reclaiming Reality* he spoke of Rorty's *Philosophy and the Mirror of Nature* as 'one of the most influential philosophical books of the post-war period' (*RR*, p. viii), and promised in this book to expand and broaden his critique of both it and Rorty's other work. Here, he reveals in more detail why he has chosen to attack Rorty further (rather than, say, Habermas, of whom he is also critical): it is because he feels that 'Rorty provides an ideology for a leisured elite – intellectual yuppies – neither racked by pain nor immersed in toil – whose lives may be devoted to the practice of aesthetic enhancement, and in particular to generating self, other and genealogical descriptions . . . [many of whom] are to be found especially in the 'soft' disciplines – the social sciences and humanities – where experimental closures are not possible and where there appear to be no criteria for rational criticism and change' (*PIF*, pp. 134–5). Rorty's arguments work in this way because, in claiming that no philosophical frameworks can be justified, he also claims that no novel proposals (philosophical or otherwise) can therefore be argumentatively justified, because argumentative justification is only possible within a framework, i.e. a 'language-game', or a systematic, rule-governed 'vocabulary'. Thus, if one cannot *argue* for novel claims, then, as Rorty sees it, they just have to be presented (asserted): you tell opponents arguing against you that you 'just don't want to talk about the topic in that way'. Indeed, in discussing the philosophers of whom he approves – such as Wittgenstein, Heidegger, and Dewey – Rorty claims that they have simply introduced another vocabulary and 'argued' for it by trying to make it 'look attractive by showing how it may be used to describe a variety of topics' (*CIS*, p. 9), and to make the vocabulary in which objections to it are phrased 'look bad, thereby changing the subject' (*CIS*, p. 44).

It is, of course, precisely claims of this kind that Bhaskar cannot stomach. Evidently, like many others of my acquaintance, Bhaskar is more than a little 'irked' by Rorty's 'kibitzing', i.e. his functioning as a philosophical 'barrack-room lawyer', giving unsolicited advice as to how properly to proceed in analysing and criticizing human affairs. For obviously, Bhaskar sees Rorty's account of paradigm shifts (especially in the social sciences) as morally and politically dangerous – because, in being essentially *poetic*, 'no overarching criteria or commensurating criteria can be given' (*PIF*, p. 135) for explanations of their occurrence, or for their rational criticism. As a respected philosopher, Rorty has thus been influential, without apparently offering any good, i.e. rational, reasons for his claims; he is enjoying power without responsibility. Thus it is not surprising that the main title of the three-volume series, of which this book is the first, is *Philosophy and the Eclipse of Reason: Towards a Metacritique of the Philosphical Tradition*.

Yet, for all the disquiet Bhaskar evinces with Rorty's views, there is also more than a little agreement between them. Indeed, as he himself claims, his study 'shares with Rorty a starting point he [Rorty] attributes to his teachers of philosophy: "that a 'philosophical problem' was a product of the unconscious adoption of assumptions built into the vocabulary in which the problem was stated – assumptions which were to be questioned before the problem itself was taken seriously" (*PMN*, p. xiii)' (*PIF*, pp. 132–3). In other words, he agrees with Rorty, that certain pervasive, but wrong, assumptions about the nature of knowledge, the world, and the relation between the two, have undergirded the philosophical tradition which informs much of contemporary culture, including the current practices of the social sciences. And it is these assumptions, implicit in the ways of talking which sustain its practices, that Bhaskar is also concerned to combat. Especially, he agrees with Rorty's assault upon its attendant ocular metaphors, mirror imagery and overseer conception of philosophy. 'Most of this I wholeheartedly endorse,' he says (*PIF*, p. 32). In fact, 'my aim is to carry the dialectic of "de-divinization" (set out by Rorty, see note 12) a stage or two further. . . . A picture has indeed held philosophy captive. It is a picture of ourselves or our insignia in any picture . . . [the ultimate mark of our escape] will be evinced in our capacity to draw non-anthropomorphic pictures of being',[3] he says (*PIF*, p. viii). Especially, he also shares with Rorty an implicit belief in the importance of conceptual frameworks, models, systematic vocabularies, or language-games, in the conduct and the settling of philosophical arguments: both seem to believe that, unless one is arguing from within an overarching framework, in terms of a general model, a systematic vocabulary, or a language-game, there are no criteria or standards against which one can judge between two (or more) ways of talking about the nature of human phenomena. Both feel, that without the prior possession of commensurating criteria, (rational) argument is not possible. Where, then, do Bhaskar's disagreements with Rorty lie?

Tensions and Their Resolutions: Theory and Ideology

Turning now to the substance of his critique of Rorty, we find that it consists in two moves: first, the discovery of certain unresolved and unresolvable tensions or aporiai in each of Rorty's different phases that lead him (Rorty) philosophically to neglect crucial aspects of human being,[4] which he covers over ideologically: and second, by Bhaskar's showing of how his provision of a framework, within which this crucial ontological and dialectical dimension neglected by Rorty can be represented, can overcome these tensions.

Let us examine the nature of this second move first. As Bhaskar sees it, all previous philosophies of science, and many current ones, Rorty's included, fall victim to what he calls the 'epistemic fallacy': 'the definition of being in terms of knowledge' (*PIF*, p. viii; *RTS*, pp. 36 ff.). In other words, in failing to make a clear distinction between epistemology and ontology, they tend to incorporate into their accounts of the being of things the very assumptions informing their epistemology. Thus as a result, in Rorty's case, he 'remains . . . a prisoner of the implicit ontology of the problematic he describes' (*PIF*, p. viii). And this is especially evidenced, Bhaskar maintains, in his failure to sustain an adequate account of human agency, which, in turn, is responsible for Rorty's failure properly to grasp the nature of human freedom as 'emancipation from real and scientifically knowable specific constraints, rather than merely the poetic redescription of an already determined world' (*PIF*, pp. viii–ix). In other words, Bhaskar's central concern is with a philosophical ontology, and 'it is Rorty's failure to thematize philosophical ontology and sociology and his subsequent subscription to the epistemic fallacy that leads to the replication of classical problems as (displaced or undisplaced) aporiai in his work' (*PIF*, p. 133).

It is the fashioning of two separate dimensions within which to talk (and to think) about science – an 'intransitive', ontological dimension existing independently of scientists and their activity, and a 'transitive', epistemological or historical sociological dimension – that Bhaskar sees as the crucial move in overcoming, not only what he sees as the aporiai and tensions in Rorty's work, but also in the reinvigorating of scientifically relevant philosophical work: it is the 'core'[5] of his philosophical research programme (indeed, he says so explicitly – p. 141). While our knowledge of the world is a social product, produced by transformational social activity from previously existing knowledge, the being of the world (including the social world) must be conceived of (at least at the moment of its scientific investigation) as existing independently of our thoughts about it. For only if this is so can we discover our theories of its nature to be wrong, thus making a scientific investigation of its *reality* a genuine possibility. Thus as a philosopher, as he freely admits, it is from within a systematic *philosophical* perspective or framework – that he has fashioned over the last fifteen years or so out of 'a Lockean underlabouring interest in the human sciences' (*PIF*, p. vii) – that he formulates the results of his criticisms of Rorty.

With regard to the tensions he finds in Rorty's work, we shall find a comment he made in his previous book relevant. There he said that 'practically, it is in the contradictions yielded by the necessity to hold two incompatible positions, as conditions of each other, that the most fertile ground of ideology lies' (*RR*, p. 57). He could have made the same comment here, because time and again, it is in what he calls the 'fault-lines' around which Rorty organizes his discourse, that Bhaskar is able to tease out aspects of his (Rorty's) ideology, and to show how his own philosophical ontology can resolve these tensions. There is not enough space to examine how Bhaskar plays out this strategy throughout the whole book, but as politics is its central focus, it will be sufficient to see it at work there.

In his criticism of *PMN*, Bhaskar suggests that it 'is a veritable tale of two Rorty's – tough-minded Humean versus tender-minded existentialist' (*PIF*, p. 47); in other words, its problem-field is defined by the tension between our determination as material bodies, and our freedom as discursive subjects, especially as poets. Turning to *CIS*, the fault-line shifts: to that between 'private irony', and public pragmatism as realized in a liberal political culture; between poetic self-invention, and the expansion of the present 'we' or moral community. Thus, 'just as in PMN Rorty neglected the material embodiment of human agency in an untenable distinction between the physical and the personal, so in CIS Rorty neglects the social realization of human agency in an untenable distinction between the private and the public' (*PIF* , p. 81). Now, it is not that Rorty himself is unaware of the tension, for as he realizes, irony, poetic redescription, in calling common sense into question, in ridiculing the taken-for-granted, can often hurt and humiliate. And in one attempt to resolve that tension, he talked of his ideal world order as being 'an intricately textured collage of private narcissism and public pragmatism' (quoted by Bhaskar in *PIF*, p. 82), while in *CIS* it is resolved by the privatization of irony, thus reserving, Bhaskar says, 'the public sphere for pragmatic social engineering' (*PIF*, p. 82). And it is in this resolution that Rorty's ideological preferences are revealed. But why, Bhaskar asks, 'should the project of self-invention be restricted to only some – a privileged elite? No wonder that Rorty has been hailed as an ideologue for "the chattering classes"'[6] (*PIF*, p. 85).

Why the fault-line creates such a gap here, is because of the rather contrived conception of private irony Rorty formulates. Again, it depends upon the simplistic view of argumentative justification he adheres to: that it is only possible within a 'language-game', or a systematic, rule-governed 'vocabulary'. In line with that view, he claims that 'all human beings carry about a set of words which they employ to justify their actions, their beliefs, their lives. . . . [And] I shall call these words their "final vocabulary"' (*CIS*, p. 73). By contrast, an 'ironist' is somebody who doubts the ultimate nature of the (supposed) final vocabulary she is currently using, and is impressed by others. But, because she sees the choice between vocabularies 'as made neither within a neutral universal metavocabulary nor by an attempt to fight one's way past appearances to the real' (ibid.), she sees the issue as simply a matter of playing off the new against the old. Yet what if, as already mentioned, 'redescription often humiliates' (*CIS*, p. 90)? The liberal ironist meets this point 'by saying that we need to distinguish between redescription for private and for public purposes' (*CIS*, p. 91). But as Bhaskar makes clear, drawing upon his transformational model of social action (TMSA) (see *PON*, Ch. 2; *RR*, Ch. 6; or *PIF*, Appendix 1), such a clear and sharp separation is untenable: 'Personal agency requires and uses social forms as its conditions, means and media and almost always has social consequences (including the reproduction or transformation of its own social structural prerequisites)' (*PIF*, p. 89). What Rorty wants here, Bhaskar would argue, makes all kinds of things we know to be possible impossible.[7] Thus, what is ideologically resolved in Rorty, is theoretically resolved in Bhaskar.

What then of politics and freedom? As far as Rorty is concerned 'freedom is the recognition of contingency' (*CIS*, p. 46). But what does he mean by contingency here? For in *PMN*, as Bhaskar points out, he has claimed that 'Physicalism is probably right in saying that we shall someday be able, "in principle", to predict every movement of a person's body . . .' (*PMN*, p. 354), thus seemingly, theoretically, we live in an already fully determined world. However, 'the danger to human freedom of such success is minimal, since the "in principle" clause allows for the probability . . . [that it] will be too difficult to carry out except as an occasional pedagogical exercise' (*PMN*, p. 354). In other words, for Rorty, contingency means not a genuine, objective indeterminacy in which, as Bhaskar says, 'events . . . are not determined before they are caused' (*PIF*, p. 50), but merely a subjective indeterminacy, an ignorance in practice. This is not enough for Bhaskar. He wants an objective freedom, one which allows 'the identification of the *source* of an experienced injustice in social reality, necessary for changing or remedying it' (*PIF*, p. 72). Does that mean that he is still proposing 'classical' kinds of solutions to social problems, i.e. analyse the situation; isolate the problem; propose a solution ; and then implement it in an active way? As we all now well know, such an approach leads to solutions confined to particular localities, or, to a particular, fragmentary aspect of a system, and such 'solutions' can thus have unexpected and unintended results – often worse than the problem itself. No, he is far too sophisticated for that, for the identification of a source of social injustice 'involves much more than redescription, even if it depends on that too centrally. It is a matter of finding and disentangling webs of relations in social life, and engaging in explanatory critiques of the practices that sustain them' (*PIF*, p. 72) – and that is a task, Bhaskar claims, that can only be undertaken from a discursive position within a theoretical framework that allows for the possibility of knowing the real nature of the constraints in question, scientifically.

BHASKAR'S METHODOLOGY AND ROLE

Unlike Rorty, Bhaskar is, of course, concerned to sustain science as *the* focal arena of cultural activity, of cultural change and criticism: without an account of the real and scientifically knowable constraints under which we live, there is, he feels, nothing to separate the poet 'who makes things new' from the demagogue.

Thus he is concerned to show (along with the fact that Rorty both misdescribes and underdescribes science), that although Rorty is careful not to denigrate science itself, he has an animus against the philosophical culture which has grown up around it. And he quotes some of Rorty's views in support of his claim. For instance, Rorty claims that '[the sciences] have receded into the background of cultural life . . . due largely to the increasing difficulty of mastering[8] the various languages in which all the various sciences are conducted. . . . We [can cope with this] by switching attention to those areas which *are* in the forefront of culture' (*CIS*, p. 52). Thus, instead of 'philosophy as science' (or Bhaskar's philosophy of and for science), he would like to see 'philosophy as art', and/or 'philosophy as utopian politics'. 'It seems clear', Bhaskar says, 'that Rorty wants a post-Philosophical but not a post-Science culture' (*PIF*, p. 19). Thus Bhaskar pays much more attention to rebutting Rorty's attempts to make a systematic, 'scientific' philosophy 'look bad' than what he says in attempting to make his own (Rorty's) preferred (conversational) alternatives 'look good' – I shall examine these in a moment, after studying Bhaskar's methodology further.

Now, in his formulation of his philosophical ontology, Bhaskar is working within a particular philosophical tradition that, because it shares many features with the physical and social sciences, can be called 'scientific philosophy'.[9] It has at least these six features: (1) It thinks of itself as solving conceptual or logical problems (as a helpful aid to factual investigations in the sciences). (2) In valuing theory over practice, it holds that to understand something requires our prior possession of a theory of it. (3) Thus, when faced with such questions as: 'What is a human agent really?' 'What is society really?' 'What is language really?' as a first step towards answering them, it provides possibly true, competing, explanatory theories or models, ones that talk about entities that can be grasped as objects of thought, i.e. which can be mentally 'seen' or 'pictured', and which make whatever is 'seen' intelligible by fitting it into a larger order or scheme of things.[10] (4) It then holds that, of all the proposed models, the true one can be discovered through philosophical discourse and argumentation, where such arguments can be 'grounded' within a logical framework of some kind. (5) Thus, rather than a montage or album of poetic metaphors, suggestive of many possible interpretations or orderings, working as a 'means' or 'tool' in the making of possibly new meanings, the models proposed must be literalized, severely limiting their possible meanings, all of which in any case must be rigorously formulated linguistically, in terms of a system of relationships between their component parts. And finally, (6) it holds that the claims made, positions outlined, arguments put forward, etc., in such discourses, are to be evaluated in terms of truth and falsity, correctness and error, and suchlike, i.e. they come to an end in our 'seeing' that something is the case.

And just to step to one side for a moment: it is important to notice that it is exactly this model of philosophy that Wittgenstein rejected in its entirety: for it cannot explain how it itself – as the kind of activity it is, involving, as it does, an advanced use of linguistic representations in both the formulation of intelligible models and in arguing for their truth – is possible. A point comes where 'we must do away with *explanation*, and description alone must take its place' (Wittgenstein, 1953: no. 109). For the problems posed by questions such as those above – to do with 'what' something 'is' – are not solved by advancing any kinds of theories at all. 'They are solved, rather, by looking into the workings of our language, and that in such a way as to make us recognize those workings: *in spite of* an urge to misunderstand them [due to the "grammatical illusions" we ourselves produce in our talk]. The problems are solved, not by giving new information, but by arranging what we have always known' (ibid.: no. 109), with the hope of arriving at a perspicuous representation. Where 'a perspicuous representation produces just that understanding which consists in "seeing connections"' (ibid.: no. 122), we cannot 'ground' our claims in any representations (mental or otherwise) of reality[11] because 'the idea of "agreement with reality" does not have any clear application' (Wittgenstein, 1969: no. 215). There are 'countless' (Wittgenstein, 1953: no. 23) ways in which we achieve the 'hook up' between ourselves and our surroundings; the 'grounds' for our claims can only be found within the context of our ongoing social practices and other activities, i.e. as Wittgenstein (1980: II, nos 625, 626) sees it, the 'bustle' of life.

Returning now to Bhaskar v. Rorty: in *PMN*, Rorty draws upon (some of!) these arguments of Wittgenstein's. And there, although seemingly arguing only against a philosophical theory of knowledge, he also argues precisely against the 'scientific' conception of philosophy – but clearly, without the same concern for the 'rootedness' of language in our social practices that we find in Wittgenstein. As he sees it, 'the desire for a theory of knowledge [of this kind] is a desire for constraint – a desire to find "foundations" to which one might cling, frameworks beyond which one must not stray, objects which impose themselves, representations which cannot be gainsaid' (*PMN*, p. 315). It is a desire which 'appears as the end-product of an original wish to substitute [undeniable, visually metaphorical] *confrontation* for *conversation* as the determinant of our belief' (*PMN*, p. 163), a desire to locate a hidden (divine) world beyond the social and the historical, either in the depths of the mind or of the body (neurophysiology), to which final appeals might be addressed.[12] Thus, if it is impossible to formulate, prior to the conclusion of inquiry, *any* framework within which all human activity (and inquiry in particular) can be said, necessarily, to take place – and Rorty seems to be claiming that it is – then the very idea of 'philosophy' in its traditional guise as the regulator of 'normal inquiry' (in science or elsewhere) is untenable. Novel possibilities cannot arise from or be encompassed within a 'logic'; new possibilities arise 'poetically' and we need another quite different, non-logical or non-systematic way of making sense of such processes, Rorty claims.

Bhaskar, however, seems to read Rorty as making a far less radical claim, i.e. as claiming only that all attempts to construct *epistemological* frameworks to 'ground' claims to knowledge must fail. And he suggest, because Rorty sees 'the only possible locus of necessity as "within the mind",'[13] that 'this prematurely forecloses the possibility of a philosophy of or for science, which was no longer concerned to "ground" knowledge or find certain foundations for it; but which was instead concerned to ask what the *world* must be like for certain characteristic (practical and discursive) social activities of science to be possible' (*PIF*, p. 27). This, then, is how he arrives at his account of this all-important ontological dimension: (1) he first offers novel transcendental arguments of the form 'what must be the case for crucial human activities that we know occur to be possible'; and then, (2) by formulating these arguments within a systematic philosophical framework (and vocabulary) in order to be able to argue for the *necessity* of his conclusions in a two-part 'deduction': (i) in a 'positive' part which shows how a proposed 'structure' (X) makes an activity intelligible, and (ii) in a 'negative' part which shows how the failure to sustain the concept of X leads to absurd or incoherent results (see *PON*, pp. 5–11). In other words, although he does not explicitly draw the parallel himself,[14] he clearly adopts a methodology similar to Chomsky (1957), Lakatos (1971), and the lesser-known psychologist Smedslund (1988), who in their own different ways want to 'explicate' what they see as the 'logical structures', e.g. the linguistic structures, human competencies or powers, etc., implicit in (or underlying) various human activities, in something like a syntax, specifying, if not in fact, at least formally, how things must 'be' in the world.[15] Claims about how-things-are-in-the-world could then be warranted, not by being 'grounded' in something ultimate or absolute, but by being 'measured' up against the theory (essentially) for their 'grammaticality'. Where any disjuncture or mismatch between the supposed real social objects (in the intransitive dimension) and people's beliefs about them (in the transitive dimension), would result, he suggests, in a 'false consciousness' (*PIF*, p. 151).

All this suggests, clearly, that the role he has assumed for himself is more than just that of an underlabourer for science. In *RR* (p. 1), he justified our 'need to take philosophy seriously', in terms of the project of winning 'the intellectual high-ground for socialism', by claiming that philosophy is the discipline that has 'traditionally underwritten both what constitutes science or knowledge and which political practices are deemed legitimate'. But Bhaskar wants more than this; he wants a 'practically-oriented' approach. In *RR* (p. vii), after having quoted Marx's eleventh thesis on Feuerbach as one of its epigraphs – that philosophers have only *interpreted* the world, in various ways: the point is to *change* it – he went on to say about the human sciences, that they will only help to interpret and change the world *rationally* 'on the condition that they interpret the world aright'. Here in *PIF*, he also clearly sees himself as a political underlabourer for socialism: hopefully providing a justified theoretical framework from within which socialist projects can be 'rationally' proposed and appraised. But is this the best way to work for a socially just society? When there are tensions between two incompatible positions which are conditions of each other, should one attempt, monologically, always to resolve them, theoretically, ahead of time? Is not such a resolution always a political matter? Hence the force of Bhaskar's claim, quoted above, that here 'the most fertile ground of ideology lies' (*RR*, p. 57). Later, I want to explore how the tensions between mutually sustaining positions or situations are in fact at work in structuring our social activities, both practically and politically. But for the moment, it is still important to study the tensions between Bhaskar and Rorty further.

ANTI-BHASKAR AND PRO-(AND ANTI-)RORTY

Against Rorty, Bhaskar feels that, rather than giving up the search for a system of linguistically formulated, logical necessities, it is possible to redirect it. They can be found within another type of systematic philosophical framework altogether. But Bhaskar, as is clear above, in being concerned to reassert the value of a science-shaped philosophy, pays little attention to what Rorty has to say in attempting to make his own preferred (conversational) alternative 'look good'; he is not himself above trying to make Rorty 'look bad'. Indeed, I also think that there is much that *is* wrong with Rorty's ways of talking, and with (some of) the terms he uses, both in their tone, and in their 'tendency', i.e. the relational form of the conversational response they 'invite': in their 'kibitzing' tone, and their 'nothing but' character, they tend to invite 'trivial', 'individualistic' and 'privatized' posturings, to close off rather than to open up a more communally extensive programme of conversational politics. As Bhaskar says regarding Rorty's talk about 'coping' with other persons: there is more to coping with social reality than just coping with individual persons; the situations in which we find ourselves, the webs of relationship (morally) sustaining us in our identities, etc., are all irreducible to dealings simply with individuals (*PIF*, p. 71). Also, I think Bhaskar is right in his negative analyses of the ideological resolutions Rorty produces of the tensions he faces. As Nancy Fraser has remarked: 'His [Rorty's] general approach is to invoke a version of the old trickle-down argument: liberty in the arts fosters equality in society; what's good for poets is good for workers, peasants, and the hard-core unemployed' (1989, p. 97).

In contrast to all this, however, I think Rorty is right in at least these respects: (1) in being critical of the primacy of the epistemological model, including the privileged place it affords representations; (2) in wanting to accord conversation a more important place in human affairs; and, (3) in distinguishing between the nature of mainstream and peripheral or marginal discourses. He is also, I think, wrong in at least these further three respects: (4) in claiming that 'at the "deepest" levels of the self there is *no* sense of human solidarity . . . [it is] a "mere" artifact of human socialization' (*CIS*, p. xiii); (5) in failing to grasp the 'negotiatory-developmental' nature of conversational understanding, which makes the existence of prior frameworks unnecessary; and, (6) in failing to appreciate the value of transcendental, conditions of possibility arguments when situated in the contexts of practical life.

Against Bhaskar (and with Rorty) then, we can remark that although he wants to carry on Rorty's project of de-divinization a stage further, to reclaim reality for itself, to make it possible 'to draw non-anthropomorphic pictures of being' (*PIF*, p. viii), he still nonetheless wants to draw pictures! Although in *PIF* (pp. 112–15), he draws an important distinction between practical (p-ref) and conversation-reference (c-ref), and suggests that *in science*, 'we must have putatively identifying descriptions [i.e. c-refs] prior to our discovery of underlying structure [i.e. p-refs]' (*PIF*, p. 121), he still thinks of conversation as working in terms of reference. Whereas Rorty, in distinguishing between participating in a conversation rather than contributing to an inquiry – for not all our actions are problematic for us – suggests that when we say something, we are not necessarily expressing a view about a subject. 'Perhaps saying something is not always saying how things are. . . . We must get the visual, and in particular the mirroring metaphors out of our speech altogether. To do that we have to understand speech not only as not the externalizing of inner representations, but not as representational at all' (*PMN*, p. 371). But what does it mean to do this?

Here we enter deep and turbulent waters. Rorty offers little help, and I have little space left to argue the points I want to make; but they are along these lines:

1. A modified 'transcendental' (Wittgensteinian) analysis of the conditions making social life possible can lead to a grasp of its 'groundings' or 'rootings' in our social practices and activities: representations are not grounded in yet further representations, but in the grasp we have of the world as socially competent agents within it. Thus, it is in the 'bustle' of social life (at the margins), not its 'order' (at the centre) that the origin of meanings is to be found (see the discussion that follows).

2. Thus Bhaskar and Rorty are wrong to believe that the meanings of our activities and practices are to be found in systematic frameworks, in 'language-games', 'normal' discourse, or whatever; *they* are all to do with the (moralistic) sustaining of various social orders – in other words, dominant discourses are used to dominate.

3. Frameworks are to do with accepted ways of problem-solving, normatively regulated modes of inquiry, etc. What are enshrined in a framework are not meanings per se, but *possible* meanings, ones which will only be fully completed when applied in practice. Thus, what is achieved within a framework is not so much meaning as *intelligibility*, i.e. certain states of affairs and circumstances become capable of being grasped reflectively and intellec- tually, as objects of thought and talk, in relation to a particular social order.

4. In the 'bustle' of everyday life, there is no order, no one single, complete order. Hence the meanings of events in the living of our lives cannot properly

be understood within the confines of an order; they are only to be found in the not wholly orderly, practical living of our lives. What retrospectively and intellectually may seem to be an unintelligible fragment of an 'underlying order', is made sense of in everyday life in different ways, in different contexts, at different moments.

5. What sustains a systematic framework is a kind of 'seeing', a seeing of certain relevant entities and objects from a 'God's-eye-view', a view from everywhere and nowhere, a constructed, disembodied, disinterested all-round view which no one could actually have. Yet, it is nonetheless 'classical' seeing, i.e. of well-defined, humanly imaginable, locatable objects and entities,[16] imagined in the literalized way required by the dominant order, not amenable to other views. We have not yet faced the possibility that non-anthropomorphic images of reality might well entail us allowing reality 'to be even more strange than we can ever imagine' (Eddington).

But what if this the case? What if no well-defined, theoretical model of locatable objects, as such, can ever capture the multivalent webs of relations in social life? What if we cannot turn the non-ordered circumstances *from* out of which we think[17] into an object of thought for us? What if society, although structured, differentiated and changing, as Bhaskar claims, is differentiated and changing to such an extent that its structure in some of its regions or moments is utterly incommensurable or incompatible with its structure elsewhere? What if, because of this, a *source* of social injustice is theoretically non-locatable, because it is distributed practically, in the political relations between such incompatible regions and moments? What if even the nature of our 'hook up' to our surroundings is also of this character, i.e. not theoretically describable ahead of time? How then are we to proceed? It is here that I think some of Rorty's comments about conversation become relevant, especially what he has to say in characterizing the distinction he draws in *PMN* (pp. 365–72), between what he calls systematic or systematizing philosophy, and edifying philosophy.

CONVERSATIONAL REALITIES

While speaking of the difference between systematic and edifying philosophy in terms of 'normal' and 'abnormal discourse', Rorty also speaks of it in terms of the mainstream and the periphery, and it is this vocabulary, of the centre and the margins, that I want to explore further. To begin with, I shall more or less precis his comments. As he describes it, mainstream philosophy is professionally accepted as *normal* philosophy. It is concerned with what is thought to be philosophy's traditional task: the search for the truth, reality. Indeed, hidden within this enterprise is the almost mystical belief that we can come 'to see' the nature of reality (independently of our talk about it) with such clarity as to make any further talk 'about it' superfluous (*PMN*, p. 375). In other words, it brings further talk to an end. Once we 'see the truth' we must *necessarily* act as the facts decree: we have no other 'rational' choice. In reality, however, such philosophy is conducted within a professional *discourse*, a systematic, canonical way of talking, regimented by an image literalized in a model, which exerts a normative pressure upon claims to truth.[18] Where the history of this kind of philosophy consists in the replacement of one relatively closed way of talking with another, different topics of inquiry – Newtonian dynamics, Darwinian biology, mathematical logic – become focal paradigms for the conduct of all inquiry. Descartes, Hobbes and Kant are the typical exponents of systematic, normal philosophy Rorty mentions.

By contrast, from within this traditional perspective, edifying philosophy is *abnormal*. Rather than a concern with truths about what is out there, with discovering what more there might actually be out in the world, it is concerned with what more there might be within us, with what more we might 'make' of ourselves. For it notes that as we communicate more, as we talk more and read more, as we create amongst ourselves more specialized forms of life – in the sciences, in the arts, in law, drama, literature, in trade and industry, in government, and so on – we become different and more differentiated people. Edifying philosophers are concerned with seeing what has not been seen before, with keeping a space open for the bringing into existence of something which in no sense was already there. Thus, rather than accepting that 'the *only* way to be edified is to know what is [already] out there (to reflect the facts accurately – to realize our essence by knowing essences)' (*PMN*, p. 360), it takes the view that the quest for truth is *just one* of the ways in which we might be edified, i.e. get to make more of ourselves. Thus, for edifying philosophers – Rorty mentions Kierkegaard, Nietzsche, the later Heidegger, Dewey and the later Wittgenstein as exemplary – the way things are said (the comparison of discourses) is more important than the possession of truths (obtained from within a particular discourse). Thus, unlike mainstream philosophy, edifying philosophy does not give rise to a discipline, to a normative, decontextualized discourse, regimented in terms of a small number of focal metaphors or figures of speech, within which reasoned arguments can be formulated, and warranted by reference to already agreed foundations. It is conversational, contextual and unregimented; figures, which at one moment in a discussion are offered as perspicuous, are abandoned, and at the next moment, others are offered, according to the requirements of circumstances.

Thus, while mainstream, systematic philosophy operates in the ordinary, orderly, normatively accountable centres of social life, and draws the authority for its claims by formulating them from within the established *discourses* which sustain in those centres a certain social order, edifying philosophy operates at the peripheries. It functions in the extraordinary, disorderly, unaccountable margins or zones between orderly centres. Thus, while mainstream talk is referential, and can be judged (from within the mainstream) for its accuracy in corresponding to a supposed reality, talk in edifying philosophy is reactive or responsive. It is a 'voice' from the margins, representing the other side of what is voiced at the centre. It has its point only as a reply to the truth-claims made there: it claims that, if we think that by knowing which descriptions within a given normal discourse apply to us we thereby know ourselves, then we are self-deceived. For, to the extent that there are other ways of talking, other ways of provoking yet further reactions from within ourselves, other ways in which we might interrelate ourselves and coordinate our activities, there is yet more we might 'make' of ourselves. Thus its aim, as Rorty says, is to keep the conversation going, to prevent open conversation[19] and debate degenerating into inquiry, into talk only within a closed discourse, thus, to prevent the freezing-over of culture and history.

Here, I would like briefly to extend these comments of Rorty's to make contact with what I had to say in a previous review of Roy Bhaskar's work (Shotter, 1990a). There, in criticizing what I called Bhaskar's socionaturalistic ontology, I pitted it against the sociohistorical ontology outlined in the work of the Russian developmental psychologist Vygotsky (1978, 1986). Here, I want to extend and deepen that confrontation. Many are now beginning to see the works of Bakhtin (1984) and Volosinov (1986) not only as a natural extension of Vygotsky's (e.g. Wertsch, 1991), but quite independently, as forming a new and much needed basis for cultural criticism (e.g. see Hirschkop and Shepherd, 1989). I also want to link Bakhtin's and Volosinov's distinction between dialogic and monologic forms of speech, to both Billig's (1987, and Billig et al., 1988) distinction between 'living' and 'official ideologies', and MacIntyre's (1981) notion of 'living traditions'. Where, as MacIntyre (1981) puts it: 'Traditions, when vital, embody continuities of conflict' (p. 206). 'A living tradition . . . is an historically extended, socially embodied argument, and an argument precisely in part about the goods which constitute that tradition' (p. 207). This is a very different idea, of course, from that which we are used to. For under the influence of modern individualism, which was meant to free us from the restrictions traditions imposed upon us, we have tended to equate the idea of a tradition with a hierarchically structured, *closed system* of knowledge that is supposed to provide the members of it with ready-made solutions to the problems they face in trying 'to be' proper members of it.

And it is indeed in this sense that Rorty and Bhaskar still seem to interpret the idea of intellectual traditions, and of the changes between them: they still see them as mainstream, monological systems pitted in a Neo-Darwinian struggle to replace each other – with Rorty seeing peripheral philosophers as failing to form such a tradition (*PMN*, p. 367). However, in MacIntyre's and Billig's view, we can see the whole process in quite a different light: as a multi-voiced activity, with both centre and margins, forming a tradition of argumentation that makes available, in Bhaskar's terms, a whole 'ensemble of position-practices and networked interrelationship' (*RR*, p. 4). Where an argumentative tradition is held together as a dynamic unity, not because it is founded upon a set of logical principles or assumptions, or constitutes a 'logic' – and thus holds together as a *system* – but because it originates in, and is directed towards, the dialogical elaboration or further specification of certain two or more sided 'topics' or 'commonplaces'. Thus within such a tradition, rather than a Darwinian struggle for the survival of the fittest, we can see a whole set of struggles of a quite different kind taking place, marked out by the tension between two quite different kinds of 'situated knowledges' (Haraway, 1991): between the realized (privileged), explicit (voiced) and orderly (professional) at the centre, and the unrealized (oppressed), implicit (silenced) and disorderly (socially unorganized) at the margins – where the stake at issue is continually and always, the degree to which those at the centre can appropriate for mere production the novel creations of those (who are hardly ever poets) on the margins; and those silenced on the margins can gain a voice at the centre in the conduct of their own lives.

CONCLUSION

Bhaskar's realism speaks from within an ordered framework of representations which, if they were to refer to existing structures, would account for the phenomena he has put in question. But this, I submit is only a theoretical realism, i.e. a realism for the doing of science. It is the dialogical dimensions outlined above – which cannot be theoretically specified before they are politically realized – not Bhaskar's transitive and intransitive, monologically articulated ones, which are, I claim, politically and practically real.

Horton Social Science Center, University of New Hampshire

NOTES

1 Abbreviations used in this article are as follows. For Roy Bhaskar's books: *PIF – Philosophy and the Idea of Freedom* (Oxford: Blackwell, 1991); *RR – Reclaiming Reality* (London: Verso, 1989); *PON – The Possibility of Naturalism* (Sussex: Harvester Press, 1979); *RTS – Realist Theory of Science* (Leeds: Leeds Books). For Richard Rorty's books: *PMN – Philosophy and the Mirror of Nature* (Oxford: Blackwell, 1980); *CIS – Contingency, Irony, and Solidarity* (Cambridge: Cambridge University Press). All other references are cited in the bibliography.

2 I have concentrated my attention only upon the Rorty/Bhaskar issue.

3 By contrast, I shall argue that it will be evinced in our being able to live without any dependence upon such 'pictures' at all: in being able to talk of a 'reality' so strange that it cannot be imagined in 'classical' terms (in the theoretical physicist's sense), i.e., by use of familiar models, at all.

4 At one point he remarks, 'Rorty is a most undialectical thinker' (*PIF*, p. 133).

5 In *RR* (p. 183), he called it the 'hard core' of a philosophical research programme.

6 *Guardian*, 23 June 1989, p. 25.

7 And vice versa: i.e., Rorty is verging on the very edge here of seemingly arguing, against all possibility, for the efficacy of a private language.

8 'Mastering' is, of course, precisely what is at issue here, in every sense of the term. Until one has satisfied the various 'gatekeepers' sustaining the 'received meanings' of certain crucial terms in a philosophical discourse, one is excluded from participation within it. One's voice is silenced as one lacks professional credentials.

9 I shall contrast it with what both Toulmin (1988) and Sullivan (1987) call 'practical philosophy', in which the perspective of the actor, who reasons practically from within a context of interaction, is given priority over the spectator, who reasons theoretically.

10 As Bhaskar himself (*PIF*, p. 31) points out, the epistemological project should not just be characterized in terms of the urge for 'philosophy as foundational', but also as conceiving of 'the mental as privileged and even incorrigible', and of 'knowledge as representational'. Although Bhaskar rejects the first two of these assumptions, he still remains (mistakenly I shall argue) partial to the last.

11 'Of course, justifications within science are a social matter – but they require and are given ontological grounds', says Bhaskar (*PIF*, p. 36).

12 In seeking to 'de-divinize' our culture, Rorty is urging that 'we try not to want something that stands beyond history and institutions' (*CIS*, p. 198).

13 'For the notion that there is such a framework only makes sense if we think of this framework as imposed by the nature of the knowing subject, by the nature of his faculties or by the nature the medium within which he works' (*PMN*, p. 9).

14 Manicas and Secord (1983) do.

15 Witness his discussion (*PIF*, pp. 147–57) of his transformational model of social action: in a way that exactly parallels Smedslund (1988) in his *Psycho-Logic*, he sketches what he calls 'the micro-logic of the theory/practice link' (*PIF*, p. 157). While Chomsky would not want to claim that his syntax was an explanatory model of a speaker's competence, Bhaskar does want to claim that such a model '*if* it were to exist and act in the postulated way would account for the phenomenon in question' (*PIF*, p. 121).

16 Recollect, Bhaskar wants to locate the '*source*' of social injustices.

17 This, I have maintained elsewhere, is a third kind of knowing, not a 'knowing-that', or a 'knowing-how', but a 'knowing-from', i.e. it is knowledge that we have from within a circumstance of what that circumstance 'is' for us, a 'situated knowing' (Shotter, 1990b).

18 On this definition, Rorty's notion of 'abnormal *discourse*' (emphasis added) is a contradiction in terms.

19 Rorty fails to distinguish clearly between conversation and discourse.

BIBLIOGRAPHY

Bakhtin, M. M. (1984) *Problems of Dostoevsky's Poetics*, ed. and trans. Caryl Emerson. Minneapolis, MN: University of Minnesota Press.

Billig, M. (1987) *Arguing and Thinking: a Rhetorical Approach to Social Psychology*. Cambridge: Cambridge University Press.

Billig, M., Condor, S., Edwards, D., Gane, M., Middleton, D. and Radley, R. (1988) *Ideological Dilemmas*. London: Sage.

Chomsky, N. (1957) *Syntactic Structures*. The Hague: Mouton.

Fraser, N. (1989) *Unruly Practices: Power, Discourse and Gender in Contemporary Social Theory*. Cambridge: Polity Press.

Haraway, D. J. (1991) 'Situated Knowledges: the Science Question in Feminism and the Privilege of Partial Perspective', in *Simians, Cyborgs, and Women: the Reinvention of Nature*. New York: Routledge.

Hirschkop, K. and Shepherd, D. (1989) *Bakhtin and Cultural Theory*. Manchester and New York: Manchester University Press.

Lakatos, I. (1971) 'History of Science and Its Rational Reconstructions', in R. C. Buck and R. S. Cohen (eds) *Boston Studies in the Philosophy of Science*, Vol. 8. Dordrecht: Reidel.

MacIntyre, A. (1981) *After Virtue*. London: Duckworth.

Manicas, P. T. and Secord, P. F. (1983) 'Implications for Psychology of the New Philosophy of Science', *American Psychologist* 38: 399–413.

Shotter, J. (1990a) '"Underlabourers for Science, or Toolmakers for Society", review essay on R. Bhaskar, *Reclaiming Reality: a Critical Introduction to Contemporary Philosophy*, 1989', *History of the Human Sciences* 3: 443–57.

Shotter, J. (1990b) *Knowing of the Third Kind: Selected Writings on Psychology, Rhetoric, and the Culture of Everyday Social Life*. Utrecht: ISOR.

Shotter, J. (1991) 'Wittgenstein and Psychology: On Our "Hook Up" to Reality', in A. Phillips-Griffiths (ed.) *Wittgenstein Centenary Lectures*. Cambridge: Cambridge University Press.

Smedslund, J. (1988) *Psycho-Logic*. Berlin: Springer-Verlag.

Sullivan, W. M. (1987) 'After Foundationalism: The Return of Practical Philosophy', in E. Simpson (ed.) *Anti-Foundationalism and Practical Reasoning: Conversations between Hermeneutics and Analysis*. Edmonton, Alta: Academic Printing & Publishing.

Toulmin, S. (1988) 'The Recovery of Practical Philosophy', *American Scholar* 57: 337–52.

Volosinov, V. N. (1986) *Marxism and the Philosophy of Language*, trans. L. Matejka and I. R. Titunik. Cambridge, MA: Harvard University Press. (Original publication 1973.)

Vygotsky, L. S. (1978) In M. Cole, V. John-Steiner, S. Scribner, and E. Souberman (eds) *Mind in Society: the Development of Higher Psychological Processes*. Cambridge, MA: Harvard University Press.

Vygotsky, L. S. (1986) *Thought and Language*, trans. A. Kozulin. Cambridge, MA: MIT Press.

Wertsch, J. V. (1991) *Voices of the Mind: A Sociocultural Approach to Mediated Action*. London: Harvester Wheatsheaf.

Wittgenstein, L. (1953) *Philosophical Investigations*. Oxford: Blackwell.

Wittgenstein, L. (1969) *On Certainty*. Oxford: Blackwell.

Wittgenstein, L. (1980) *Remarks on the Philosophy of Psychology*, Vol. II. Oxford: Blackwell.

HISTORY OF THE HUMAN SCIENCES   Vol. 5 No. 3

© 1992 SAGE (London, Newbury Park and New Delhi)   pp. 175–184

Organicism, pluralism and civil association: some neglected political thinkers

CHARLES TURNER

Otto von Gierke, *Community in Historical Perspective*. Cambridge, Cambridge University Press, 1990. £35.00, xxxiii + 267 pp.

Paul Q. Hirst (ed.), *The Pluralist Theory of the State*. London, Routledge, 1989. £40.00, 240 pp.

Paul Franco, *The Political Philosophy of Michael Oakeshott*. New Haven and London, Yale University Press, 1990. £20.00, vii + 277 pp.

> An appreciable part of the interest of the French revolution seems to me to be open only to those who will be at pains to give a little thought to the theory of corporations. (F. W. Maitland, 1900)

When the intellectual history of the Eastern European revolutions of 1989 comes to be written it will, one suspects, be rather brief. Whether one describes them, with Claus Offe, as 'exit' revolutions,[1] with Jurgen Habermas as 'retrieving' revolutions,[2] or with Paul Hirst as the belated, mistaken and possibly dangerous attempt to buy in on the enlightenment,[3] their contribution to the history of ideas is likely to be negligible. This does not mean that they have no lessons to teach. The lesson that a rejection of the idea of progress can have revolutionary force is perhaps the most significant.[4]

Not far behind is the lesson that the democracy to which the West thought it was committed during the Cold War requires urgent redefinition in the face of its sudden expansion and the loss of the Other which once gave it a stable boundary. The literature on post-1989 Eastern Europe, now mushrooming as fast as satellite dishes in nightmare Eastern German villages, is dominated by the question of the foundation for a stable post-revolutionary democracy. And if there is a single concept whose history is being retrieved, and to which appeal is being made in an attempt to address it, it is that of 'civil society'. In its least interesting sense, civil society is the rallying cry of those who believe that markets have personalities, who would give the history of charisma one more stage than Max Weber gave it.[5] It would hardly be worth mentioning if the Finance Minister of Czechoslovakia, among others, did not subscribe to it, advocating a 'market economy without the adjective', where the adjective is 'social', and rejecting the corporatism which underpins the most powerful economy in Europe as 'the Rhine model'. In a related sense, civil society refers to the critical public sphere envisaged by discourse ethics, one of private persons coming together as argumentative reasoners. In the long run, it is unlikely that the future of Eastern European democracy will depend upon the development of civil society in either of these individualistic senses. More important is the sense of civil society which pertains to the nature and status of intermediate groups, to those forms of association lying between the individual and the state. While liberals may conceive of the life of groups in terms of voluntary associations and clubs, and theorists of new social movements understand it in a more directly political sense, they share the belief that state and civil society are antagonists.

As the need for an independent countervailing civil society as a solution to the dilemma of democracy competes with the ideology of the free market, their combination almost drowns out the voice of those western neo-Marxists who, having adopted a fall-back corporatist position, retain the hope that the countries of Eastern Europe will transform themselves into something resembling Sweden. The distinction between state and societal corporatism notwithstanding, the majority of contributors to the debate on Eastern Europe have disdained the language of corporatism, not least because many of the old regimes attempted to legitimate themselves through it.

For western intellectuals, the task of retrieval or exit has been as urgent as it is for those in the East attempting to lock on to what *they* take to be a western democratic tradition. What are we to read or reread, where are we to find the conceptual resources with which to construct a political theory adequate to the events of 1989? A brief *Begriffsgeschichte* of 'civil society' quickly throws up the names of Hegel and Tocqueville for those who take the state/civil society relationship to be one of antagonism, Hegel for those who favour a neo-corporatist solution, Tocqueville for more traditional liberals. But beyond their obviousness as great political thinkers, are they the most appropriate for an understanding of 1989? In particular, if those who see state and civil society opposed take seriously the idea of the flourishing of voluntary associations within a constitutional state, what legal and moral status is to be accorded those associations? If the ultimate aim of the emerging democracies is decentralization, what is to be the precise relationship between the state and non-state groups?

There is a widespread assumption that, since the old regimes were centralized states, decentralization of state authority is consistent with individualism. The books reviewed here contain the strongest types of argument against this view, and for the view that the individualism which *is* consistent with decentralization entails a rather different account of the character of the state than that subscribed to by those engaged currently in debate about Eastern Europe. Each of the thinkers concerned attempts to defend the integrity of intermediate groups and of associational life in general, yet they receive scant attention among contemporary theorists of democracy and the modern state. There are good reasons of an historicist kind for this – Otto von Gierke (1841–1921) suffered in his own lifetime from having his ideas associated with republicanism by monarchists and with conservatism by social democrats, and his emanationist account of social wholes is sometimes seen as anticipatory support for national socialism. The British pluralists' concept of a divided state authority and advocacy of a functional mode of representation had lost its voice by the late 1920s. And the publication in 1975 of *On Human Conduct*, while confirming Michael Oakeshott as the greatest writer of English philosophical prose this century, seemed to his critics and former admirers to mark a shift towards an impossibly libertarian vision of conservatism.

While the neglect of these thinkers may have respectable theoretical reasons, too, converging perhaps in the concept of nostalgia, be it for the depths of the German forest, for medieval guilds or for Montaigne, and while the magpie's accumulation of resources for a never-to-be-achieved synthesis has never been an engaging spectacle, this literature provides, if not individual ideas which chime with those of today, a body of material which combines practical urgency with theoretical sophistication.

Community in Historical Perspective is a translation of some of the first volume of Gierke's massive and never-to-be-completed *Das deutsche Genossenschaftsrecht*. It appeared in 1868 when Gierke was 27. It is a legal, philosophical and political history written as the history of a struggle between two principles of association, a horizontal principle of *Genossenschaft*, or fellowship, and a vertical principle of *Herrschaft*, or lordship. He divides German history into periods during which first one, then the other, is predominant. In the dispute between Romanists and Germanists which raged during the latter half of the 19th century, Gierke's work was an attempt to vindicate an essentially egalitarian and Germanic law of fellowship in the face of a Roman law which served only to sanction the principle of *Herrschaft* opposed to it.

> . . . even today the German system of fellowship is confined in both theory and practice in the strait-jacket of the Latin corporation – not . . . that of the

ancient Romans, but that which was debased in the shadow of its former
independence under the Byzantine empire. (Gierke, p. 5)

The key to the difference between them is the concept of personality. Gierke was
convinced that the unity of German fellowship was grounded in its having a real,
moral personality irreducible to its individual members and constituting the real
source of their individual actions. By contrast, Roman law could attribute to the
group nothing more than a personality in law, a fiction. Which meant, in effect,
that whether there existed a system of group-life between the individual and a
higher power depended upon a concession from that power. Roman law
sanctioned an *Obrigkeitssystem* in which intermediate groups were no more than
subjects of private law.

In his second period (800–1200), though 'the patrimonial and feudal [i.e.
herrschaftlich] principle dominates the life of the nation', the feudal idea is never
fully realized, so that the corporate idea of fellowship lives on 'in the
consciousness of the people', both in the lordship groups themselves and in a
principle 'which finally reduces the feudal state to ruins' (p. 10), the principle of
free association. Its prototype was the Germanic guild system, and in combining
with the 'natural' fellowship of market community it was the foundation of the
towns of the 11th and 12th centuries. The medieval guild existed not for a single
purpose, but 'was an association based on a union which was entered into freely
. . . which, like other guilds, encompassed the whole person as today only family
and state do' (p. 47). In contrast to the modern system of association, 'which
resembles a great number of infinitely intersecting circles', and in which one
belongs to an association with only a part of one's being, 'the empire remained
the sum total of these circles, of which one might encircle the other without
intersecting them' (p. 23).

The period from 1200 to 1523 represents the final collapse of feudalism and the
creation of 'the most magnificent organisations from below by means of *freely
chosen fellowships*' (p. 10). Yet these lack the strength to break through the
system of estates. Indeed, the increasing importance of territoriality transforms
lordship over land into the territorial state.

The period 1525–1806 represents the triumph of territorial independence,
sovereignty and enlightened despotism. The system of fellowships, in which
fellowships united with similar groups to form a greater whole, gave way to one
of privileged and separate corporations. Corporative egotism resulted in a desire
'to perceive the corporation as a unique individual, where it had formerly
perceived itself as also being a member of a higher universality' (p. 106). It was no
longer a vital organism, but a dead mechanism confronting its members. And
hand in hand with this descent into particularism went the elevation of the
sovereign state which, while being unable to avoid its own articulation into lesser
associations, seeks to 'absorb the public significance of communities and
fellowships into the concept of the state, and . . . to reduce whatever remains in

these groups of innate importance to the level of a state-owned capacity' (p. 112). The reception of Roman law greatly enhanced this development. For Roman law knows only private and public law, and conceives only a right which is unlimited in itself and has to be checked by an external right opposed to it. Gierke's lasting significance was to have reasserted a third category of law, Germanic social law (*Sozialrecht*) for which each right contains its own limit. For Roman law a collectivity could be one of only two things: a *societas*, having no real existence outside that of those who compose it, or a *universitas*, a corporate group with a legal personality based on a concession from the state which could be withdrawn at any time.

Nineteenth-century Germany saw a flourishing of clubs, societies and producers' cooperatives with which socialists, liberals and conservatives alike had to reckon. Gierke's response was to see in these modern associations something much closer to the medieval concept of free union. It 'comes from within the people and builds upwards from below. . . . As the medieval union was set against the idea of lordship and service, so the modern association sets its face against the idea of a sovereign standing above and beyond the whole. . . . The privileged corporation's corporative separateness . . . is no less alien to it' (p. 119). The major difference concerns the singularity of purpose of modern associations. 'Even the highest association – the state – has its purposes' (p. 120). The state is the highest form of association, not in the sense peculiar to the *Obrigkeitsstaat* of 1525–1806, but in that sense provided for by the non-exclusivity of lower-level, single-purpose associations, which together 'construct one collective unity out of single groups interlocking with one another in a hundred different ways' (p. 122). The idea of the modern German state is that the state is one with the people as that people's organized form, grounded in the fellowship of citizens of the state. The significance of the modern principle of association is that it provides for this idea's future realization. While in the 18th century the state stood over against civil society as an institution (*Anstalt*), now it is to grow out of it as an association (*Verein*). And yet, just as the principle of fellowship was never fully suppressed even by feudalism at its height, so its modern victory is not complete. The state is a fellowship in its foundation. At its summit, it develops the old idea of lordship. The modern state as a whole is the final resolution of their opposition.

Through his account of the *Obrigkeitsstaat*, Gierke was able to attack both socialism and liberalism for being ideologies foreign to the legal consciousness of the German people. Socialism promised an administrative state consistent with a centralist doctrine of sovereignty, liberalism the particularism which opposed it. But while he opposed to both of them the allegedly German idea of the state as grounded in fellowship, thereby distinguishing him from social democracy, this failed to establish his conservative credentials. Between 1871 and 1918 the struggle against 'Manchesterism', and a concomitant extension of the activity of the German state, turned the study of history towards political and *constitutional* history and away from the social history which Gierke wrote. Gierke's theory of fellowship seemed increasingly to contain democratic and republican strains which sat uneasily with his manifest monarchism.

Gierke was an openly organicist thinker in two senses. First, he located the unity of groups in a principle of life and conceived of them as living organisms. But secondly, he secured the link which connected the medieval and modern associational principles by asserting that in both cases the relationship *between* groups was one of organic unity. Yet despite his appeal to a distinction between organism and mechanism, he was not the type of political romantic of which Carl Schmitt wrote. His work contains none of romanticism's irony and paradox and, despite the postulated similarity of organizational principle between medieval and modern associations, this is not a backward-looking glorification of medievalism.

Responsibility for Gierke's reception in Anglo-Saxon scholarship lay with F. W. Maitland, who in 1900 translated a fifth of Volume 3 (!) of *Das deutsche Genossenschaftsrecht* as *Political Theories of the Middle Age*,[6] describing it as the greatest book he had ever read. Yet the Gierke Maitland introduced was of interest as one who provided the resources for a pluralist interpretation of the relationship between the state and non-state groups, the Gierke of the real personality of voluntary associations, but not of the organic relationship between associations, or of the state as the highest form of association in which a single people, united in fellowship, expresses itself. This contrasted markedly with Germany, in which, with the possible exception of Hugo Preuss,[7] subsequent writers developed the organic-authoritarian aspects of his work.

The effect of this partial reception is evident in the writings of those most deeply influenced by what they took to be Gierkean arguments, the British pluralists G. D. H. Cole, Harold Laski and John Neville Figgis. All thought it necessary to defend the independence of civil society by insisting upon the theoretical homogeneity between the state and non-state groups. The modern combination of the indivisibility of state sovereignty and of the right- and duty-bearing individual threatened to undermine the integrity of intermediate associations. The individual comes to him/herself only as a member of such a group, a principle denied by the individualist representation peculiar to liberal democracy. The point of emphasizing that the voluntary association has a personality, 'a life that glows beneath' (p. 179), that it is 'a living social union of men bound together by specific ties . . . and acting by virtue of an inherent spontaneity of life which is not improvised but original'[8] was twofold. First, it was necessary to take up Maitland's point that the threat to modern associations came as much from the possibility of individual lawsuits against them as from state pressure, and that the state's refusal to find in favour of the association when its purposes begin to differ from those of its voluntary members would spell the death 'of all the political clubs that ever existed'.[9] Second, contrary to Gierke's postulation of an organic link between the numerous intersecting circles associational purposes formed, the pluralists wished to show that the purposes for which associations are formed are expressed as interests, and to propose a functionalist system of representation based on the coordination of those interests.

There is something incongruous about the appeal, within the British pluralist idiom, to Gierke's real personality of groups. The collection recently edited by Paul Hirst, being devoted largely to the two leading exponents of that idiom, Cole and Laski, adds to this impression. Figgis, who warrants fewer than 20 pages, was far more at home than they in the 'continental' tradition of social and political theory, his exposure to Gierkean arguments and formulations was more direct, his arguments tighter and his style considerably more elegant. A familiarity with organicist and life-philosophical formulations may be an oddity in one credited with the most coherent understanding of what it is to be an Anglican, but Figgis knew perhaps better than Cole and Laski what he required of them, and how they should be put to work to show that the state cannot be the origin of whatever life associations have.

The pluralists shared the view that a flourishing civil society was possible only on the basis of clarity about the authority of the state. The view of state sovereignty to which they objected was repeatedly traced to Hobbes, who conceives of the authority of the state as an indivisible unity, and who therefore has no place for corporations with competing authority, and to a lesser extent to Hegel, for whom the corporation is nothing more than the root which the state extends downward into civil society. Since the future of Eastern European democracies is held by most western commentators to depend upon the rebirth or reinvention of an autonomous civil society, fairly short shrift is being given to anyone who, on the basis of Hobbesian or Hegelian arguments, suggests that the state is the highest form of human association. The old regimes were, after all, centralized states which granted little independent life to non-state groups. The official rhetoric of the German Democratic Republic may have been organicist and explicitly *genossenschaftlich* (party members regularly addressed each other as '*Genosse*', industrial and agricultural production was exclusively organized on a cooperative basis), but this was simply the state articulating itself into its lesser associations.

In the face of this, the appearance of the first monograph encompassing the whole of the corpus of Michael Oakeshott is as timely as a renewed interest in organicist or pluralist theory. For although Oakeshott's major influences in political philosophy were Hobbes and Hegel, and his most sustained piece of political theorizing, *On Human Conduct*, can be read as an attempt to reconcile them, his concept of civil association is intended to provide for precisely what neither Gierke nor the pluralists thought a Hobbesian theory of the state could, the integrity of non-state groups. What matters here is less what the pluralists called the authority of the state than its character.

Oakeshott had his first spat with the pluralists in the late 1920s, in 'The

Authority of the State', in which the idea of illegitimate or limited authority is dismissed as meaningless.

> That which is authoritative is . . . absolute and unlimited, not in the sense of embracing every detail, but because there can be no appeal from it. The real authority of all belief and action is that which can show itself to be absolute, irresponsible, self-supporting and inescapable.[10]

Cole and Laski could only conceive of state authority as anything else because they defined the state in terms of the abstractions of 'government' or 'territoriality'. But government never deals with the whole of life, only with an aspect of it. The state is only a concrete fact rather than an abstraction if it is self-subsistent and requires to be linked to no other whole to be understood. The authority of the state resides neither in government nor in a people conceived of as a homogeneity, but in the totality of conditions under which the satisfaction of the needs of concrete persons, a satisfaction towards which state activity is directed, takes place. This totality cannot be the object of approval or disapproval.

This formalist vision of the state received its fullest expression in *On Human Conduct*, in which Oakeshott offers less a theory of the state than a history of the modern state in terms of rival 'intimations' of its 'character' as a mode of human association. As Gierke writes of history as a struggle between lordship and fellowship in order to vindicate the Germanic concept of the personality of the group, so Oakeshott writes of history as a struggle between *societas* and *universitas* as two Romanist understandings of the character of the state. As *universitas*, the state is enterprise association with a substantive purpose. As *societas*, it is civil association, with a formal, moral, non-instrumental character, having no purpose and prescribing no action, and an authority residing in the conditions to be subscribed to in action. A state understood as *universitas* will have no place for collectivities pursuing purposes at variance with its own. Its members are not intelligent agents but members of a mass. Oakeshott contends that it is primarily as *universitas* that modern Europeans have suffered the character of the state to be understood, an understanding given succour by modern warfare. A state at war is a state under mass mobilization, having less room than ever for autonomous corporate association. By contrast the absolute, unlimited and indivisible authority of *lex* in a state understood as *societas* implies a theory of sovereignty in which the identity of the state depends neither upon an external threat, nor upon the homogeneity of the people. The conditions which specify the modality of political experience are not and cannot be encapsulated in written constitutions or Bills of Rights, which latter may be perfectly consistent with the state understood as enterprise association.

There is nothing in Oakeshott's concept of *societas* to suggest the type of hostility towards corporate bodies such as universities or trade unions which Hirst, in his introduction to the pluralism collection, identifies with Thatcherism and which, he proposes, is best opposed by pluralist arguments. In fact, he takes it to be their best defence. To be sure, unlike Gierke and the pluralists, he did not believe it necessary to defend the autonomy of corporate groups by attributing to them a personality, and he rejected the idea that the interests to which corporate purposes gave rise could be coordinated in a functionalist system of representation. But it is odd that Hirst, having referred to the shocking neglect of Collingwood's political philosophy, should not have mentioned Oakeshott in an account of the renewed topicality of pluralism.

Oakeshott never thought of civil association as a standard against which to 'measure' existing states, but as the intimation of a colloquial understanding of the conditions of a type of practice. Yet, as the emerging democracies in Eastern Europe throw off the legacy of absolutism, write their constitutions and rediscover lost and short-lived republican traditions, we might reflect on the consequences of the fact that what they are not throwing off is the legacy of the state as an enterprise. Oakeshott's description of the voice which Europeans addressed to new African and South American states might still apply to the voice Western Europeans are addressing to Eastern Europe:

> . . . what they have learned from us is an understanding of a state as a compulsory corporate association and the notion of ruling as the management of a corporate enterprise, which they called 'nationalism'. What these states have never heard is the voice of civil association because we ourselves long ago suffered it to be confused with the 'liberal' concern for constitutional devices. When the President of Malawi said, 'I don't care what the world calls me, a dictator or what, my job is to develop this country', he spoke in a European voice.[11]

University of Cambridge

NOTES

1 C. Offe (1991) 'Das Dilemma der Gleichzeitigkeit', *Merkur*, April.

2 J. Habermas (1990) *Die Nachholende Revolution*. Frankfurt: Suhrkamp.

3 P. Hirst (1991) 'State, Civil Society and the Collapse of Communism', *Economy and Society* 20(2).

4 U. K. Preuss (1990) *Revolution, Fortschritt und Verfassung*. Berlin: Wagenbach.

5 Perhaps it is no accident that for Weber the last stage was the charisma of reason under Robespierre. See *Economy and Society* (1978) Berkeley: University of California Press, p. 1209.

6 O. von Gierke (1988) *Political Theories of the Middle Age*. Cambridge: Cambridge University Press.

7 For an early example of Gierke's influence see H. Preuss (1990) 'Über Organpersönlichkeit', *Schmollers Jahrbuch für Gesetzgebung, Verwaltung und Volkswirtschaft* 26. Jahrgang.

8 J. N. Figgis (1913) *Churches in the Modern State*, p. 33. London: Longman's, Green.

9 ibid., p. 45.

10 M. Oakeshott (1929–30) 'The Authority of the State', *The Modern Churchman* XIX: 316.

11 M. Oakeshott (1975) *On Human Conduct*, pp. 296–7. Oxford: Clarendon Press.

Contributors

PETER BARHAM is a psychologist who studied at the Universities of Cambridge and Durham. Presently he is visiting senior lecturer in mental health, Goldsmiths College, University of London, and chairman of the Hamlet Trust. He and his colleagues are currently engaged in a project on mental health reform in Poland. His publications include: *Schizophrenia and Human Value* (Blackwell, 1986); *From the Mental Patient to the Person* (with Robert Hayward, Routledge, 1991); and *Closing the Asylum* (Penguin, in press).

ZYGMUNT BAUMAN is Emeritus Professor of Sociology at the University of Leeds. Recent publications include *Modernity and Ambivalence* (Polity Press, 1991) and *Intimations of Postmodernity* (Routledge, 1992).

RONALD BEINER is a professor of political science at the University of Toronto. His publications include *Political Judgment* and an edition of Hannah Arendt's *Lectures on Kant's Political Philosophy*. His most recent book is *What's the Matter with Liberalism?* (University of California Press, 1992).

IAN BURKITT lectures in sociology and social psychology at the University of Bradford, where he is British Academy postdoctoral research fellow in the department of social and economic studies.

DIANA COOLE is lecturer in political theory at the University of Leeds. Her interests include feminist theory, postmodernism and postwar French thought. She is the author of *Women in Political Theory* for which she is currently writing a second edition, and she is also writing a new book on the politics of negativity.

GEOFFREY HAWTHORN teaches sociology and politics at Cambridge University. His most recent book is *Plausible Worlds: Possibility and Understanding in History and the Social Sciences* (Cambridge University Press, 1991).

PETER LASSMAN teaches political and social theory in the Department of Political Science and International Studies at the University of Birmingham. His current interests are in problems of contemporary liberal political philosophy and Max Weber's political writings.

CHARLES MARTINDALE is Reader in latin and comparative literature at the University of Bristol. He has a special interest in applying new theoretical approaches to the study of antiquity, and his latest book *Redeeming the Text: Latin Poetry and the Hermeneutics of Reception* will be published by Cambridge University Press in 1992.

DAVID OWEN teaches politics at Queen Mary and Westfield College, University of London, and City of London Polytechnic. He has published on Nietzsche, Weber and Foucault, and is currently completing a book on these three thinkers.

RAYMOND PLANT is Professor of Politics at the University of Southampton since 1979. He is the author of: *Hegel, Community and Ideology, Modern Political Thought* (with K. Hoover); *Conservative Capitalism in Britain and the United States: A Critical Appraisal* (with A. Vincent); *Philosophy, Politics and Citizenship* (with H. Lesser and P. Taylor-Gooby); and *Political Philosophy and Social Welfare*.

JEREMY RAYNER has published articles on conservatism and political language. He currently teaches politics at Malaspina College in British Columbia.

JOHN SHOTTER is a professor of interpersonal relations in the Department of Communication, University of New Hampshire. He is the author of *Images of Man in Psychological Research* (Methuen, 1975), *Human Action and its Psychological Investigation* (with Alan Gauld, Routledge, 1977), *Social Account-ability and Selfhood* (Blackwell, 1984), and *Knowing of the Third Kind: essays on Rhetoric, Psychology, and the Culture of Everyday Social Life* (ISOR, Utrecht, 1990). He is also the editor with Kenneth J. Gergen of *Texts of Identity* (Sage, 1989) and with Ian Parker the editor of *Deconstructing Social Psychology* (Routledge, 1990).

TRACY B. STRONG is professor of political science at the University of California, San Diego and editor of *Political Theory*. He is author, most recently, of *The Idea of Political Theory, Reflections on the Self in Political Time and Space* (University of Notre Dame Press) and is at work on a book on the relation between political thought and aesthetics in the early 20th century.

CHARLES TURNER lives in Cambridge. His book *Modernity and Politics in the Work of Max Weber* will be published by Routledge in October 1992.

MARK E. WARREN is Associate Professor of Government at Georgetown University, Washington, DC. His areas of interest include continental political thought, democratic theory and Marxism. He is author of *Nietzsche and Political Thought* (MIT Press, 1988), and has recent articles on democratic theory, Marx, Weber, Habermas and Nietzsche in *Political Theory, The American Political Science Review, Philosophy of the Social Sciences, Theory and Society*, and *Political Studies*. He is now working on a book entitled *Democratic Transform-ations of the Self*, which draws on continental political thought to rethink assumptions about the self in participatory democratic theory.

Modernity and Political Thought

A major new series

THE AUGUSTINIAN IMPERATIVE

A Reflection on the Politics of Morality

William E Connolly *Johns Hopkins University*

Volume 1 / May 1993 • 176 pages
Cloth (8039-3636-2) / Paper (8039-3637-0)

THOMAS HOBBES

Skepticism, Individuality, and Chastened Politics

Richard E Flathman *Johns Hopkins University*

Volume 2 / May 1993 • 160 pages
Cloth (8039-4080-7) / Paper (8039-4081-5)

G W F HEGEL

Modernity and Politics

Fred R Dallmayr *University of Notre Dame*

Volume 3 / May 1993 • 264 pages
Cloth (8039-3615-X) / Paper (8039-3616-8)

READING 'ADAM SMITH'

Desire, History, and Value

Michael J Shapiro *University of Hawaii*

Volume 4 / May 1993 • 176 pages
Cloth (8039-4584-1) / Paper (8039-4585-X)

SAGE Publications Ltd
6 Bonhill Street
London EC2A 4PU
England

SAGE Publications Inc
2455 Teller Road
Newbury Park
CA 91320 USA